"Neither life nor scholarship occurs in a political vacuum. True for Paul, Elliott insists, and true no less for his modern interpreters. In these intellectually impassioned and morally lucid essays, Elliott summons his reader to approach Paul's letters with critical historical imagination; to place Paul in his Roman no less than in his Jewish context; to think historically when thinking theologically. *Paul the Jew under Roman Rule* is an exciting exploration of the ethics of New Testament interpretation."

—PAULA FREDRIKSEN
Author of *Paul: The Pagans' Apostle*

"It is of immense benefit to scholarship to have these innovative, carefully reasoned essays, the fruit of Neil Elliott's groundbreaking research here in one volume. Convincingly, Elliott demonstrates from various angles that Paul's Jewish identity and the fact that he lived and worked under Roman rule are so intertwined that one cannot be separated from the other. Insights otherwise hidden unsettle any and every perspective and challenge us to consider with methodical and hermeneutical rigor approaches old and new to Paul and his legacy. This is an indispensable contribution and relevant for today."

—WILLIAM S. CAMPBELL
Research fellow, Faculty of Theology, University of Basel

"The intersection of Jewish concerns and practices in antiquity with the rise of Roman imperialism and 'empire' is a major interest in ancient world studies. This crucial intersection is too often separated in Pauline studies: numerous scholars either situate Paul in his 'Jewish' context or within the wider 'Roman world.' However, the interlocutions between the two are insufficiently investigated. Neil Elliott's masterful volume of essays is a scintillating scholarly and exegetical contribution to the field."

—JAMES R. HARRISON
Professor of biblical studies, Sydney College of Divinity

"Neil Elliott is known as one of the most prominent interpreters of the apostle Paul, and his research has been of extraordinary importance for the emergence and development of the so-called Paul-within-Judaism perspective. This collection of state-of-the-art articles and essays is an excellent example of this. This is a must-read for pastors, students, and fellow scholars."

—MAGNUS ZETTERHOLM
Associate professor of New Testament studies, Lund University

Paul the Jew under Roman Rule

Paul the Jew under Roman Rule

Collected Essays

NEIL ELLIOTT

CASCADE *Books* • Eugene, Oregon

PAUL THE JEW UNDER ROMAN RULE

Collected Essays

Copyright © Neil Elliott 2024. All rights reserved. Except for brief quotations in critical publications or reviews, no part of this book may be reproduced in any manner without prior written permission from the publisher. Write: Permissions, Wipf and Stock Publishers, 199 W. 8th Ave., Suite 3, Eugene, OR 97401.

Cascade Books
An Imprint of Wipf and Stock Publishers
199 W. 8th Ave., Suite 3
Eugene, OR 97401

www.wipfandstock.com

PAPERBACK ISBN: 978-1-6667-5267-0
HARDCOVER ISBN: 978-1-6667-5268-7
EBOOK ISBN: 978-1-6667-5269-4

Cataloging-in-Publication data:

Names: Elliott, Neil, 1956–, author.

Title: Paul the Jew under Roman rule : collected essays / Neil Elliott

Description: Eugene, OR: Cascade Books, 2024. | Includes bibliographical references and indexes.

Identifiers: ISBN: 978-1-6667-5267-0 (paperback). | ISBN: 978-1-6667-5268-7 (hardcover). | ISBN: 978-1-6667-5269-4 (ebook).

Subjects: LCSH: Paul, the Apostle, Saint. | Bible.—Epistles of Paul—Criticism, interpretation, etc.

Classification: BS2650.2 E451 2024 (print). | BS2650.2 (epub).

Contents

List of Figures | vii
Acknowledgments | ix
List of Abbreviations | xi

Introduction: Paul, the Jews, and the Nations, and Empires,
    Then and Now | 1

1. Situating the Apostle Paul in His Day and Engaging His Legacy in Our Own | 10

2. Taking the Measure of an Earthquake: Comments on the Fortieth-Anniversary Edition of *Paul and Palestinian Judaism* | 43

3. The Anti-Imperial Message of the Cross | 53

4. Paul and the Politics of Empire: Problems and Prospects | 70

5. The "Patience of the Jews": Strategies of Resistance and Accommodation to Imperial Cultures | 94

6. The Apostle Paul's Self-Presentation as Anti-Imperial Performance | 104

8. Paul and Empire in Romans, 1 and 2 Corinthians | 124

9. The Question of Politics: Paul as a Diaspora Jew under Roman Rule | 144

10. *Qui Bono*? Power Relations and the Work "within Judaism" Language Does | 174

Bibliography | 193
Ancient Documents Index | 213
Author Index | 223

Figures

Fig. 1.1.   A basic chronology of Paul's life and career | 22
Fig. 9.1.   The *kata sarka* interpretation of Paul's Judaism | 149
Fig. 10.1. A tension in "within Judaism" scholarship | 175

Acknowledgments

ANY SCHOLAR'S WORK DEPENDS upon a host of connections, older and newer, with friends and critics alike (often the same people). In gathering this collection of essays I have been happily reminded of conversations, many of them ongoing over the years, with Roland Boer, William S. Campbell, W. Royce Clark, Kathy Ehrensperger, Pamela Eisenbaum, Robert Ellsberg, Paula Fredriksen, Jione Havea, Richard A. Horsley, Wes Howard-Brook, Richard Hughes, Brigitte Kahl, Davina A. Lopez, Mark D. Nanos, Steve Newcom, Todd Penner, Adele Reinhartz, Grant Stevenson, Diana Swancutt, Larry L. Welborn, Vincent L. Wimbush, Karin Hedner Zetterholm, and Magnus Zetterholm, among many others. Of course, none of them bears responsibility for judgments expressed in the following pages.

I am particularly grateful for the interest and persistence of K. C. Hanson, longtime friend and worthy colleague in scholarship and academic publishing alike, in bringing this volume to life.

Chapter 1 was first published in the *Fortress Commentary on the Bible: The New Testament* (2014) and is reprinted here with permission of Fortress Press. I thank my esteemed Fortress Press colleague Scott Tunseth for the invitation to write the essay.

Chapter 2 was published in *Journal for the Study of the Jesus Movement in Its Jewish Setting* 5 (2018) 21–31. It represents remarks given at an SBL session marking the 40th anniversary of E. P. Sanders's *Paul and Palestinian Judaism*.

Chapter 3 began as a chapter in my *Liberating Paul: The Justice of God and the Politics of the Apostle* (Maryknoll, NY: Orbis, 1994; Minneapolis: Fortress, 2007); it was republished under the title that appears here in the collection *Paul and Empire: Religion and Power in Roman Imperial Society*, edited by Richard A. Horsley (Harrisburg, PA: Trinity, 1997). Reprinted with kind permission of Fortress Press.

Chapter 4 began as an address to the Paul and Politics Group of the SBL; it was first published in *Paul and Politics: Ekklesia, Israel, Imperium, Interpretation,* edited by Richard A. Horsley (Harrisburg, PA: Trinity, 2000), and is reprinted with kind permission of Continuum.

Chapter 5 appeared in *Pauline Conversations in Context: Essays in Honor of Calvin J. Roetzel,* edited by Janice Capel Anderson, Philip Sellew, and Claudia Setzer, JSNTSup 221 (Sheffield: Sheffield Academic, 2002); reprinted with kind permission of Continuum.

Chapter 6 appeared in *The New Testament: Introducing the Way of Discipleship,* edited by Wes Howard-Brook and Sharon Ringe (Maryknoll, NY: Orbis, 2002), and is reprinted with kind permission of Orbis Books.

Chapter 7 appeared in *Paul and the Roman Imperial Order,* edited by Richard A. Horsley (Harrisburg, PA: Trinity, 2003); reprinted with kind permission of Continuum.

Chapter 8 appeared in *The New Testament and Empire: An Introduction,* edited by Adam Winn (Atlanta: SBL, 2016), and is reprinted with kind permission of SBL Press.

Chapter 9 first appeared in *Paul within Judaism,* edited by Mark D. Nanos and Magnus Zetterholm (Minneapolis: Fortress, 2015); reprinted with kind permission of Fortress Press.

Chapter 10 is an expanded version of an essay appearing in abbreviated form in *Within Judaism? Jewish, Christian, and Muslim Perspectives from the First to the Fifth Century,* edited by Anders Runesson and Karin Hedner Zetterholm (Lanham, MD: Lexington Books/Fortress Academic, 2023), published with kind permission of Lexington Books/Fortress Academic.

Abbreviations

BibInt	Biblical Interpretation Series
JBL	*Journal of Biblical Literature*
JSNT	*Journal for the Study of the New Testament*
JSNTSup	Journal for the Study of the New Testament Supplements
LCL	Loeb Classical Library
LNTS	Library of New Testament Studies
NovT	*Novum Testamentum*
NTS	New Testament Studies
SJLA	Studies in Judaism in Late Antiquity
SNTSMS	Society of New Testament Studies Monograph Series
TDNT	*Theological Dictionary of the New Testament.* 10 vols. Edited by Gerhard Kittel and Gerhard Friedrich. Translated by Geoffrey W. Bromiley. Grand Rapids: Eerdmans, 1964–1976
WUNT	Wissenschaftliche Untersuchungen zum Neuen Testament

Introduction
Paul, the Jews, and the Nations, and Empires, Then and Now

THE ESSAYS GATHERED HERE concern two areas that continue to occupy the best efforts of the apostle Paul's interpreters today and, often enough, to set them at odds with one another. One is the effort to understand Paul's relationship to his ancestral religion, where we can find some who understand Paul as a "convert" from Judaism to Christianity posed over against others who seek to understand the apostle "within Judaism," without remainder. The second area seeks to set the apostle in the context of the early Principate and to understand him as engaging imperial claims; that is, as some would have it, to read him "politically." Here, the range of interpretation involves not only questions of substance (for example, did Paul mean a blanket endorsement of governing authorities in Romans 13, or did he not?), but also self-critical questions of interpretation: however we read Romans 13, mustn't we regard Paul as an irreducibly *theological* thinker, so that any attempt to understand him from a political point of view is inevitably an anachronistic projection of our own prejudices?

Both conversations have involved not just serious methodological reflection, but also a respectable measure of *ad hominem* argument and invective. We are told that the "within Judaism" crowd has been blinded to hard historical realities by their "misty-eyed" sentimentality regarding the horrors of the Shoah; conversely, we hear their opponents are merely dressing up their own presumptuous Protestantism in period costume when they claim to interpret Paul historically. Here, we read that "empire-critical" interpreters are disgruntled Leftists who take their frustrations out in essays on the apostle; there, that the conventional reading is but the projection of the Constantinian cooptation of Christianity as perpetuated through centuries of imperial-colonial privilege.

As the essays that follow reveal, I cannot present myself as floating calmly above the fray in either area of contestation. My purpose is more modest, but, I hope, significant nonetheless. I argue that these questions are so intertwined that they cannot be adequately grasped separately. Understanding Paul *as a Jew* requires understanding him as a Jew *under Roman rule*.

~

At the risk of self-indulgence, it may be helpful for me to give the reader of these essays a sense of where their author is coming from. I discovered E. P. Sanders's *Paul and Palestinian Judaism* soon after its publication in 1977, while still an undergraduate. I recognized its significance because I had already been introduced to Rosemary Radford Ruether's *Faith and Fratricide* (1974), and had come to recognize how much was at stake in the investigation and exposure of anti-Judaism in the New Testament.

As I pursued an MDiv, then entered the PhD program at Princeton Seminary, intent on studying biblical theology, I increasingly found it impossible to separate *exegetical* endeavor from questions about the energies at work in contemporary interpretation. The neat distinction between "what the text meant" and "what the text means" seemed an evasion. Surely the primary task of biblical interpreters, whether academics or clergy, was to exercise a self-critical honesty: not only to seek to understand biblical figures and texts in their own contexts, but to take full responsibility for the consequences of our readings in our own (see chapter 1).

Though I had not planned on a career in Paul scholarship, undergraduate and graduate courses on Romans showed me that Christian interpreters too often perceived the letter generally as something of a theological "white paper," without recognizing the way it worked *as argumentation*—the subject of my dissertation in 1989.[1] Observing the centrifugal trajectories of scholarship in the wake of Sanders's explosive work led me to wonder about the politics of interpretation (see chapter 2).

Nor had I entered seminary with the goal of political activism. But these were tumultuous years. Iranian revolutionaries seized the U.S. embassy in Tehran during my first semester at Princeton; Salvadoran Archbishop Oscar Romero was assassinated during my second. Officials of the newly elected administration lied about the rapes and murders of four U.S. churchwomen in El Salvador, blaming the victims themselves,[2] even as they

---

1. Elliott, *The Rhetoric of Romans*.
2. Jeane Kirkpatrick, soon to be Reagan's ambassador to the UN, insisted the women

dissembled about the murder of Romero and misrepresented the cause of liberation theology. Suddenly our class readings had clear and contemporary life-and-death significance.

A few activist Presbyterian student peers slipped petitions "for the people of El Salvador" into their prayers in chapel. I joined the campus Plowshares group and spent a number of Sunday mornings in area churches, discussing the U.S.-sponsored wars in Central America.

Having found my way across Mercer Street to Trinity Episcopal Church, I discovered a communion that took its justice-oriented theologians as a matter of course. These included William Stringfellow, whose *Ethic for Christians and Other Aliens in a Strange Land* I'd read in college. At Evening Prayer on the day his death was announced in 1985, I listened as Trinity members rose to their feet spontaneously, one after another, to offer testimonials of their personal encounters with "Bill."[3] The Rt. Rev. Desmond Tutu adorned the church bulletin board, in a *New York Times* photo showing him standing defiantly, arms crossed, in his bishop's robe as he faced down a heavily armed South African policeman. I learned of the Rev. Carter Heyward, heralded as one of the "Philadelphia Eleven" of 1976, who named the U.S. church's challenge as "doing theology in a counter-revolutionary situation."[4] The Rev. Carol Stoy, Trinity's own formidable deacon, introduced me to the Episcopal liturgy, the Coalition for Nuclear Disarmament, the community food bank, and the Sanctuary Movement as parts of a seamless fabric of life.

The notion that theology and political commitment were related was tested as I began my first full-time teaching position at a Roman Catholic women's college. My first semester there began just weeks after Iraqi President Saddam Hussein sent his tanks across the border into Kuwait. Despite the U.S. ambassador having assured Hussein that Kuwait was of no concern to Washington, George H. W. Bush and members of his cabinet began a relentless mobilization toward war. I joined protest marches in the Twin Cities, even as the largest anti-war movement in history surged around the world, *in advance* of military action. I was unsuccessful in persuading my senior theology department colleagues to organize a teaching moment around the Christian "just-war" tradition, however, because, as I was told, "the case against Saddam is so clear": raising questions in the classroom would needlessly confuse our students.

---

were "political activists"; Reagan's Secretary of State Alexander Haig would testify to Congress that they had died in a "shootout" after trying to run a roadblock.

3. Stringfellow, *An Ethic for Christians and Other Aliens in a Strange Land.*
4. Heyward, "Doing Theology in a Counterrevolutionary Situation."

I frequented the Minneapolis-based Resource Center of the Americas, abuzz with weekly presentations regarding U.S. covert policy in Central America and beyond. At the RCTA, I helped organize the Haiti Justice Committee after the 1991 military coup against democratically elected Haitian president Jean-Bertrand Aristide (a coup orchestrated, we later learned in Congressional testimony, by the CIA).[5] At the RCTA, I met brilliant, impassioned activists, lawyers, social workers, university professors, and engaged laypersons—and heard a number of them declare that their faith commitments informed their work, even as the clergy of their churches had discouraged them from "getting political."

When a more conservative Roman Catholic archbishop was appointed, the theology department chair advised that the word "feminist" should be stricken from our course descriptions, lest conservative students from "outstate" read the term as code for "lesbianism" and create trouble for the college. (I wish I were making this up.)

Later, I served on a faculty committee charged to develop a college-wide course on "the global search for justice." I saw the new curriculum as an opportunity to build the legacy of Catholic Social Teaching into every graduating student's coursework. The committee brought figures like Noam Chomsky, Paul Farmer, and Denis Halliday to campus to speak. Though none was a trained theologian, Chomsky and Farmer spoke eloquently on the theology of liberation; Halliday evoked its preferential option for the poor in explaining his resignation from the UN in protest of the "genocidal" sanctions program against Iraq.[6] Such events created something of a groundswell of interest in theology among faculty and students in other departments—but some of my own theology department colleagues disapproved. No matter that the curriculum revision put Catholic Social Teaching on the agenda of every senior: it also took away a theology requirement that allowed my colleagues to teach their own favorite electives. Meanwhile, a senior theology colleague stumped for neoconservative Michael Novak's argument that the only "preferential option" needed in the United States was already provided by free-market capitalism.[7]

---

5. See Ridgeway, ed., *The Haiti Files*.

6. Chomsky quoted the Reagan national security document declaring war on "the weapons of liberation theology"—meaning, Chomsky pointed out, the *minds* of liberation theologians, which the assassins of Nov. 16, 1989, had directly targeted. Farmer was director of Partners for Health and a superb epidemiologist who had demonstrated that AIDS did not originate in Haiti but spread outward there from U.S. military stations. Halliday resigned in 1998, after a 34-year career at the UN, one of two directors of the "oil-for-food" program to resign in protest.

7. Novak, *Will It Liberate?*

Introduction

These tensions were played out on campus and in churches in the Twin Cities, and of course beyond. They informed my 1994 monograph, *Liberating Paul*, which sought to relate a theological theme, "the justice of God," to "the politics of the apostle." Several currents flowed together in that book. One was concern for the "effective Paul"—the actual ways phrases and concepts from the Pauline corpus (including genuine and pseudepigraphic epistles) were being deployed around us, usually in authoritarian and repressive ways. Robert McAfee Brown had just published the first three Kairos documents, from "third-world" theologians, protesting "state theology" under repressive regimes that relied on snatches of the Pauline letters for sacred legitimacy.[8] Susan Faludi's *Backlash*, also published in 1990, exposed the usefulness of other Pauline texts in "America's undeclared war against women."[9] I knew that the "paper trail" in scholarship on many of the relevant passages did not support the more injurious ways they were customarily deployed.

I also knew that large swaths of Paul scholarship remained preoccupied with other matters, especially with a Protestant agenda that set Paul's lofty spiritual insights high above the supposed ethnocentric and materialist preoccupations of Judaism. That bifurcation, I knew, overlapped with a calm preference for proper "theological" over improper "political" interpretation. And I knew that such scholarship was vulnerable to challenge.

I was stung when several reviewers of *Liberating Paul* avoided questions of substance, where I expected challenges, and instead criticized me for bringing political concerns to the interpretation of Paul's letters instead of sticking properly to *theology*. In a personnel review, my department chair dismissed the work as "not serious scholarship" and mused that it represented "unresolved psychological issues" on my part. (Meanwhile, I found Elisabeth Schüssler Fiorenza's critique of my effort to "rehabilitate" the apostle far more intelligent and on-target; I cited it in a later edition of the book.)[10]

Theology and politics *were* connected, then, but often, in what seemed an inverse relationship. To some, including some of the academics around me, it seemed that "sticking to theology" was a way to avoid political controversy; the status quo was apparently tolerable enough to them. On the other hand, those whose theological convictions led them to work for social change tended not to hold established positions in churches or academic

---

8. Brown, ed., *Kairos*.
9. Faludi, *Backlash*.
10. Elliott, *Liberating Paul*.

departments of religion or theology; they often had no "voice" in theological interpretation.

I was especially gratified, then, when *Liberating Paul* came to Richard A. Horsley's attention at the University of Massachusetts in Boston. Horsley's scholarship had long been inflected by attention to political realities, and his voracious intellectual appetite had recently brought him to consider the latest scholarship on the economy and culture of the Roman Empire, including Simon Price's work on "rituals and power" and Paul Zanker's work on the "power of images."[11] He found a congenial interest in my *Liberating Paul*, and he invited me to work with him and others to organize a new unit at the Society of Biblical Literature on "Paul and Politics." The Consultation (the first stage in development for a group in the SBL) was launched as Horsley published *Paul and Empire* (1997), bringing together recent essays and excerpts from relevant scholarship.

Horsley invited me to contribute a chapter from *Liberating Paul* (see chapter 3 below). At the inaugural session of the Consultation, I gave the address that appears here as chapter 4, laying out something of a program for the political interpretation of Paul. (I had already presented many of its ideas at a conference panel on Paul organized by William S. Campbell at the University of Birmingham, U.K., where Elisabeth Schüssler Fiorenza and I had the first of several very fruitful exchanges.)

The early years of the Consultation, then Group, were productive ones, bringing together a spectacular array of creative scholars. (The Group has continued to the present, under the able leadership of new teams of interpreters.) Horsley approached these academic explorations with the zeal of a community organizer, constantly strategizing how best to bring in new voices, always asking what marginalized perspectives could be brought forward, what new insights needed to be foregrounded.[12] Often, his own explorations were suggestive for the Group's direction and related publication projects—regarding Roman imperialism, the range of "political" interpretations, ancient slavery, "people's history," James C. Scott's work on the partially "hidden transcripts" of subordinates, and more.[13]

My own attempts to extrapolate from Scott's work led me to a new understanding of Jewish experience under Roman rule (see chapter 5). The

---

11. Price, *Rituals and Power*; Zanker, *The Power of Images in the Age of Augustus*.

12. See the appreciative essays gathered in Horsley's honor in Elliott and Kelber, eds., *Bridges in New Testament Interpretation*.

13. Horsley, ed., *Paul and Empire*; Horsley, ed., *Paul and Politics*; Horsley, ed., *Paul and the Roman Imperial Order*; Horsley, ed., *Hidden Transcripts and the Arts of Resistance*; Horsley, ed., *Christian Origins*; Horsley and Callahan, eds., *Slavery in Text and Interpretation*.

Paul and Politics Group's continuing efforts led, in turn, to further insights into Paul's apostolic work as praxis engaged with aspects of imperial culture and ideology (chapter 6). Even Paul's self-presentation as apostle—the subject of older scholarship on his "apostolic *parousia*"—appeared in new light when set in comparison with the contours of imperial claims (chapter 7).

∽

Looking back on the Group's work, I am impressed by the disciplined effort of so many to think carefully through the various dimensions of power relationships and, consequently, of political interpretation—dimensions of ideology and class, persuasion and force, identity and ethnicity, sex and gender, and so much more. I have been just as impressed by how blithely some academic peers have brushed these explorations aside as failures to recognize the sublime *theological* nature of the biblical materials, beside which all else was but chaff. On several occasions I have heard, or read, our work dismissed as the tendentious preoccupation of disgruntled American Leftists frustrated by George W. Bush's war in Iraq. I still marvel: does that accusation mean we should presume that more narrowly *theologically-*minded scholars are more sanguine regarding that, or other military and paramilitary adventures?

∽

I learned of the attacks of September 11, 2001, during the course of an extended phone conference as one of several U.S. staff for a Haitian NGO. It seemed clear to me and my colleagues that our nation was under a systematic attack, of a scope still unknown. We also were keenly aware that our work to get desperately needed funds and equipment to several peasant cooperatives might well prevent the deaths of several thousand Haitian men, women, and children over the coming months, as famine in the Artibonite valley and the callous neoliberal policies of the "Washington consensus" combined to effect what the United Nations declared the most severe "depth of hunger" in the hemisphere. So, we continued our phone call. The training for my staff position had included rounds of policy briefings with development officers and NGO officials in Washington, but I had heard the most succinct analyses of the neoliberal order from women in cooperatives in the Artibonite—some of them learning to read for the first time. *Plan Gwangou*, they called it: "the starvation plan."

My experiences in and around Haiti brought home to me the depth of material realities involved in proper political interpretation. They also made me acutely receptive to arguments by scholars like Justin Meggitt and Stephen Friesen, who challenged fundamental assumptions regarding the social and economic location of Paul and the members of the assemblies to which he wrote. Instead of little gatherings of middle-class artisans and shopkeepers, entrepreneurs happily competing in the "marketplace" alongside a sprinkling of the very rich and poor—assumptions prevalent enough, comfortable enough, in what Friesen aptly called "capitalist criticism"[14]—their scholarship was attuned to the dynamics of poverty and the strategies of survival employed among the poor. Their work had a significant impact on my understanding, as evident in chapter 8, which returns to questions of "Paul and Empire" but with greater attention to economic realities.

Those insights also gave focus to my monograph *The Arrogance of Nations: Reading Romans in the Shadow of Empire* (2008), an initial volume in the Paul in Critical Contexts series. Romans had never been far from my sight, and *Arrogance of Nations* relied on other previous essays that are now gathered into other volumes from Cascade Books.[15] This volume revolves around the interplay of "Paul within Judaism" and "Paul and Empire" research, as the two final essays here make clear. Chapter 9 argues that addressing the second area, "the political question," is key to making sense of the first. Chapter 10 is a fuller version of an essay for a volume dedicated to the question "what does 'within Judaism' scholarship mean?" My own answer is that a Marxist approach to historiography requires attending to the dynamics of power—and that, in turn, must reorient our discussion of the New Testament writings—Paul in particular here—toward a thick description of ancient Judaism.

Throughout this volume, I hope also to argue that an adequate historical understanding—of the apostle Paul, but also of ourselves—will remain elusive unless and until we recognize and push against the powerful conforming pressures of a dominant form of Christian theology in the Capitalocene. That conviction continues to inform and motivate my work.[16]

---

14. Meggitt, *Paul, Poverty, and Survival*; Friesen, "Poverty in Pauline Studies"; Friesen, "The Blessings of Hegemony."

15. See Elliott, *Currents in the Interpretation of Paul: Collected Essays*; and Elliott, *Paul against the Nations: Soundings in Romans*.

16. See the superb treatments by Keller, *Political Theology of the Earth*; and Rieger, *Theology in the Capitalocene*, with which I am in complete sympathy. I anticipate joining their cause with a new monograph, *Bodies of Christ: A Materialist Theology of the New Testament*, in the near future.

Given the focus of these essays, some overlap and repetition are perhaps inevitable, but not, I hope, distracting. Except where I have noted, I have not edited the essays beyond bringing them into some stylistic conformity, especially regarding citations.

The reader will also observe some terminological variation over the years in which these essays were written. I have translated the Greek *Ioudaioi* as "Jews" but also as "Judeans," meaning with the latter word to indicate the geographic and ethnic sense of the term but without restricting it to those meanings. (The effort of some interpreters to render *Ioudaioi* as a merely geographic term used by "Israelites" elsewhere, e.g. in Galilee, seems to me transparently to serve theological or apologetic Christian interests, and I find it unconvincing.) Although I used the term "Gentile" or "Gentile-Christian" in earlier essays, it has always troubled me: the Roman world knew no ethnic identification of "Gentiles," and Paul's use of the plural *ethnē* fairly clearly continues the Septuagintal use that is almost always rendered "nations," i.e. "the nations other than Israel."

Finally, while some theologically minded Paul scholars cavil at any discussion of the Roman Empire because the apostle did not name any Emperors or officials directly, I argue that in specific cases he seems clearly to have imperial theopolitical claims—to authority, to justice, to mercy, to destiny, to divine approval—in mind; but readers will judge for themselves whether these arguments are compelling. I have also sought, in referring to contemporary realities, to use the language of "empire" with more restraint than it is often used in contemporary political, philosophical, and, yes, theological discussions. My goal has been to be as precise and transparent as possible in moving between our judgments regarding the ancient world and those regarding our own.

1

Situating the Apostle Paul in His Day and Engaging His Legacy in Our Own

AFTER JESUS OF NAZARETH, the apostle Paul is the most significant figure in the New Testament. The letters he wrote, other letters attributed to him, and the portion of the Acts of the Apostles dedicated to him together account for about a third of its pages. In Christian churches that read the Bible according to lectionary cycles, Paul's is the single voice more often heard than any other, as his Epistles are read in all three years of a cycle. Throughout Christian history, Paul has been revered as one of the chief witnesses of the risen Christ (1 Cor 15:3–8) and as his "apostle to the nations" (Rom 1:1–5, 13; 11:13; 15:16–18; Gal 2:8). (The Greek word *apostolos* means one "sent," as on a mission; the translation "nations" will be discussed below.)

But from the beginning, Paul was also opposed, and today he is held by many men and women in suspicion, within the churches as much as outside them. Paul has been reviled—and not only in the modern age!—as a religious huckster who betrayed the teaching of Jesus, concocted a mythology of heavenly redemption through his death, and, in his enthusiasm for that religion, imposed on his converts a harsh doctrine of subordination to gender and social hierarchies.[1] His detractors have regarded him as a spiritual charlatan at worst, a deeply flawed personality at best, and have regarded his letters as a toxic residue still leaching into contemporary culture with harmful consequences. Even in churches where his figure elicits deep devotion, Paul also evokes wariness, even antipathy, among men and women who have suffered real injuries under the invocation of his name.

---

1. Famously, Kazantzakis, *The Last Temptation of Christ*, 473–77.

To the historian of Christian origins, and of the relationship between early Christianity and Judaism in particular, Paul's letters are indispensable. But because the information they provide is partial and far less than the historian would like to produce a convincing picture, we are compelled to fill in the blanks with educated, but nonetheless imaginative reconstructions. Not surprisingly, historians draw different conclusions, due to the different weights they give to various aspects of the evidence and to their assumptions about the scope and significance of their subject—assumptions shaped as much by social location as by the scientific aura of historiography.

Paul's letters also present considerable challenges to readers seeking spiritual inspiration or theological clarity. They may be surprised how uninterested Paul actually appears to have been in explaining metaphors or themes that have subsequently proven important for Christian doctrine. The obvious explanation is that Paul wrote his letters for others, far removed from us in historical circumstance and cultural presuppositions, and simply did not explain what he presumed his readers would understand. But because Paul himself repeatedly declares that scripture (by which he meant Israel's scripture) was "written for our sake" and provides examples "for us" (1 Cor 9:8; 10:1–11), and a later Pauline letter declares that "all scripture is inspired by God and useful for teaching, for reproof, for correction, and for training in righteousness" (2 Tim 3:16), the rehearsal of such phrases have encouraged many modern readers to expect that his words (which, after all, are "scripture" for many in our day) should be completely transparent and self-explanatory to the spiritually discerning. These readers will often be disappointed. Unfortunately, too few churches today regard complicating such expectations as part of their agenda.

Beyond the confines of Christian churches as well as within them, statements from Paul's letters have come to be woven into the fabric of social roles and expectations in contemporary life, in the public sphere and domestic spaces alike. Modern readers may well find ourselves chafing against those statements. Much of the contemporary interest in Paul—in scholarly circles as well as beyond them—is driven by concerns to address the sometimes ambivalent, sometimes acutely painful legacy of his remarks, most often by seeking to set them into one or another historical context in Paul's life or the life of one or another assembly. None of these efforts have yet won universal acceptance, however, for reasons that cannot be attributed solely to the agendas—or the obstinacy—of the apostle's various interpreters. Paul's letters themselves present a confounding array of puzzles and problems. Even if a particular reconstruction of the past should prove convincing, its significance for the present would remain a conundrum, for Paul's letters are accorded very different levels of authority in different churches, let alone in a putatively secular society.

This entry will not attempt to resolve these interpretive questions or to set out a definitive portrait of Paul. To the contrary, one of its themes will be the remarkable variety of alternative interpretations on offer today. The task will instead be to identify some of the most important questions raised in the encounter with Paul and to discuss the sorts of decisions readers must make in the attempt to answer them. We will proceed in an order corresponding to the sequence in commentary entries in this volume.* First, we will explore aspects of Paul's letters and of his apostolic work in their ancient context. Next, we will consider some of the varied ways Paul has been remembered, and appropriated, through history. At last, we will turn to questions of Paul's legacy, and the interpreter's responsibility, today.

HISTORICAL PUZZLES IN THE LETTERS

Paul's letters are important to the historian for several reasons. They offer the only direct access to a first-person voice in the New Testament. (Jesus left behind no writings; the Gospel narrators are anonymous; and the Epistles that appear under the names of Peter, James, and John are considered by many scholars to be pseudonymous: see the introductions to those writings).* They are also the earliest writings from the nascent movement of believers in Christ (with the possible exception of the hypothetical document Q: see the Introduction to the Gospels).*

But it is the powerful quasi-biographical story that lies behind Paul's letters that attracts and intrigues the historian, no less than the Christian believer. It is the story of a Pharisee, "zealous" for the law and ardent in his opposition to the earliest followers of Jesus, who was caught up short when "God revealed his son" to him and "called" Paul to be Christ's apostle (Gal 1:13–17). That language evokes Israel's prophets, who were "called" and "sent" to deliver God's word; and if Jeremiah could speak of the Word of the Lord like a fire "burning" irrepressibly in his bones (Jer. 20:8–9), Paul could declare that he had been "crucified with Christ; and it is no longer I who live, but Christ lives in me" (Gal 2:19–20). The intensity of the experience to which Paul repeatedly alludes has long attracted the attention of theorists of religion, whether or not they are sympathetic to Christian belief.[2] Further,

---

* Throughout this essay, cross-references marked with asterisks are to other essays in Aymer, Kittredge, and Sánchez, eds., *Fortress Commentary on the Bible: The New Testament* (2014).

2. Meeks and Fitzgerald, *The Writings of Paul*; Ashton, *The Religion of Paul the Apostle*.

Paul's sharp juxtaposition of his "earlier life in Judaism" (Gal 1:13–14) with his newfound life "in Christ" has long been read as evidence of his "conversion," his abrupt and total reversal from life under Torah to life in a new reality, though that understanding has been challenged and largely undermined, at least in scholarly circles, in the last half of the twentieth century.[3]

Whatever its nature (a question to which we return below), the intensity of Paul's experience is echoed in the intensity of concern he expresses for "all the churches" (2 Cor 11:28), the assemblies that he founded in various cities in Asia Minor, Macedonia, and Achaia. (The Greek word *ekklēsia* is usually translated "church" in English Bibles, and the Latin loanword *ecclesia* gives us the adjective "ecclesiastical" for all things churchly, but *ekklēsia* was also used in Paul's day for a civic assembly in a Greek city, and so a growing minority of interpreters prefer the translation "assembly.") The letters provide us tantalizing glimpses onto landscapes of community life in very different congregations, landscapes that defy easy description or even harmonization with each other. Because Paul addresses a bewildering assortment of issues in his correspondence with the Corinthian believers, our 1 and 2 Corinthians, which probably represent a compilation of earlier, more fragmentary letters (see the entries for each letter), are irresistible to the historian, and have often been used as the primary evidence for generalizations about "Pauline Christianity."[4] —But what situation should we imagine prompted these letters: a rift between Paul and the (more law-observant) Jerusalem apostles and their adherents (C. K. Barrett)? The impulses of an incipient Gnosticism among the Corinthians (Walther Schmithals)? Differences in economic status, reflected in theological conflicts (Gerd Theissen)? Tension between Paul's social experience and that of inspired women in the congregations (Antoinette Clark Wire)?[5] Each of these answers (and there are more!) grasps at real clues in the letters, but none has won universal recognition for its capacity to explain the whole. And the issues Paul encountered in Corinth are quite different from those he addressed in letters to other cities!

And how should we understand Paul himself? To take a single question as an example, Paul tells the Romans that the horizon of his concern for the assemblies is not just the calling to secure "the obedience of faith among all the nations" (Rom 1:5, my translation): that obligation is based in a deeper anguish for his "own people," that is, "Israelites" (Rom 9:1–5).

3. Stendahl, *Paul among Jews and Gentiles*; but see Kim, *The Origins of Paul's Gospel*.

4. Meeks, *The First Urban Christians*; Theissen, *The Social Setting of Pauline Christianity*.

5. Barrett, "Cephas and Corinth"; Schmithals, *Gnosticism in Corinth*; Theissen, *Social Setting of Pauline Christianity*; Wire, *Corinthian Women Prophets*.

It is the clashing juxtaposition of what generations of readers have taken as Paul's "conversion," or from another perspective, his apparent *apostasy* from Judaism, with such expressions of abiding *loyalty* to the people Israel that generates some of the liveliest controversies in biblical scholarship today. Should we understand Paul as having left central aspects of his former life in Judaism behind, or, as a matter of principle, interpret his work and thought *within* Judaism?[6]

STORIES WE TELL ABOUT PAUL

In the mid-twentieth century, Rudolf Bultmann wrote what stands as a crisp summary of Paul's place in early Christianity: "Standing within the frame of Hellenistic Christianity, he raised the theological motifs that were at work in the proclamation of the Hellenistic church to the clarity of theological thinking; he called to attention the problems latent in the Hellenistic proclamation and brought them to a decision; and thus—so far as our sources permit an opinion on the matter—became the founder of Christian theology."[7] This summary makes clear that Paul did not develop his views from nothing, as some sort of theological genius: he joined a movement already in the lively process of developing beliefs and practices, and he received its most important traditions (see 1 Cor 11:2, 23–26; 15:3–7). Scholars differ, however, among themselves and with Bultmann, regarding the key phrase in this summary. What *were* "the problems latent in the Hellenistic proclamation"? Bultmann recognized that Paul did not invent a movement that welcomed non-Jews without requiring Torah observance of them; that is, he already stood "within the frame of Hellenistic Christianity." But that frame appeared more a strategy of opportunity than a theological principle, and talk of freedom from the law could easily be construed as mere libertinism. For Bultmann (as for many Protestant interpreters before and after him), Paul's grappling with the Hellenistic church required him to resolve tensions inherent in the characteristically Jewish understanding of the human before God, which *had* been Paul's own understanding, and the understanding to which Paul had been brought "in Christ," especially regarding the role of the law in the human's obedience to God's claim. Even "within the frame of Hellenistic Christianity," then, the apostle was preoccupied in letter after letter by an implicit debate *with Judaism*. The eventual prevalence of a law-free "Gentile" church is not a historical accident or an aberration, but the triumph of Paul's own ideas: thus, although he did not write the letter to the

---

6. Nanos and Zetterholm, eds., *Paul within Judaism*.
7. Bultmann, *Theology of the New Testament*, 1:187.

Situating Paul in His Day and Engaging His Legacy in Our Own

Ephesians, its calm assurance of the Torah's irrelevance to those who are "in Christ" can be regarded, on this view, as "the quintessence of Paulinism."[8]

(Here a note on the translation of a Greek term, *ethnē*, is important. The word, a plural, literally means "peoples" or "nations," and is used throughout Jewish scripture to mean the nations *other than Israel*. In many English New Testament translations, however, it is rendered "Gentiles." The capitalized form is potentially misleading since it suggests a coherent ethnic identity, like "Scythian" or "Egyptian," though no individuals in the ancient world called themselves "Gentiles." Furthermore, the same word is sometimes translated two different ways in the same Bible. For example, the NRSV uses "nations" in Isaiah, but "Gentiles" in Romans 15:9–12, *even where Paul is quoting the same passages from Isaiah*. The effect is subtle, but meaningful: it suggests that Paul imagines two sorts of people in the world, "Jews" and "everyone else," and is preoccupied with the boundary line that distinguishes them.)

Just this understanding of Paul has been hotly contested in the late twentieth and early twenty-first centuries, however. At the risk of an inevitable measure of imprecision, we may broadly distinguish three "stories" that interpreters now tell about the apostle.

Paul as Convert from Judaism

The first story prevailed in Bultmann's day, as it still does today in much of Christianity. Paul received a preeminent education as a Jew (Acts names him "Saul" in this period and makes him a student of the famed rabbi Gamaliel II: Acts 5:34; 22:3). Indeed, his self-professed credentials, "as to the law, a Pharisee; as to zeal, a persecutor of the church; as to righteousness under the law, blameless" (Phil. 3:5–6), "zealous for the traditions of my ancestors" (Gal 1:14), are an accurate self-appraisal as an exemplary Jew. It is as a representative Jew that he sought "a righteousness of [his] own that comes from the law" (Phil. 3:9), for all Israel characteristically strove for "the righteousness that is based on the law, . . . as if it were based on works" (Rom 9:31–32). On this view, Paul (Saul) the Pharisee persecuted the early believers in Jesus because they had, in some way he found intolerable, flouted or ignored the law. The reversal occasioned by the "revelation" of Christ to him was nothing less than a conversion, a personal about-face from one who now abandoned any effort at achieving his own righteousness through works of law and accepted instead the righteousness "on the basis of faith," meaning trust in Jesus (Rom 9:32). From this point on, Paul was opposed

---

8. Peake, "The Quintessence of Paulinism."

by other Jews because he adamantly insisted the law had no positive role in salvation: it provided only the knowledge of sin (Rom 7:7). His resolve to approach those outside the law "as one outside the law" (1 Cor 9:19–21) and his judgment that "nothing is unclean in itself" (Rom 14:14) show his rejection of the Torah's binding authority. Even the Jerusalem apostles (and their delegates) fought Paul on these points, refusing to accept shared meals between Jews and "Gentiles" at Antioch (Gal 2:11–14; on the view that the law forbade even social "associations" between Jews and Gentiles, see Acts 10:28). Paul saw this failure as hypocrisy on the part of the apostles (Gal 2:14), and could only regard with anguish his fellow Jews' stubborn insistence on that righteousness "as if based on works." Though Paul (in Gal 2:1–9) and Acts (15:1–29) agree that the Jerusalem apostles accepted his mission to the "uncircumcision," they apparently acquiesced when Paul was accused by other Jews of flouting the law himself and teaching other Jews to do the same (see Acts 21:17–36). Jewish antagonists further accused Paul (falsely, according to Luke) of bringing Gentiles into the Temple court, a capital offense—but James and the other apostles play no further role in Luke's narrative. Paul's subsequent pleas before "kings and governors" (see Luke 21:12) are eloquent arguments that he represents the true legacy of Israel's scriptures, but by the end of the story he has convinced only a minority of Jews who hear him. The "parting of the ways" between Judaism and Christianity is already evident in the response to Paul, and the anguish he expressed for his "kindred according to the flesh" (Rom 9:1–4) was his response to their final failure to obey his gospel.

    This is the account most familiar to readers today, and still predominates in Christian preaching. Since the last quarter of the twentieth century it has been challenged, however, ultimately because of several landmark developments. One is the discovery in the 1940s and 1950s of the Dead Sea Scrolls, which bore abundant witness to a form of Judaism that could not be identified with the "works-righteousness" Paul presumably opposed, and that often sounded "Pauline," as in its insistence that "by [God's] righteousness alone is a human righteous" (11QH 5.18; 8.12; etc.). Because the Scrolls also included multiple copies of some Jewish texts that had previously been known, but marginalized in biblical interpretation (e.g., *Jubilees*, *1 Enoch*), they sparked renewed interest in such "pseudepigraphic" writings and a growing awareness that second-Temple Judaism was a far richer and more complex array of religious expressions than the traditional account had allowed.

    Second, in the wake of the mass murder of European Jews (the Shoah or "Holocaust"), many European and U.S. churches turned to processes of institutional soul-searching, seeking to identify and repudiate aspects of

Christian teaching that traded in stereotype and caricature of Jews and Judaism (see, notably, the Roman Catholic document *Nostra Aetate*). In this changed environment, older Jewish objections to Paul's rhetoric suddenly gained new attention from Christian and other interpreters. Third, these developments provided the space in which new and innovative scholarly monographs appeared that reconfigured the relationship of Paul, Judaism, and the origins of Christianity.[9] E. P. Sanders' demonstration in 1977 that the traditional understanding of "works-righteousness" was *not* current in Paul's day issued in a changed climate, sometimes called the "post-Sanders era," in which a "new perspective on Paul" began to take shape.[10]

Paul the Champion of a Law-Free Church

The "new perspective" (now more than thirty years old!) actually includes a variety of different interpretations, united by their acceptance of the agenda posed by Sanders.

We may nevertheless sketch the outlines of a coherent second narrative in this array of "new perspective" readings. Here, Paul is *not* assumed to have been a representative Jew, but (taking him at his word) is seen to have persecuted the early churches out of an extreme hyper-observance, having been "*far more* zealous for the traditions of my ancestors" than his peers (Gal 1:13–14, emphasis added). Paul did not suffer the sort of introspective anguish regarding his own salvation that would later preoccupy Martin Luther and subsequent Western interpreters; rather than being "converted" to a new understanding of redemption, Paul experienced a "call" similar to the call of Israel's prophets.[11] This calling was specifically to bring a *biblical*, i.e., *Jewish* message of salvation to the nations (or "Gentiles"). The proper focus of interpretation, on this view, is thus not "soteriology" (the salvation of individuals) but the sociological behavior of groups. The "works of law" against which Paul repeatedly inveighed (Gal 2:16; 3:2, 5, 10; Rom 3:27–28; 4:2, 4–6; 9:32; 11:6) are now relieved of the burden of summarizing a Jewish theology of redemption; they should instead be identified with specific "boundary-maintaining" practices that distinguished Jews from their non-Jewish neighbors, especially circumcision, kosher diet, and sabbath observance. Rather than opposing a Jewish understanding of "redemption" or "justification from works," Paul was defending the "Gentile church" from

9. Ruether, *Faith and Fratricide*; Stendahl, *Paul among Jews and Gentiles*; Sanders, *Paul and Palestinian Judaism*.

10. Dunn, "New Perspective on Paul"; Dunn, *Theology of Paul the Apostle*.

11. Stendahl, *Paul among Jews and Gentiles*.

Jewish opponents who sought to incorporate Paul's converts into Jewish life according to more traditional channels—the acceptance of circumcision and observance of Torah. The difference between Paul and other Jews, then, involved a question of the scope of salvation, rather than its mechanism. Was the covenant people limited to Israel (and "converts" or proselytes to Judaism), or did it, on Paul's innovation, include non-Jews as full members?

Challenges have been raised to this second narrative as well. Except for a few voices who have concluded that Paul's own thought was "inconsistent" or "incoherent,"[12] many "new perspective" interpreters still put Paul forward as the pioneer of an intelligible and appropriately inclusive faith—the indispensable ancestor of contemporary Christianity. But this also means that Paul is not infrequently contrasted with negative characterizations of Jewish "ethnocentrism" or exclusivism. His identity as a Jew is affirmed and his conflicts with other Jews are regarded as "inner-Jewish" controversies, but the often unavoidable implication is that Paul and his associates alone represented the open, inclusive, "right" legacy of Judaism, in contrast to the narrow and ill-fated insistence of his contemporaries on ethnic boundaries to the covenant people. The "parting of the ways" between Christianity and Judaism still appears here to be foreshadowed in Paul's controversies with other Jews.

Paul the (non-Christian) Jew

A third narrative has emerged from a small group of interpreters—many of them Jewish New Testament scholars—who seek thoroughly to interpret Paul's work and thought within Judaism, without appeal to a dramatic interruption (Paul's vision of Christ) that somehow set him on a course that necessarily led him away from it. On this account, Paul the Pharisee persecuted the early *ekklēsiai* not because of any halakhic deviation on their part, but because their (thoroughly Jewish) proclamation of a messiah who had been crucified by Rome was potentially threatening to the precarious stability of other Jewish communities under Roman rule.[13] Paul's vision of the crucified Jesus in heaven (as obliquely reported in 2 Corinthians 12) was formally similar to other Jewish visionary experiences;[14] and while Segal himself did not pursue the implications, it is possible to regard the vision of Christ as impelling Paul to conclusions regarding God's sovereignty over the nations

---

12. Paul "thought backward" (Sanders, *Paul and Palestinian Judaism*); see also Räisänen, *Paul and the Law*.

13. Fredriksen, *From Jesus to Christ*, 133–76.

14. Segal, *Paul the Convert*.

that fit on the spectrum of conclusions drawn by other Jewish apocalyptists.[15] This vision involved no halakhic "conversion": Paul remained a Jew (and never became a "Christian").[16] These interpreters point out that there is no evidence anywhere in his letters that Paul himself relinquished observance of Torah (1 Cor 9:19–21 describes only a rhetoric of empathy, not a change of identity), or taught other Jews to do so. It did involve Paul's perception of non-Jewish adherents to the proclamation of Jesus as the fulfillment of biblical prophecy: they were the "nations" who would turn to Israel and Israel's messiah at the last day. (Note here that the term *ethnē* is given its more natural meaning "nations": Paul's concern is not with the un-Jewish ethnic identity of individuals, but with relations between the world's nations and Israel and the biblical vision of international harmony to be achieved in the messianic age.)

Paul's resistance to the pressure to "normalize" these converts by making them Jews had nothing to do with any perceived insufficiency in Judaism or the law. It had everything to do with his expectation that *morally* converted non-Jews—rare enough, in diaspora Jewish eyes—*united around obedience to Israel's Messiah, and in solidarity with Israel*—would be as clear a signal to other Jews as they were to him that the messianic age had dawned. His organization of a collection for "the poor among the holy ones" in Jerusalem (Rom 15:25–28), which he perceived both as a gesture of reciprocity and as a sacred "offering" that he presented as a priestly service (Rom 15:14–16, 27), was motivated by this expectation.

On this interpretation, already foreshadowed in some ways by Johannes Munck, Paul's disagreements with the Jerusalem apostles (e.g., in Antioch: Galatians 2) are not deep theological fissures, but tactical or rhetorical differences.[17] His differences from Jews outside the assemblies arose, on one side, from his belief that the messianic age has arrived, and on the other, from the concern of Jews who did not share that belief to protect their communities from the sort of scrutiny or suspicion that messianic agitation on the part of Paul's almost-unwashed newcomers might prompt. As to the question of justification from works of law, interpreters in this third perspective hew methodologically to the principle that any of Paul's statements regarding the law *made in letters addressed primarily to non-Jews* should be read narrowly as statements about the significance of the law *for non-Jews*, rather than universal statements about the Torah's role in salvation

---

15. Elliott, *Liberating Paul*, 140–80.

16. Eisenbaum, *Paul Was not a Christian*.

17. See Munck, *Paul and the Salvation of Mankind*; now Nanos, *Mystery of Romans*; and Nanos, *Irony of Galatians*.

generally. The nature of *Jewish* opposition to Paul is less the focus of attention here than in the preceding two perspectives; on the other hand, the possible motivations of *non-Jews* in Paul's assemblies to adopt *some* Torah observances—but not all (see Gal 5:2–3)—is a paramount consideration. Here, interpreters explore possible reasons for anxiety on the part of non-Jews who may have seen in the Torah the promise of achieving the goal of "self-mastery" (*enkrateia*) so highly prized in post-Augustan culture (Stowers), or (in Galatia) might have sought to "pass" in Roman society, taking on some of the mystique of the synagogue in order to make their refusal of customary Roman worship ("idolatry") more palatable to their Roman neighbors.[18] Paul's resistance to "Judaizing" is seen here as his thoroughly Jewish reaction to aberrant behavior on the part of non-Jews.

Similarly, the letter to the Romans has been read as an admonitory warning to non-Jews not to show disdain or contempt for Jews. That warning is evident enough in Rom 11:13–32, but in earlier interpretation was often seen as an isolated aside. When chaps. 9–11 are read as the "climax" of the letter and the whole letter is read as rhetoric directed to a primarily non-Jewish audience, the brief address to a hypothetical Jew in Romans 2–3 no longer is seen as an attempt to "explode Jewish privilege"; rather it supports the overarching purpose of the letter to correct non-Jewish error. Here, too, Paul appears to offer a fundamentally Jewish response to aspects of the emerging Hellenistic church.[19]

Paul against Roman Imperial Ideology

If, in service of the last-named narrative, interpreters have tried in different ways to understand Paul within Judaism, that effort seems also to have involved understanding Judaism not just as a *religion* or an *ethnic identification* (it was, of course, both in Paul's day), but also as participation in an identity construed in different ways by outsiders. The experience of Jews *under Roman rule*—as a minority population seeking civic recognition in different Roman cities and under different imperial regimes—becomes a central requirement of such interpretation of Paul.[20] A new field of study has sprung up since the late 1980s around the relationship between "Paul and Empire," initially seeking to challenge the apolitical character of previous "theological" scholarship and to wrest Paul from what had become a fairly

---

18. Gaston, *Paul and the Torah*; Nanos, *Irony of Galatians*, 257–71; Stowers, *A Rereading of Romans*; Kahl, *Galatians Re-Imagined*.
19. Elliott, *Rhetoric of Romans*; Elliott, *Arrogance of Nations*.
20. Smallwood, *Jews under Roman Rule*.

tight grip on his legacy on the political right. "Paul and Empire" scholarship and the adjacent field of postcolonial study of Paul have now become themselves the object of scrutiny and debate, which is all to the good.[21] It bears note, however, that these areas are not only concerned with the ways Paul is interpreted and appropriated for political purposes today. They also inform, and necessarily so, the investigation of Paul as a member of the Jewish diaspora in the Roman world.[22]

THE PARADOX OF READING PAUL'S LETTERS TODAY

Many, perhaps most readers of Paul's letters come to them with religious interest. Paul's letters have long offered Christianity a rich resource for devotion and for theological reflection. As mentioned above, the letters are the most frequently encountered vein of scripture in many churches. At least some of the more lyrical passages in them, such as Paul's assurance that "nothing will be able to separate us from the love of God in Christ Jesus our Lord" (Rom 8:28–39) or his praise of love as the "better way" (1 Cor 12:31—13:13), are among the most cherished passages of scripture for many people. Metaphors that appear in Paul's arguments have exercised powerful and decisive influence in Christian theology: that of baptism as a "dying with Christ," for example (Rom 6:3–11), or of the church as the "body" of Christ (Rom 12:3-7; 1 Cor 12:4–30), or the Lord's Supper as a proclamation of the death of Jesus (1 Cor 11:17–34). Paul's use of an apparently preexisting Christian hymn in Philippians has shaped Christian understanding of the divinity of Christ as one who, though "in the form of God," "emptied himself" to accept "the form of a slave" and humbled himself even further, in obedience to God, to the point of "death on a cross" (Phil. 2:6–8).

This familiarity makes for a remarkable paradox: When we read these letters today, we do so with purposes Paul never imagined, and may grant them an importance they never enjoyed in Paul's own day. They are our primary source for understanding Paul; that was not true for Paul's first readers. The possibility of reading the letters anachronistically inevitably increases when they are incorporated into modern worship as "scripture."

It is customary in modern scholarship to distinguish the letters whose authenticity has only rarely been questioned from other letters that appear under his name, but are regarded by many scholars as pseudepigrapha—"falsely

---

21. See Horsley, ed., *Paul and Empire*; Horsley, ed., *Paul and Politics*; Horsley, ed., *Paul and the Roman Imperial Order*; Stanley, ed., *Colonized Apostle*; McKnight and Modica, eds., *Jesus Is Lord, Caesar Is Not*.

22. Nanos and Zetterholm, eds., *Paul within Judaism*.

attributed" writings by others, after Paul's death, who traded on his name to win acceptance for their ideas. The genuine (or "unquestioned") letters are Romans, 1 and 2 Corinthians, Galatians, Philippians, 1 Thessalonians, and Philemon. (This is their order of appearance in our New Testament, based originally on decreasing length; their chronological order is indicated in the timeline below.) The pseudepigrapha include Colossians and Ephesians (but see the entry on Colossians),* 2 Thessalonians, and the Pastoral Epistles (see the introduction to those letters).* The genuine letters are premiere sources for understanding the beginnings of Christianity, but are puzzling and paradoxical sources, nonetheless. But the New Testament collection makes no distinction between "genuine" and pseudepigraphic letters, presenting all alike as "Pauline Epistles" and as scripture.

Fig. 1.1. A Basic Chronology of Paul's Life and Career[23]

33	The crucifixion of Jesus
34	Paul's "conversion" (or, better, call)
35–38	Missionary activity in Arabia (including escape from Damascus and from the ethnarch Aretas IV)
38	First visit to Jerusalem
38–48	Missionary activity in Syria and Cilicia
48	Second visit to Jerusalem (the "Apostolic Council")
48–52	Missionary activity in Asia Minor (Galatia), northern Greece (Philippi, Thessalonica, and Beroea), and Achaia (including Corinth)
	50–56 Writing of 1 Thessalonians
	51–52 Hearing before Gallio
52–55	Missionary activity centered in Ephesus. Writing of Galatians, 1 Corinthians, portions of 2 Corinthians, Philemon, perhaps Philippians
55–57	Final missionary activity in Greece (Macedonia and Achaia). Writing of other portions of 2 Corinthians and, from Corinth, Romans
57–59	Journey to Jerusalem with offering; arrest and imprisonment
59–60	Journey to Rome as prisoner

23. After Taylor, *Paul, Apostle to the Nations*.

60–62   Imprisonment in Rome; perhaps writing of Philippians and Philemon

ca. 62   Execution under Nero

The Paradox of "Theological" or "Pastoral" Readings

It is a little incongruous for readers today to approach even Paul's genuine letters to discover his "theology." We do not have a sample of the message Paul initially proclaimed to gather a community (although many interpreters have tried to read Romans as such). Rather, all of the letters were written to assemblies some time *after* Paul, or, in the case of Romans, others, had founded them. In his letters, Paul sought to strengthen or occasionally, as he saw it, to correct their adherence to Christ, and as a consequence, the letters have a theological character, but they never spell out his convictions in any systematic way. Paul often leaves a key conviction unspoken, since he could presume his audience already had heard, or heard about, his proclamation. The letters are therefore problematic sources, at best, for describing "Paul's theology."

The passage from Philippians cited above, for example, shows that Paul's understanding of the death of Jesus already depended on traditions he received from early assemblies that preceded him. He explicitly acknowledged as much when he wrote to the Corinthians, "I handed on to you as of first importance what I in turn had received: that Christ died for our sins in accordance with the scriptures . . ." (1 Cor 15:3). Note that Paul does not explain here which scriptures he has in mind, or just what dying "for our sins" meant. In fact, Paul could describe the salvific value of Christ's death in very different ways: as a "sacrifice of atonement" (*hilastērion*, Rom 3:24–25), though Paul never elaborates a comparison with the ritual of the Day of Atonement (as does Hebrews); or as the slaughter (NRSV: "sacrifice") of a Passover lamb (1 Cor 5:7)—a very different ritual!—or as deliverance from the "curse" of Deut 21:23, though, again, this reference seems to have played no larger part in his thinking (Gal 3:13). Surprisingly, amid these diverse and conflicting metaphors, Paul never offers even a rudimentary explanation of just *how* he understands Christ to have "died for our sins." He is more concerned, in Romans, to insist that those who have "died *with* Christ" in baptism (another dramatic metaphor that is simply asserted, not explained) can no longer live in sin, having been joined to Christ's obedience (Romans 5–6).

His purpose in these letters (and in the apostolic work of which they are occasional instruments) has been described as "pastoral," but Paul was not evidently interested in the sort of long-term spiritual accompaniment of individuals and families in settled congregations that we associate today with pastoral ministry. (Indeed, he seems intentionally to have left such work to others whom he described as his "coworkers," *synergoi*.) The "daily pressure" about which Paul complained to the Corinthians, caused by his "anxiety for all the assemblies" ("churches": 2 Cor 11:28, NRSV), was less oriented to the self-fulfillment of individuals than to the sanctity in which they were to maintain themselves. ("Saints"—literally, "holy ones" [*hagioi*]—was Paul's preferred designation for members of his assemblies.) Looking at the non-Jewish world through the eyes of a Hellenistic Jew, Paul regarded the hallmarks of such holiness in the avoidance of the vices characteristic of that world—the worship of other gods, using tangible forms ("idolatry"), and a range of sexual transgressions to which he simply referred as "immorality" (*porneia*)[24]—and the maintenance of an ethos of affectionate mutual regard characteristic of the idealized Roman household. Paul sought to establish a sort of baseline of such holiness and then, on an ad hoc basis, to perform whatever corrections were needed to maintain it. We might consider Paul "pastoral," then, to the extent that he was an "advisor" who "counsels" his congregations, "in order to be able to present them to Christ at his coming, which Paul expected in the near future."[25]

He described his work to the Romans in terms of priestly service (*latreuein*, Rom 1:9; *diakonos, leitourgos, hierourgōn*, 15:8, 16, terms associated with public ritual action). He sought to present to God "the obedience of the nations" (Rom 15:17; see 1:5–6), represented in each city by the holy living of individuals on whom he called to present their bodies as "a living sacrifice, holy and acceptable to God" (Rom 12:1–2), and on an international scale by the sanctified "offerings [*prosphora*] of the nations" (Rom 15:16–17). The latter phrase rang with the language of the prophet Isaiah's vision in which the earth's nations streamed to Jerusalem, bearing tribute and joining in the worship of Israel's God (see Isaiah 60, and Paul's quotations in Rom 15:8–13); but also with echoes of an imperial vision in which conquered peoples offered their gifts to Caesar (for example, Virgil, *Aeneid* 8.720–23). More prosaically, it referred to the collection of money Paul had gathered from various assemblies in Achaia and Macedonia as "aid for the poor among the saints" in Jerusalem (Rom 15:25–26). Paul hoped those

---

24. See discussions in Gaca, *The Making of Fornication*; and Ruden, *Paul among the People*.

25. Dahl, *Studies in Paul*, 73, citing Rom 15:16; 2 Cor 11:2; Phil 1:10–11; 1 Cor 1:8; 1 Thess 3:13; 5:23.

funds would be received as more than relief, as evidence of a fulfillment of messianic prophecy.

The "pastoral" aspect of Paul's work, then, had a much nearer eschatological horizon than many church leaders acknowledge today as they plan decades-long ministerial careers. Even Paul's expression of concern for "all the assemblies" in 2 Corinthians comes at the end of a recital of dangers Paul had faced *in travels abroad* (11:23-27). His letters responded to situations that arose after Paul had *departed* from one city or another, usually after a relatively brief stay—just sufficient to inaugurate an assembly. (Note that Paul's longest stay in one place, according to the book of Acts, was eighteen months in Ephesus—what some denominations would consider a carefully bounded "interim" ministry today.) Neither did Paul apply himself to what we might call "church growth." To judge from one admittedly conflictual, but nonetheless telling situation, he gave thanks that during his initial stay in Corinth he had baptized only Crispus and Gaius, and the household of Stephanas (1 Cor 1:14—16); the increase of the Corinthian congregation under the baptismal ministry of Apollos, and the lively competition of perspectives that increase generated, precipitated a crisis for him (1 Cor 2:1—3:15). Paul seems to have regarded innovation with suspicion: his interventions were intended to preserve the assemblies in an initial, pristine state of "holiness" as they awaited the imminent return of Christ.

This aspect of Paul's work might be compared with a Vaudeville performer whose act was to set plates atop slender poles and keep them spinning in place as long as possible. The thrill of such an act is the anticipation that eventually, everything must come crashing down. The culmination of Paul's story, however, was a series of disappointments bordering on the tragic. We cannot say whether his views immediately prevailed in controversies in Corinth or in Rome. We do know, however, that the anxiety he expressed concerning his last journey to Jerusalem, bearing the collection, was more than warranted. The story told in Acts 21 describes controversy in Jerusalem over Paul's allegiance to the Torah and the accusation—which Luke considers false—that Paul had brought some, at least, of his non-Jewish delegates into the precincts of the Temple reserved for Jews alone (21:28-29). The riot that ensued set Paul on a narrative road that ends in Rome, whither he was sent on charges of civil unrest that he was compelled to appeal before the Emperor (Acts 22-28).

The deep symbolic significance Paul attached to the collection, his reason for being in Jerusalem, goes unmentioned in Acts; so also, then, is any hint at the impact of its failure on him. Also missing is any account of Paul's subsequent hearing before Nero, or any reference to Paul's execution on the Emperor's authority, events reported (however reliably) in other sources

(*Acts of Paul* 10.6; Eusebius, *E.H.* 2.25.5). Instead of these catastrophes, Luke offers the reader the triumph of Paul speaking the word of proclamation boldly before assembled philosophers in Athens (17:16–34); before the Roman procurators Felix and Festus and the Judean king Agrippa (chapters 24–26), and—for the first time in the narrative—before an unbiased synagogue audience, in Rome itself (28:17–22). These accomplishments fulfill Jesus' prophecy that his followers would take his word "before kings and governors" (Luke 21:12), and incorporate Paul's last days in Rome within Luke's theme of the inexorable spread of the word "to the ends of the earth" (Acts 1:8). But these triumphant notes come at the cost of what Luke must suppress. The reader will not learn from Acts how much hung, for Paul, on the journey to Jerusalem. Nor does Luke convey the purpose behind Paul's fervent attempts to conform the non-Jews in his assemblies to a life of holiness: namely, in order to impress upon his fellow Jews that they were living in the last days (see Romans 11).

It appears enough for Luke that Paul helped to inaugurate the church of Jews and non-Jews (though he is careful to stipulate that the important first steps were taken by Peter in Joppa, Acts 10). Just so, in the generation after Paul's death, another writer represented the core of Paul's gospel as the "mystery" that God intended Jews and non-Jews to worship together in the name of Christ (Eph 3:1–6). But while Paul had hoped the "obedience of faith among the nations" would manifest the fulfillment of scriptural promises to Israel, the author of Ephesians understood the Pauline "mystery" to involve the dispensability of Torah itself, its having been "abolished" by Christ (*katargēsas*, Eph 2:13–16)—an idea that was unthinkable for Paul himself (see Rom 3:31).

The attention given to reading and interpreting Paul's letters today, especially in churches, may then be described as paradoxical. The paradox lies not just in the fact that these letters were manifestly written to others, centuries ago; it is a matter of the letters being directed to achieve specific ends that made sense within an eschatological scenario that has not just been "delayed," but has manifestly failed. When Paul is read today simply as the champion of a law-free, "Gentile" Christianity, he is being read through the lens of Ephesians and Acts. But this is to impose onto Paul's letters the "perfect hindsight" that our place "downstream" from him allows us. The temptation for those of us who find our place in the current of Gentile Christianity is, to paraphrase Carly Simon, to be so vain that we imagine the apostle was talking about *us*, and to imagine Paul as the founder of our religion.

The Paradox of Paul's Authority

Some passages in the letters suggest that Paul may have not been the clearest of communicators. In places, Paul seeks to "correct" or manage what he considers his audience's mistaken apprehension of his own earlier teaching (see 1 Thess 4:13–18; 1 Cor 2:1–6; 5:9–13), or hints at obligations that were perhaps not explicit earlier (e.g., the master's "duty" in Philemon 8). He admonishes the Corinthians for grievously misunderstanding the nature of the Lord's Supper, though he had passed along to them traditions he obviously considered important (1 Cor 11:17–34). He is "astonished" at how quickly the Galatians have deserted his teaching (Gal 1:6–9), though he refers obliquely to having taught something else earlier (did he once "preach circumcision," 5:11? Is he now "building up" what he once "tore down," 2:18?). In none of these passages does Paul admit that he has changed his mind, or that he might not have spoken clearly in the first place—even when his advice appears to remain contradictory (compare his advice on food offered to idols in 1 Corinthians 8 and 10:14–22). Further, his readers may well have been confused when he took a different tack than what they may have heard from the tradition of Jesus' words—regarding questions of marriage and divorce, for example (1 Corinthians 7), or his refusal of the support to which apostles are entitled (1 Corinthians 9). They might have been as vexed by his sometimes-cavalier attitude to the authority of other apostles (Gal 2:11–14; 2 Cor 11:1–6), or his fierce denunciations of "other" gospels (Gal 1:6–9; 2 Cor 11:4). If Paul had such difficulty communicating with his first hearers, perhaps the contemporary reader may be forgiven for not finding the meaning of his letters transparent!

Precisely because Paul's letters have been read, preached, cherished, annotated, and exposited over centuries of Christian practice, they present their contemporary readers with another paradox that we might call a "lexical illusion." Put simply, we *read* Paul, and more, we read Paul as a part of the Bible. We thus may think of him as an influential and articulate *writer*, picking up his pen to express sublime thoughts. This would have surprised many of Paul's contemporaries, however, for whom Paul was not, first of all, a writer. (Some adversaries in Corinth contemptuously declared that his letters were the weightiest aspect of his work, and even these were unimpressive: see 2 Cor 10:9–10.) Nor would many of those who knew him best have regarded him primarily as a "thinker," and certainly not one whose authority was unquestioned. Indeed, one of the most vivid impressions one gets from these letters is that of an ardent and often scrappy polemicist. Paul appears frequently to argue for a viewpoint or a practice that he *expects* to be controversial, at least, and likely contested by at least a few of his hearers. The

Corinthian correspondence shows that Paul faced considerable opposition from some of the more influential members of that assembly who found his arguments unconvincing. Paul's prominence in our New Testament hardly justifies the assumption that his voice normally prevailed in his own day!

It is a commonplace that as readers of Paul's letters, we are "listening in" on only one half of a conversation, but even this is putting the matter too simply. We are listening to an intensely opinionated correspondent! The reverence Paul is accorded in the Christian tradition for his role as paramount guide into the practices of new life "in Christ" is, in large part, the mirror image of the significance Paul claims for himself as he addresses "his" congregations. They may have "many guides in Christ, but not many fathers," he tells the Corinthians (a characteristic claim: 1 Cor 4:15); he is an example to be imitated (Phil 3:17). His letters often give a contemporary reader the sense of riding an emotional roller coaster. In the rhetoric of 1 and 2 Corinthians, for example, Paul alternates between assuring a community that the Spirit of Christ dwells among them, guiding them and guaranteeing their holiness, and shaming them for not living up to even the rudimentary standards of the pagan world (1 Cor 5:1-8). To contemporary readers more accustomed to modern ideals of mutual respect and equality among persons, Paul's rhetoric may come across as authoritarian, perhaps even coercive or abusive. It is the enduring gift of feminist scholarship to have clarified that in his letters (and, we may presume, in his initial face-to-face efforts as well), Paul may *claim*, but can never *presume* his authority. Indeed, in correspondence like the Corinthian letters, he appears to be scrambling to find the rhetorical ground from which to assert a right to a hearing. We must take into account, then, not only the existence of another "half" of a conversation, but the possibility that Paul's construal of one or another situation was a minority opinion and may even, on occasion, have been unintelligible to his readers. The point may seem subtle, but it is an important principle to which feminist interpretation calls much-needed attention. A view of biblical authority that *presumes* Paul's voice would have prevailed, simply because it was his, is anachronistic. It takes Paul's letters "out of the public domain where argument is in order and where Paul's strong arguments could have social impact." Careful attention to the way Paul argued shows that he never presumed his voice was sufficient to settle an issue. Rather, he hoped to gain the assent of his hearers to his arguments "*because they are convincing.*"[26] Today as well, when various and competing appeals are made to this or that passage in Paul's letters, the same principle suggests that mere resort to biblical authority is insufficient and inappropriate: thoughtful and

---

26. Wire, *Corinthian Women Prophets*, 10 (emphasis added).

ethical discernment remains our shared responsibility, within the churches no less than in the public square.

SEEING PAUL THROUGH A GLASS, DARKLY

I have been dwelling on the challenges and complications of understanding Paul quite deliberately. Any hope that we will arrive at a single understanding of the apostle that will convince everyone must be tempered by recognizing the divergent responses Paul received in his own day and the significant variety of portrayals of Paul that have been cherished over the centuries—beginning with writings found in our New Testament.

The Pauls in the New Testament

We do not have all of Paul's letters to the assemblies: we do not have what he says he earlier wrote to the Corinthians, for example (1 Cor 5:9). The reference in Col 4:16 to a letter to the Laodiceans, not otherwise attested, prompted a Christian in the third or fourth century to supply one by patching together phrases from the available letters of Paul. We have Paul's letters, we may presume, because after they were first given the hearing for which Paul wrote them, some persons in the assemblies thought them worth preserving, exchanging with others (see Col 4:16 again), and collecting. We should also presume that Paul wrote for the purposes that are evident in the letters themselves; the *subsequent* work of preserving, exchanging, and collecting was done by others, for their very different purposes. The letter form became a popular device by which others disseminated the apostle's thought, *after* his own letters had won whatever (probably mixed) reception they were given. The *Epistle to the Laodiceans*, a third letter to the Corinthians, and correspondence with the philosopher Seneca are examples of letters written by other Christians, living long after the apostle's death, to achieve results for which Paul should hardly be held responsible.[27] The technical term for such "falsely signed" writing is *pseudepigraphy*.

Today, many interpreters are convinced that pseudepigrapha appear in our New Testament as well as outside it. The "Pastoral" Epistles (1 and 2 Timothy and Titus) are different enough in vocabulary, writing style, and mood, and seem to address so different a situation from the other letters, that they are the most widely considered to be pseudepigrapha. Ephesians

---

27. For texts discussed here, see Elliott and Reasoner, *Documents and Images for the Study of Paul*; for further discussion, Pervo, *The Making of Paul*.

is also widely questioned, and after it, Colossians and 2 Thessalonians (but see the entries on these letters).* It is a principle of scholarship that judgments about Paul's own thought should be based first on the genuine (that is, the unquestioned) letters, Romans, 1 and 2 Corinthians, Galatians, Philippians, 1 Thessalonians, and Philemon, and that the other, possibly pseudepigraphic letters should be used only when they corroborate what has been found in the genuine letters. From the scholarly viewpoint, the appearance of some pseudepigrapha in our New Testament should not cloud this principle. After all, various writings that are now universally recognized as pseudepigraphic, like the *Acts of Paul* (in which *Laodiceans* and *3 Corinthians* appear), were once not only popular, but frequently copied and regarded by some Christians as part of the New Testament. Hebrews was often copied after Romans in collections of Paul's letters, on the assumption (now almost universally rejected) that Paul wrote it; the Epistle to Barnabas, a pseudepigraphon bearing the name of Paul's erstwhile companion, also was included in some copies of the New Testament. Furthermore, while the shape of our New Testament gives the impression of continuity, leading some interpreters to describe the "canonical" pseudepigrapha (Colossians, Ephesians, and the Pastorals) as appropriate "adaptations" of Paul's legacy by faithful "Pauline churches" or a "Pauline school," there is no *external* basis for establishing only some pseudepigrapha as the creations of such "faithful" disciples of Paul, and rejecting others as betrayals.[28] The scholarly principle holds that each writing should be evaluated in terms of its own similarity to or difference from the genuine letters.

But letters were not the only way Paul's legacy was fashioned and refashioned in early Christianity. At one point in his controversy with some members of the Corinthian assembly, Paul wrote, "I have become all things to all people, that I might by all means save some" (2 Cor 9:22-23 NRSV). His immediate purpose was apparently to defend his refusal of financial patronage from wealthy members of the church; but his words have floated free of their original context to become something of an emblem for what his sympathizers might consider his strategic skill, and what less charitable interpreters might consider an unscrupulous ambition. Even in the first few centuries of Christianity, Paul seems, chameleon-like, to have taken on a wide variety of guises, depending on who held him in their gaze.

The Acts of the Apostles was only the first of several narratives that gave Paul, or one version of Paul, pride of place. Written decades after Paul's death, Acts purports to continue the authoritative account begun in the Gospel of Luke of "the things that were fulfilled among us" (Luke 1:1). The

---

28. See Elliott, *Liberating Paul*, 25-54.

narrator is never identified. In some dramatic passages, the narrator suddenly shifts to the first person plural ("we"), giving rise to the belief that the account is eyewitness testimony of a companion of Paul: traditionally, Luke, the "beloved physician" of Col 4:14. But the abrupt use of the first-person was a stylistic device in Hellenistic historiography (to which one might compare the intended effect of television dramas that declare, "You are there!" when, of course, you aren't). The narrator strikes a number of notes in describing Paul that are not found, or are in some tension, with Paul's own letters. In Acts, Paul is first named "Saul" (many Jews bore both Hebrew and Greek names), and identified as a native of Tarsus (9:11) and a student of Rabbi Gamaliel (22:3), who is revered in the Mishnah as well. Acts reports that Paul's actions as a persecutor of the followers of Jesus were authorized by the high priest (9:1-2). And Acts narrates—three times, twice in recitals by Paul himself!—the dramatic reversal in his course on the road to Damascus, where he is blinded by a bright light and hears the commissioning voice of the risen Jesus (chaps. 9, 22, 26). Here, Paul is also a Roman citizen, a piece of information that arises at a crucial plot point to deliver Paul from an angry mob in the Temple and set him on the protracted course that ends in Rome (22:25-29).

All of these pieces of information appear only in Acts, and serve to present Paul dramatically as a faithful and observant Jew. Here he is also an indefatigable missionary, proclaiming Christ in cities in Syria, Cilicia, Galatia, Asia Minor, Achaia, and Macedonia, and at last, in chains, in Rome. In the adventurous style common to Hellenistic novels, his travels are recounted as accompanied by miraculous healings and deliverance from shipwrecks, imprisonments at the hands of corrupt magistrates, and attacks from jealous Jewish rivals, all of which give Paul occasions to make his case in eloquent speeches in synagogues, theaters, and the court of the Temple, and before philosophers, governors, and kings (in explicit fulfillment of Jesus' words in Luke 21:12).

What is left unsaid in Acts is just as interesting. As mentioned above, although Acts narrates Paul's final visit to Jerusalem, we learn nothing of his collection or how it was received. Instead, hostile "Jews from Asia" stir up mob action by making a false accusation, that Paul has brought non-Jews into the Temple itself (21:27-29). And Acts ends on a triumphant note: Paul has at last reached Rome and has opportunities freely to address the city's Jewish leaders without interference from his antagonists (28:21-22; perhaps mirroring Luke's own narrative purpose). Though living under Roman guard there for two years, he welcomes inquirers and preaches and teaches "without hindrance" (28:30-31). We know from other sources, and Luke's readers must have known, that Paul was martyred under Nero, probably in 64, but that event has no place in the story Luke wants to tell.

Competing Memories

The multiplicity of portraits of Paul—which is to say, the multiplicity of "Pauls" effective in particular historical situations—did not end with the diversity in the New Testament; it was only sparked by that diversity. For example, the author of 1 Timothy assumed Paul's identity (though writing, most scholars agree, decades after his death) to exhort the subordination of women and to extol marriage (2:12–15; 4:1–4)—in some tension with Paul's own commendation of women colleagues (and superiors: Rom 16:1–7), and his exhortation to the Corinthians that he wished all people could remain unmarried as he was! (1 Cor 7:1–7). Whether Paul himself encouraged the silencing of women is a matter of still-unresolved controversy around the status of 1 Cor 14:33–34 (are these lines genuine, or a later interpolation into the text?). Regarding marriage, 1 Timothy and 1 Corinthians seem to offer contradictory advice, but set together in the New Testament as equally letters of Paul, they provide a sort of ranked hierarchy: the ideal is celibacy; second-best, but still good, is a single monogamous marriage. Other variations—suffering divorce and even remarrying, provided it is within the assembly—are acceptable, but clearly represent failures to achieve the ideal. The "biblical" Paul is effectively conformed to the moral expectations of the Roman household (see the entry on the Pastoral Epistles).*

But a different memory of Paul persisted: perhaps a hundred years later, the anonymous author of the *Acts of Paul* described the apostle as teaching a "gospel of virginity" and leading the Iconian noblewoman Thecla, as she then led other women, to break off engagements and even leave husbands. Tertullian repudiated the *Acts of Paul* because it so clearly endorsed the ordained leadership of women, but could not declare the document a forgery (it does not claim to be written by Paul); instead, he attacked the impudence of its author. His attack shows us, however, that in the third century a priest was able to compile such a portrait and do so "out of love for Paul" (*On Baptism* 17). Nor did the *Acts* represent one man's idiosyncratic perspective: it appeared in manuscripts of the New Testament as late as the sixth century and was a widely popular text long afterward, to judge from the proliferation and variety of manuscripts of the writing.

Other such contrasts could easily be multiplied. (1) In the early second century, Marcion championed Paul as "*The* Apostle," who had rightly taught Christians to reject Jewish law and Jewish scripture. Marcion was condemned as a heretic, but his claim regarding Paul is only a little more extreme than that of Ephesians, where we see formulated another early synthesis of Paul's gospel, now as the unification of Jews and Gentiles into one people through the "abolishing" of the law through Christ's death (2:13–16). Decades later, the anonymous author of an early Christian novel apparently shared this basic understanding of Paul as an opponent of the law, but bitterly opposed it, casting a Paul-like figure as the wicked mortal enemy of the properly law-abiding apostles Peter and James in terms that evoke Paul's confrontation with Peter in Galatians 2 (Clementine *Recognitions* 1.70–71). According to Irenaeus, the Ebionites, too, repudiated the apostle, "maintaining that he was an apostate from the law" (*Against Heresies* 1.26.2). Another writing, the *Ascents of James*, alleged that Paul was an impostor, a Greek who came to Jerusalem and accepted circumcision only to woo the high priest's daughter; when his prospective father-in-law spurned him, "he became angry and wrote against circumcision and against the Sabbath and the law" (Epiphanius, *Panarion* 16.6–9). Heated arguments about Paul's view of the law are not a recent innovation!

(2) The pseudepigraphic letters between Paul and Seneca depict warm mutual respect between the apostle and the Emperor Nero's closest advisor, who even brings Paul's letters to the Emperor's attention; they commiserate over the unfairness of Nero blaming the Christians for the great fire in 64. Paul counsels a policy of quiet life, rather in keeping with Rom 13:1–7 and 1 Tim. 2:2. In the *Martyrdom of Paul*, however (which was incorporated in some versions of the *Acts of Paul*, but also traveled separately), the apostle speaks defiantly to the Emperor, warning that his lord comes "to wage war upon the world with fire." After being put to death, Paul returns in a resurrected state to warn Nero that he faces eternal judgment; in terror, the Emperor releases Paul's companions. The defiant tone stands in contrast to the perception among many contemporary readers of Rom 13:1–7 as a quietist, even abject endorsement of governing authority as established by God. It is noteworthy, then, that the earliest reports of Christian martyrdoms—apparently composed and circulated to present an "ideal" protocol for extreme circumstances—portray Christians citing or quoting the apostle, indicating that "we have been taught to render honor . . . to princes and authorities appointed by God" (*Martyrdom of Polycarp*); "we give honor to our emperor" (*Acts of the Scillitan Martyrs*), even as they offer resolute defiance. (The site of Paul's own martyrdom and his tomb "outside the walls" were sites of Christian worship from very early on.) Romans 13:1–7 appears to

have been read, at least by some Christians, as a script for respectful refusal to obey authority.[29]

(3) Paul's oblique reference to a heavenly vision (2 Corinthians 12), his description of seeing Christ raised in a "spiritual," rather than a "physical" body (1 Cor 15:50), and his insistence that "flesh and blood cannot inherit the kingdom of God" (1 Cor 15:50) stand in contrast with the depiction in Acts of Paul's remarkable, but clearly terrestrial audition of the heavenly Christ (Acts 9; 22; 26), and in even more pointed contrast with the terrestrial and quite tangible appearances of the risen Jesus to his disciples in Luke 24:36–43 or John 20:26–29 or 21:1–14. We know that some Christians took the language of Paul's own letters further because their opponents appropriated Paul's memory or voice to denounce them. In the *Acts of Paul*, men who declared "that there is no resurrection of the flesh, but that of the spirit only, and the human body is not the creation of God . . ." come to Corinth and trouble Paul's church; the narrator includes a transcript of Paul's response as *3 Corinthians*, universally regarded today as a pseudepigraphon, in which Paul affirms not only the bodily life, death, and resurrection of Jesus, but his miraculous birth from Mary (something Paul never mentions in the unquestioned letters).

(4) As a final example, Paul's own comments on slavery are maddeningly brief and enigmatic. The two-word slogan in 1 Cor 7:21 is characteristic: "if you can gain your freedom, *mallon chrēsai*"—alternatively translated, "take advantage of the opportunity!" and "make use of your present condition instead!" His letter to the owner of Onesimus is rhetorically powerful but cryptic (see the introduction to Philemon).* Later writings sought to clear up the mystery by attributing to Paul a clear endorsement of the master-slave relationship, though tempered with Christian kindness (Eph 6:5–9; Col 3:18–4:1), and 1 Timothy went further, insisting that slaves in the churches should not "be disrespectful on the ground that they are brothers: rather they must serve all the better since those who benefit by their service are believers and beloved" (6:1–2). (The author is also concerned to limit support for widows to only the impeccably worthy: 5:3–16.) The risk that slaves might consider their status changed once they stood alongside their masters in the assembly may have arisen from Paul's own language in Gal 3:28: "there is no slave nor free . . . in Christ Jesus." Some early Christian communities did in fact practice the manumission of slave members (Hermas, *Mand*. 8.10, *Sim*. 12.8; *1 Clem*. 55.2). But Ignatius, bishop of Smyrna, who presented himself as an ardent follower of Paul, specifically rejected the practice: "Do not be haughty to slaves, either men or women; yet do not let

---

29. See Schottroff, "Give to Caesar What Belongs to Caesar."

them be puffed up, but let them rather endure slavery to the glory of God, that they may obtain a better freedom from God. Let them not desire to set free at the church's expense, that they not be found slaves of desire" (*To Polycarp* 4). Centuries later, John Chrysostom complained from the pulpit that Christian efforts to redeem slaves constituted "violence" against masters, "the subversion of everything." He cited "Paul"—that is, 1 Timothy 6:1—to denounce the practice as inciting "blasphemy" against Christianity (*Homily on Philemon*).

These examples suffice to show that throughout the early centuries of Christianity, Paul was remembered in very different ways.[30] While a few of these memories have ended up in our New Testaments today, it is just as remarkable that the variety *persisted* so long: there simply was no single, "authoritative" version of Paul from whom all the alternatives could be imagined simply as divergences. Just as remarkable as the fact of diversity is the determination with which Christians have, in so many diverse ways, clung to a perceived continuity with Paul as an important warrant for their own actions. For every bishop like Chrysostom, whose homilies were gathered reverently and published in handsome volumes, we have indirect evidence for other, anonymous Christians (whom we would not know except for Chrysostom's protest!) who practiced the manumission of slaves, quite possibly in Paul's name and quite possibly aware that they were practicing an "alternative" Christianity opposed by their bishop!

PAUL THE PROBLEM: APOSTLE OF THE STATUS QUO?

Our efforts to understand Paul's thought and work in his historical context and to wrestle with his legacy today are of importance far beyond the bounds of church life. Paul merits thoughtful attention wherever Christianity has played a role in shaping contemporary cultures. My goal here is not to resolve the numerous questions that continue to occupy Paul's interpreters—or even to name them all!—but to describe the most important patterns into which the answers continue to fall.

Many of the apostle's critics—and even a few of his champions, who appear to consider this a virtue—would agree that Paul was largely unconcerned with the social inequities and injustices of his age. To many contemporary ears, the New Testament letters that now appear under his name include some of the most offensively retrograde passages in scripture. These letters are among the most cited parts of the Bible (and remain influential even when they are not cited!) when a variety of questions regarding civil

30. Pervo, *The Making of Paul*.

rights, gender equality, economic justice, and other areas of public life are discussed today.

The Pauline letters have played a dismal role in many of the most grievous episodes of modern history. For example, the nineteenth-century movement to abolish slavery in the United States faced steep challenges, not least because the Bible nowhere condemns slavery. To the contrary, letters appearing under Paul's name explicitly exhorted slaves to obey their Christian masters (Eph 6:5-8; Col 3:22-25; Titus 2:9-10), and not to assume that being members of the church together (literally, "brothers") constituted genuine equality with their masters (1 Tim 6:1-2). At a time when questions about the authenticity of these letters were rare, the presumption that the apostle Paul condoned slaveholding was inevitably powerful, and for that reason, specific letters proved inestimably useful to slaveowners in the U.S. South who recruited preachers to indoctrinate their slaves regarding their spiritual "duties." But this woeful situation cannot be explained simply as resulting from a naïve acceptance of letters that many scholars today consider pseudonymous. Even a century after the passage of the Thirteenth Amendment to the U.S. Constitution, the Civil Rights movement faced fierce opposition among twentieth-century American Christians who read Paul as enjoining quiet submission even to fiercely segregationist government (see Rom 13:1-7), and exhorting believers to "remain in the state in which [they were] called" (1 Cor 7:17-24, RSV). Martin Luther King, Jr.'s "Letter from a Birmingham Jail," in which he challenged white clergy not to be "more devoted to 'order' than to justice" and lambasted appeals for Negro "patience," had this legacy of Paul as one of its targets.

For another example, the women's suffrage movement in the United States faced tremendous obstacles in the clear and ostensibly Pauline admonitions that women should keep silence in the assembly and submit to their husbands (1 Cor 14:34-35; Eph 5:22-24; Col 3:18; 1 Tim 2:11-15). Almost a century after U.S. women won the right to vote, these passages continue to exercise a baleful influence in the cultural "backlash" against women's ongoing struggle for equality. Advocates for women and their children who suffer violence at the hands of the men in their homes candidly point out that these passages are now woven into a culture of rape, of silence, and of terror,[31] yet Christian clergy are often reluctant to denounce these texts from their pulpits. Like the passages exhorting subordination of slaves, verses encouraging women's subordination continue to hold powerful sway through the presumption, alive and well in some corners of American society, that striving for equality between genders or among races somehow

---

31. See Faludi, *Backlash: The Undeclared War against American Women*.

springs from an inordinate self-indulgence. Both these sets of passages are hard to square with Paul's own declaration that in Christ "there is neither slave nor free, neither male nor female" (Gal 3:28). But this only intensifies the question: *If* Paul wrote all these passages, was he unaware of the tensions between them? Or (as some more conservative Christians today would have it) did Paul wisely see, from the first, that freedom and equality could properly be exercised only within very straitened limits?

Paul presents other problems as well, to which we have already pointed. His retrospective comments about his "former life in Judaism" (Phil 3:4–7; Gal 1:11—2:10) have often been read as flat dismissals of an obsolete and ineffective religion ("loss," "rubbish"). Alongside Gospel narratives assigning blame for Jesus' death to the "crowds" or "people" of Jerusalem, these passages have provided impetus not just for Christian supersessionism, but for centuries of violence against Jews that came to a terrible climax under Nazism. Yet as the historical record shows, even some Christian pastors in Nazi Germany who recognized that their government was perpetrating grave evils were often reluctant actively to resist it, not only out of fear but also from an exaggerated concern to obey the apostle's admonition to "be subject to the governing authorities" (Rom 13:1).

Those same words from Romans served to quell Christian resistance to Apartheid in South Africa and to the national security regimes of Central America in the 1980s.[32] They have been cited to deflect pacifism and conscientious objection to combat in every U.S. war to date, and, with Paul's exhortations (as they are usually translated) to "remain in the life the Lord has assigned," the "condition in which you were called" (see 1 Cor 7:17–24), have proven a powerful inhibition of Christian involvement in every progressive movement down to the present.

But Paul's legacy has not always been read in so monochromatic a way. S. Scott Bartchy has shown that the now-standard reading of those exhortations in 1 Cor 7:21–24, in which the Christian's "calling" (*klēsis*) is understood as a calling *to a particular social location*, a "state" or "condition," is lexically and exegetically impossible: the Greek simply does not say what the English represents.[33] In subsequent work, he has traced the decisive (mis)translation to the period of the Peasants' Revolt in Germany and Martin Luther's response to it—hardly a situation conducive of objective, dispassionate exegesis! But the translation persists, and exercises decisive control over the assumptions that modern readers bring to Paul. Indeed, we perceive a much narrower range of possible meaning in Paul's letters than

---

32. See Brown, ed., *Kairos*.
33. Bartchy, *Mallon Chrēsai*.

our predecessors may have done. For example, some clergy were ranged with the poor in the fourteenth-century Peasants' Rebellion in England, including a bishop who publicly read Paul's declaration that "there are divisions of work, but all of them, in all men, are the work of the one Lord" (1 Cor 12:6) as showing clearly that God did not intend disparities of wealth in creation (Thomas Brinton, *Sermon* 44). For another example, the words in 2 Thess 3:10—"if any will not work, neither let them eat!"—have been quoted by right-wing pastors and politicians in order to vilify families seeking state-provided food or medical assistance, with such regularity that the verse has become a banner of what one journalist calls "poverty denialism" in government.[34] But a century ago, V. I. Lenin quoted the same verse as exemplifying "the prime, basic, and root principle of socialism: 'He who does not work, neither shall he eat.'" It was obvious to Lenin, just as it was to a number of anonymous Russians who made the slogan into banners plastered around Petrograd, that those who "would not work" were the bourgeois profiteers, who exercised monopoly control over grain markets and used their power to suffocate labor. "Every toiler understands that," said Lenin, and "in this simple, elementary and perfectly obvious truth lies the basis of socialism."[35]

Particular challenges to a received understanding of Paul's "social conservatism" have been posed especially from Latin American interpreters working in the context of the theology of liberation. One of the earliest in a line of philosophical interpreters of Paul, José Miranda read Romans in terms of the contemporary tension between justice and "law and civilization."[36] Elsa Támez has argued that "in societies where poverty and marginalization abound," evangelistic misreadings of the Protestant understanding of justification by faith "can be inappropriate and even violent"; Paul's thought, she continues, was in fact "markedly utopian: Paul longed for a society of equals where solidarity would reign."[37] Néstor O. Míguez has read 1 Thessalonians in terms of the strategies needed to keep hope vital in a situation of imperial oppression.[38] Indeed, Luise Schottroff argued years ago that the pivotal theme of liberation theology, the preferential option for the poor, was simply an elaboration of Paul's conception of the *ekklēsia*.[39] One

---

34. Goldberg, "The GOP's Poverty Denialism."

35. Lenin, "On the Famine: A Letter to the Workers of Petrograd."

36. Miranda, *Marx and the Bible*, 109–200; see more recently Jennings, *Transforming Atonement*; Frick, ed., *Paul in the Grip of the Philosophers*.

37. Támez, *Amnesty of Grace*, 23, 49.

38. Míguez, *The Practice of Hope*.

39. Schottroff, "Give to Caesar What Belongs to Caesar," 249.

of the most important efforts on the part of a North American to synthesize a liberative theology of the New Testament relies on the Pauline language of "powers and principalities" to describe the need to name, engage, and unmask systems of domination in our own day,[40] and others have sought to describe a more emancipatory understanding of Paul's thought.[41]

THE PROMISE OF A CRITICAL HISTORICAL IMAGINATION

Such widely divergent interpretations, or appropriations, of a text can leave many a reader perplexed: "but what did Paul really *mean*?" Were the busybodies rebuked in 2 Thessalonians the indolent recipients of some imaginary Roman antecedent of the modern welfare state, or were they people of means who could pursue lives of leisure, presuming that their social inferiors would attend to their needs? (The latter attitude is in fact well documented among the Roman aristocracy.) Was the letter to Philemon most like the genre of the *amicus* ("friend") letter, which we know from a number of Roman examples, in which a social peer would appeal to an angry slaveholder to extend leniency to a slave who had disobeyed or run away, then had a change of heart? Or was it simply a request to "borrow" a slave's services for a time; or a carefully leveraged appeal to a master to fulfill an otherwise unspecified "duty" by granting a slave his freedom?

On these and many other points of interpretation, the *promise* of historical criticism is to describe a range of possible meanings that may be drawn, through inference, from the available data and, on occasion, to identify some as more or less probable (or even to rule some out as impossible). The *temptation* of historical criticism, however, is to exaggerate that promise: to imagine that once the right methods and instruments have been deployed, a single "right" interpretation, *what the text really meant*, can be determined. As the diversity of current interpretations of Paul shows, however, things rarely work out that way.

One reason is simply the limits of our evidence (and thus of the inferences we can draw from it). Another is that "we" contemporary readers do not agree on what should be done with whatever results might be achieved, because "we" actually encompass a variety of different subjectivities and purposes. Some of us presume the authority of Paul's voice because it is scriptural; we want to use historical-critical method to fix the single,

---

40. Wink, *Naming the Powers*; Wink, *Engaging the Powers*; Wink, *Unmasking the Powers*.

41. Elliott, *Liberating Paul*; Lopez, *Apostle to the Conquered*; Zerbe, *Citizenship*.

authoritative meaning of his words. Others of us want to qualify or mitigate the consequences of one or another pronouncement in Paul's letters and use historical-critical method to circumscribe Paul as a man of his own age, *rather than* a transcendent voice of revelation, binding on all generations.

And many of us are frankly inconsistent about just when or how historical considerations should matter. For example, Paul is often cited most vociferously today by individuals who insist that *some* of his words, at least, enjoy timeless and universal authority. In the still-roiling debates over equal protection under law and marriage equality for same-sex couples, a few select passages (Rom 1:24–27; 1 Cor 6:9–10; 1 Tim 1:8–11) are regularly invoked by some Christians to argue that God considers homosexuality, and even homosexual persons, an "abomination" (though that specific language is drawn from Leviticus, not Paul). My purpose here is not to adjudicate the issue but to point out that such appeals to Paul are necessarily selective: that is, most of these same Christians would presumably *not* argue analogously that the comments on slavery discussed above had an eternal validity, binding on twenty-first-century American society, any more than of the other "abominations" mentioned in Leviticus might. Such appeals also necessarily avoid historical investigation. "Homosexuality" is a modern conception; we know, from abundant and intersecting data, that people in the ancient world did not recognize what we call "sexual orientation," and so Paul simply could not have commented on it.[42] This has not stopped the appearance of some recent Bible translations, however, where Paul's Greek is rendered—quite improbably—with interpretive paraphrases like "active and passive partners in homosexual relations." Whatever Paul *did* mean to comment on in these passages (and this remains a matter of debate among scholars)[43] is clearly abusive and outrageous, but this might suggest that to equate Paul's target with contemporary same-sex couples seeking a church's recognition of their love seems both exegetically specious and morally gratuitous. Regrettably, with regard to this unfinished debate, it seems that setting the Pauline letters in their historical context is the last thing some readers wish to do!

Some of us have used the historical-critical identification of Pauline pseudepigrapha to disqualify certain letters, or verses in them, as tendentious adaptations of Paul's own voice, which in contrast is more liberative than has usually been perceived.[44] Others point out that the attempt

---

42. Nissinen, *Homoeroticism in the Biblical World*.

43. See for example Boswell, *Christianity, Social Tolerance, and Homosexuality*; Scroggs, *New Testament and Homosexuality*; Martin, *Sex and the Single Savior*, 37–64; Countryman, *Dirt, Greed, and Sex*; Ruden, *Paul among the People*.

44. Elliott, *Liberating Paul*; Elliott, *Arrogance of Nations*; Lopez, *Apostle to the Conquered*; Zerbe, "Politics of Paul"; Zerbe, *Citizenship*.

to isolate the "genuine" voice of Paul only reinforces the problematic and too-prevalent assumption of "the 'masculine' hegemonic voice inscribed in kyriarchal Pauline or other ancient source-texts,"[45] and the problematic aura of Paul himself as a "heroic" figure.[46] It is worth notice that the plea to "decenter" Paul is based, in part, on a historical-critical argument that contextualizes Paul precisely as one voice among many on a crowded and complex Roman landscape.[47] Resistance to "kyriarchal" aspects of Paul's legacy involves recognizing the actual character of Paul's own appeals for obedience, submission, and imitation as rhetoric—patterns that were reinscribed in successive generations.[48]

Historical criticism, then, is neither a panacea that will reliably deliver us from the tyranny of an oppressive text *or* an obsolete means of holding on nostalgically to the same text—though it can be used for either purpose. The important consideration is what the interpreter's purposes are, for these will determine just how one or another method of biblical study will be used. The twin virtues of responsible interpretation are honesty with regard to the data (or lack of it) on a specific question, and accountability with regard to the purposes toward which we invoke it. In this light, the scientific mystique that the historical criticism of scripture has long enjoyed is rather like the insistence of the Professor who manipulated the voice and smoke mechanisms of the Great Wizard of Oz: "pay no attention to that man behind the curtain!" More recent criticisms of classical historical criticism, whether they have gone under the names "post-modern," "post-critical," "contextual," "deconstructive," or "minority" or "minoritized" interpretation, have sought to pull back the curtain to reveal the identity, standpoint, and intentions of the interpreter.

That gesture remains one of contestation, however. That is, attention to the social location of the interpreter is most pronounced when members of a marginalized group seek to identify the power relations inscribed in the dominant discourse. Greg Carey has argued that in biblical studies, a "common-sense" interpretation that privileged the biblical text as floating above ambiguity coincided with the culture of white privilege in the United States; thus, he observes, it remains the case today that "'minority' criticism is performed almost exclusively by minorities," while the analysis of white

---

45. Schüssler Fiorenza, "Rhetorical Situation and Historical Reconstruction," 187.
46. Johnson-DeBaufre and Nasrallah, "Beyond the Heroic Paul."
47. Wire, *Corinthian Women Prophets*.
48. Schüssler Fiorenza, "Rhetorical Situation and Historical Reconstruction"; Castelli, *Imitating Paul*; Kittredge, *Community and Authority*; Marchal, *Politics of Heaven*.

interpreters is also performed, "well, almost exclusively by minorities."[49] Nor is race the only modality in which questions of power relations are usually effaced by the scholarly mainstream. In his slender 2005 book on Paul, N. T. Wright discussed the state of Pauline interpretation by identifying the social location of various alternative viewpoints. Narrative criticism precipitated, as naturally as dew, in "the postliberal and canonical air of New Haven"; secular Copenhagen gave rise, unsurprisingly, to readings of Paul "which owe little to traditional Jewish or Christian ideas and much to first-century pagan philosophy"; and political interpretation distilled, almost inevitably, from the context of "below-the-tracks university" life in Blue-State Massachusetts, where deep suspicion of American empire is presumably at home. Similarly, suspicion of the authenticity of Colossians and Ephesians derived from "a particular kind of German existentialist Lutheranism . . ." But if those specific contexts produced the readings that Wright considered eccentric, social location had nothing to do, so far as he admits, with his own theological approach, except in so far as he speaks from "[his] own acquaintance with Paul"; and he attributes the same innocence to "the vast majority of Christians in the world today" who "read Paul with blissful ignorance" of those other, peripheral, situationally contingent "movements and counter-movements."[50]

In contrast, the interpretation to which a number of voices call us in the twenty-first century will require habits of candid self-awareness. Alongside historical questions about the apostle Paul and lexical, exegetical, and rhetorical-critical questions about the range of possible meanings of his words, we will need to ask what is at stake for our engagement with the apostle and his legacy. In what ways do we "use Paul to think with"? Are there more direct and honest ways to think through our responsibilities together?

---

49. Carey, "Introduction and a Proposal."
50. Wright, *Paul in Fresh Perspective*, 16–18.

2

Taking the Measure of an Earthquake
Comments on the Fortieth-Anniversary Edition of *Paul and Palestinian Judaism*

IT WAS AN HONOR to be part of the distinguished panel that gathered in Boston on November 17, 2017, to offer critical appreciation of the significance of E. P. Sanders's magisterial *Paul and Palestinian Judaism* on the fortieth anniversary of its publication and to mark the publication of a new edition of the work, which included a valuable new foreword by Mark Chancey.[1]

Although, like many biblical scholars, I have known E. P. Sanders as an author for decades, only in the last two years have I had the pleasure of making his acquaintance, and that of his wife, Dr. Becky Gray, and electronically, that of Professor Chancey. As an academic editor at Fortress Press, it was my charge to make sure there was enough "value added" to encourage people who already owned *Paul and Palestinian Judaism* to pick up a new edition. Professor Sanders immediately suggested that Professor Chancey offer a substantial new foreword to the book. As a scholar and a sometimes teacher, I am delighted that the foreword offers a superb description of the importance of the book and a critical review of the forty-year history of its reception. "Value added," indeed!

What follows are admittedly impressionistic observations about an academic career in the "Sanders era." (Though it is common enough practice,

---

1. I thank the organizers, Professors Paula Fredriksen and Emma Wasserman, for their invitation, and Professors Ed Sanders and Mark Chancey for the occasion.

it has always seemed peculiar to speak of a "*post*-Sanders" era, especially—as was the occasion in Boston—when *he's in the room*.)

Perhaps no one has stated the impact of this book better than Andreas Detweiler, who wrote in 2003 that the landscape of Pauline studies today resembles a city "devastated by an earthquake," in the aftermath of which "people scurry about in every direction, some assessing the damage, others verifying what still stands. Everyone takes the measure of the changes to come, but no one dares to build again, out of fear of a new shock."[2]

Well, that's not exactly right.

My older son is a seismologist, and he points out that in many parts of the world, after a population has been displaced by a catastrophic earthquake, the humanitarian imperative is to provide adequate housing, quickly. Having strong building safety codes in place only means that fewer people will be able to afford expensive new construction. Having corporate developers in the picture means that there may be plenty of new construction for sale, standards be damned. So, it's usually *not* the case that "no one dares to build again," unless there is a clear and coherent public commitment to the highest standards.

There may be a parable in there.

My seismologist son also complains about the sort of crowd-sourced data compiled on websites like "DidYouFeelIt.com," where, invariably, there's a small set of responses, even near the epicenter, in which people say, "I was washing my dog" or "playing a video game" or "just got home from the club—and didn't feel a thing."

Here, too, I find a parable. It's amazing, even decades later, how much of Pauline scholarship proceeds as if nothing in particular happened in 1977.

I began my graduate studies just a few years after *Paul and Palestinian Judaism* appeared, at Princeton Seminary, where it seemed that every other dissertation in biblical studies was written on the letter to the Romans (including mine). My cohort studied the architecturally magnificent scholarly works of our professors, some of which had been under construction before the earthquake hit in 1977, and we noticed places where they were newly patched with fresh plaster (if I may overextend the metaphor); I mean, scattered footnotes indicating that Sanders was right or wrong about this or that detail. But no one, it seemed, had stopped construction to inspect their foundations thoroughly; to relocate; or to tear down and reevaluate and redesign before building again.[3]

---

2. Marguerat, "Introduction," 9; my translation.
3. In J. Christiaan Beker's magisterial work (*Paul the Apostle*), to take just one

Reading and writing as graduate students in those early years, we had a vague sense that our "new construction" would be held to different standards. We had to be particularly alert as we picked our way through the secondary literature. Only a few earlier scholars had noticed the problems that Sanders had put front and center.[4] Now, suddenly, there was intense effort all around us to shore up aspects of Protestant interpretation, in what was soon branded the "new perspective" on Paul. In his foreword to this anniversary edition, Mark Chancey offers acute and important distinctions between the views of James D. G. Dunn, N. T. Wright, and other champions of the "new perspective" on one hand and Sanders himself on the other, but in the early 1980s, there were precious few voices making such clear discriminations.

In *The Origins of Anti-Semitism* (1985), John G. Gager published with permission a personal message from Lloyd Gaston in which Gaston wrote,

> I suddenly find that I have great difficulty in reading the standard literature on Paul: Why do other interpreters miss the obvious while spending much time on matters not in the text at all? I find that I cannot even trust such "objective" works as lexica on some points. It's almost paralyzing when it comes to writing, for so little can be assumed and all must be discussed.[5]

I copied that quote onto an index card that I carried with me on every trip to Speer Library, to work on my own dissertation. But of course, the lesson is right there on every page of *Paul and Palestinian Judaism*: Every primary source must be examined, and examined again, on its own terms

---

(particularly erudite) example, there are nine citations of Sanders, several of them apparently added after typesetting (so included as footnotes, not endnotes that would have required renumbering). There is a single extended discussion (pp. 235–43) where Sanders is mentioned several times, in passing, as one among a host of scholars dismissed for failing to grasp Paul's *Christian* understanding of Judaism. It is only at p. 340—in another late-added footnote—that we read that "one of the great merits" of Sanders's work is that "he destroyed the anti-Jewish bias in scholarship once and for all." That is remarkable news, surely, to many of us working in the twenty-first-century. My more immediate point is that this "great merit" did not apparently lead Beker—himself keenly sensitive to the importance of representing early Judaism accurately—to reconsider either his argument or the organization of his book.

4. Sanders himself points to the work of G. F. Moore (*Judaism in the First Centuries of the Christian Era*), among others, as an important predecessor. Another scholar alert to the rampant prejudicial slant to Protestant Paul scholarship was William S. Campbell, who has written that "the literature on Romans was very different" in the 1970s, when he began his research—far narrower, and constrained by a presumed theological agenda—than in the 1990s (*Paul's Gospel in an Intercultural Context*, iii). In the 1980s, we could at least rely on Campbell—and on Sanders.

5. Gager, *The Origins of Anti-Semitism*, 198.

and in its own context. The "assured results" of scholarship need always to be measured against the evidence; "received wisdom" may be anything but wise. And given the history of Christian anti-semitism and supersessionism, the more confident the generalization—the more heartwarming the doxological gloss—the greater the need to test for implicit biases, to read with suspicion. Although I never studied with Professor Sanders, this book (and others of his books that would follow) taught me—as they taught many in my generation—what scholarship would require of us.

If the landscape is different today, it is in no small part a measure of the importance of Sanders's work.

The "New Perspective," especially identified with the work of Dunn and Wright, remains a powerful and alluring paradigm for many, in part because it promises to restore something that Sanders seemed to remove from the Christian theological arsenal: a theologically coherent, rhetorically compelling apostle. But others have raised protests that (in Thomas Deidun's words) the New Perspective allows "practically all the old Lutheran demons" of Jewish caricature "to return unabashed to the Judaism which Sanders had by all accounts meticulously swept and put in order," though now "exclusivism" and "ethnocentrism" replaced works-righteousness as the fatal flaw at the heart of Judaism—a flaw that Paul alone could allegedly diagnose.[6]

For a brief while, the work of René Girard held out the promise of revealing Paul as the master diagnostician of lethal mimetic desire—again, nestled at the heart of Judaism.[7] In more recent years, the enthusiasm of Neo-Marxists Alain Badiou and Slavoj Žižek for the apostle Paul has offered Pauline scholars the prospect of sudden relevance, if they will look beyond the way these authors trade in theologically prejudicial caricatures of Judaism.[8] To the question at the heart of Sanders's simple formula—for Paul, what was wrong with Judaism?—there are still crowds of theologically minded Christian scholars who reject his succinct answer, "it was not

---

6. Deidun, "James Dunn and John Ziesler on Romans in New Perspective"; see also Nanos, *The Mystery of Romans*, 88–95; Boyarin, *A Radical Jew*, 209–24.

7. Hamerton-Kelly, *Sacred Violence*; the book was criticized by several scholars for its almost-covert anti-Judaism at the 1992 Colloquium on Violence and Religion and, memorably, by Daniel Boyarin at the 1993 Annual Meeting of the SBL. I offered a critique in "Paul and the Lethality of the Law," now chapter 1 in Elliott, *Currents in the Interpretation of Paul*.

8. Badiou, *St. Paul: The Foundation of Universalism*; Žižek, *The Puppet and the Dwarf*. The literature on these and other contemporary philosophers expands monthly; I commented on Badiou's reliance on old (one wishes one could say, *obsolete*) stereotypes of Judaism in "Ideological Closure in the Christ Event," now chapter 7 in Elliott, *Currents in the Interpretation of Paul*.

Christianity," and stand ready to explain just what really *was* wrong with Judaism that Paul alone so brilliantly exposed. (It seems it's easy enough to deny an earthquake if *your* people weren't involved in it.)

There are other scholars, however, who have presented new possibilities for interpreting Paul that both respect and presume the destruction caused in 1977. I wish to name four different approaches—we might say, four architectural schools—that didn't exist before the publication of *Paul and Palestinian Judaism*, and that quite possibly would not have emerged, at least as quickly or coherently, without the stimulus Sanders's book offered.

First is an approach that simply follows the consequences of Sanders's argument. Here the chief example is Heikki Räisänen, for whom the apostle remains theologically "incoherent." What Sanders could *understand* as the rhetoric of a convert, Räisänen rejects as rhetorical question-begging: Only another convert would find Paul's twisted and caricatured depiction of Judaism convincing. We should get along without him.[9]

A second "school" is represented by John G. Gager and Lloyd Gaston. Both scholars follow Sanders's lead and argue that Paul was not diagnosing an actual defect in Judaism. Both foreground as a methodological principle that everything Paul writes to Gentile churches should be read as addressing Gentile-Christian theology and practice, often as a theological corrective, and that nothing Paul writes should be read as a criticism of Jews or Judaism. That's an important methodological divergence from Sanders's work; it constitutes a decision point for interpreters. Gager and Gaston went on to propose that Paul imagined two "tracks" of salvation: salvation through the covenant in Torah for Jews, salvation through Christ for non-Jews; and most scholars have found this "two-track" model unconvincing.[10]

A third approach is well represented by some scholars in this room; I think of Professor Fredriksen as first laying out its basic lines, and Mark D. Nanos as perhaps its most indefatigable apostle. It has more recently been labeled the "Paul within Judaism" approach. Advocates also respect and assume Sanders's demonstration that Paul was not analyzing a genuine defect in Judaism, but they demur from the conclusion that Paul "thought backward, from solution to plight." On this view, Paul continues to think—coherently—as a Pharisaic and apocalyptically-minded Jew, who believes he is living in the day, long prophesied, when the nations would turn in obedience to the Messiah; indeed, Paul thinks he is the instrument of that turning. All his fulminations about the Torah are aimed at preventing non-Jews from

9. Räisänen, *Paul and the Law*. Räisänen's resolute effort to interpret the New Testament historically, independently of theological bias, was well honored in the volume *Moving beyond New Testament Theology*, ed. Penner and Vander Stichele.

10. Gager, *The Origins of Anti-Semitism*; Lloyd Gaston, *Paul and the Torah*.

blurring the lines by adopting marks of Jewish identity. For these scholars, as for Gaston and Gager, the "fault" Paul exposes lies not in Judaism, but in the temptation to Judaize in the nascent Gentile church. Instead of "two tracks," however, we might imagine that the "Paul within Judaism" crowd envision one track, but two different cars on the train, one for Israel, another for the nations, and Paul as the conductor trying to keep everyone in their separate compartments until everyone reaches their destination.[11]

So far, so good. I would identify a fourth school of interpretation that emerges from the aftermath of Professor Sanders's work: what has come to be called "empire criticism" or, more colloquially, the "Paul-against-empire" crowd. I realize this claim sounds counter-intuitive: Professor Sanders is on record in finding precious little justification for any political argument in Paul's letters. The apostle himself was a "social conservative"; his un-nuanced exhortation to be subject to the governing authorities (Rom 13:1–7) is "enthusiastic, idealistic, or perhaps naïve," but hardly troubled by shadows of unjust tyranny. Paul expected an imminent end, and "while Christians awaited the return of the Lord, they should not attempt to change the status quo by (for example) campaigning for the freedom of slaves and opposing unjust laws and rulers."[12]

That has proved a sturdy enough reading in modern interpretation, and it's not my purpose here to quarrel with it.[13] My point is that some people who spend their time detecting implicit or even "hidden" political agendas in Paul's rhetoric have *Paul and Palestinian Judaism* to thank, in part, for the inspiration. At least, I do.

I'm aware that's not how the guild views empire criticism. No less omniscient a scholar than N. T. Wright has explained that political interpretation of Paul originated in "below-the-tracks university" life in Boston, just as other specialized perspectives have a readily identifiable social location

---

11. Perhaps the most energetic advocate of this approach has been Mark D. Nanos, in *The Mystery of Romans* and subsequent publications, most recently the collection he edited with Magnus Zetterholm, *Paul within Judaism*. Four volumes of Nanos's collected essays are being published now by Wipf & Stock: *Reading Paul within Judaism* and *Reading Corinthians and Philippians within Judaism* (2017), *Reading Romans within Judaism* and *Reading Galatians and Corinthians within Judaism* (forthcoming). The general approach I am describing was pioneered by Paula Fredriksen, however, in *From Jesus to Christ*, a work that makes transparent the significance of Sanders's argument. Also relevant here are Eisenbaum, *Paul Was Not a Christian*; Zetterholm, *Approaches to Paul*; and Boccaccini and Segovia, eds., *Paul the Jew*.

12. Sanders, *Paul: The Apostle's Life, Letters, and Thought*, 692–96.

13. On recent developments in "Paul vs. empire" scholarship, see the essays on "Paul and Empire" by me (now chapter 8 in this volume) and James R. Harrison in *An Introduction to Empire in the New Testament*, ed. Adam Winn.

that produced them.¹⁴ Others have attributed empire-critical readings to the frustration of left-leaning U.S. scholars who were agitated by President Bush's war in Iraq; these scholars are accused of reading their own political preoccupation into Paul's letters and thus drowning out the apostle's voice with their own.¹⁵

Speaking only for myself, I'm happy to own my leftist inclinations. I don't know why they should be limited to opposition to George W. Bush in particular; in between *two* wars in Iraq, launched by *two* Presidents Bush, a Democratic administration conducted an eight-year-long sanctions program that killed half a million Iraqi children, according to United Nations estimates, and from which two U.N. directors resigned, calling its effects "barbaric." I don't know why anyone should be contented with those facts. I wonder whether people who attribute politically interested exegesis to opposition to such policies would assume the converse proposition, that "normal," that is, ostensibly apolitical, theological interpretation implied the practitioner's satisfaction with, or indifference toward, such policies. Would I read Paul differently if I stopped worrying and learned to love the bomb, the drone strike, or waterboarding?

That rhetorical question aside: I didn't come to the search for implicit anti-imperial themes in Paul's letters because I was stewing over Republican presidents. Rather, I read *Paul and Palestinian Judaism*, close to forty years ago. I quickly came to realize that most of the other books on the library shelves had Paul wrong, at least in significant part. These elaborate treatments of Paul's theological and rhetorical brilliance were all upended by Professor Sanders's elaborate, methodical demonstration that Paul *should not* have meant what he said, if he was trying to describe the inadequacies of Judaism.

But what, I wondered, if Paul had been trying to do something else?

Here I might assign some of the "blame" for my own interpretive wanderings on my dissertation advisors, particularly Paul W. Meyer, who from

---

14. Wright, *Paul in Fresh Perspective*, 16–18; he presumably has the work of Richard A. Horsley, retired from the University of Massachusetts in Boston, in mind. Wright doesn't explain how his own ecclesiastical or civil location, for example, occupying a seat in the British House of Lords, might have shaped his perception of the apostle (though in another place he told an interviewer that his episcopacy gave him the distinct advantage over his Peers of knowing just what "ordinary members of the people" thought: "we're coming hot from the coalface, as it were, to say 'This is what's actually going on'" [Oct. 25, 2010, interview with the online resource *Faith and Leadership*, https://www.faithandleadership.com/nt-wright-working-building]). To the contrary, he declares that he simply speaks from "[his] own acquaintance with Paul," as do "the vast majority of Christians in the world today" (*Paul in Fresh Perspective*, 18).

15. Burk, "Is Paul's Gospel Counterimperial?" and Kim, *Christ and Caesar*.

the start directed me to immerse myself in the rapidly developing field of rhetorical criticism and the "New Rhetoric." I realized soon enough that everything the ancient rhetorical handbooks and contemporary rhetorical theorists alike had to say about rhetorical competency crashed into Professor Sanders's presentation of the apostle Paul as someone who "thought backward, from solution to plight."

It wasn't just that, following Sanders's view, what Christian scholars had learned to read as Paul's theological sophistication collapsed into the rationalizations of an enthusiastic convert. He also would have been rhetorically incompetent before any audience other than a self-satisfied group of converts who already shared all of his conclusions. That judgment is, of course, plausible. In recent history, we've seen bombastic, intellectually incoherent figures amass tremendous popularity and political power on the basis of their ability to incite the emotions of like-minded citizens, in the absence of any but the crudest form of rhetorical ability. It is perfectly plausible—I would argue, *probable*—that the apostle Paul's canonical legacy was shaped, after his death, by a Gentile-Christian church that heard in his letters just what they wanted to hear: congratulatory assurances of their place in God's good favor apart from the law (so much is the message of Ephesians, for example). But that possibility does not require that Paul *himself* meant no more than what the Gentile church took him to mean.

Of course, without direct access to Paul's own performance (or that of his representative) and the reaction of the audience, as well as a "thick" understanding of the original rhetorical situation surrounding the composition, sending, and reception of a particular letter, any historically valid judgment of the Paul's rhetorical competence is impossible. "Rhetorical criticism" of the New Testament inevitably proceeds on the premise—itself unprovable—of rhetorical competence on the part of its various authors, and Sanders has done us the great service of pointing up the possibility that just that premise may, in some cases, be false.

But before accepting that conclusion, it has seemed to me from the beginning of my scholarly career, we should ask, what if Paul was up to something else than explaining Christianity's superiority to Judaism? What if talk about "God's justice" wasn't primarily a category of religious inclusion, of "getting in" (as Sanders seemed to agree with the established Protestant reading), but instead engaged what other voices around Paul meant when they used the language of justice, faithfulness to divine purposes, or the "obedience of the nations"?[16]

---

16. These paragraphs summarize my approach in *The Rhetoric of Romans*.

I found a pointer to an answer in Professor Fredriksen's *From Jesus to Christ*. She patiently walked the reader through Sanders's demolition of Protestant interpretation, with its devoutly intoned caricatures of Judaism, but she went further, to ask what stood behind Paul's supposed conversion to the perspective of the Gentile church (something that in Sanders's work seemed to me to remain a black box). She found a ready explanation in Jewish restoration eschatology, which shaped Paul's insistence that the righteous among the nations remain righteous among *the nations*.[17] (I consider this a cornerstone of the "Paul within Judaism" paradigm.) She also argued, convincingly, that Paul's former harassment of the churches had been motivated, not by some halakhic objection to Messianic belief, or hostility to an incipient abandonment of Torah observance among the earliest believers in Jesus, but by Paul's fierce, thoroughly Jewish concern to safeguard Jewish communities in the midst of larger and potentially hostile Gentile populations. "The enthusiastic proclamation of a messiah executed very recently as a political insurrectionist—a *crucified* messiah—combined with a vision of the approaching End *preached also to Gentiles*—this was dangerous. If it got abroad, it could endanger the whole Jewish community."[18]

Professor Fredriksen has elaborated on these early lines of interpretation in her important recent monograph *Paul the Pagans' Apostle*. Here she gives greater depth and color to her earlier depiction of the fundamental threat the early proclamation of the risen Christ would have posed to Diaspora synagogues—and by extension, the alarm Paul's own gospel would have evoked on the urban landscape of the Roman world. Fredriksen never speaks of the apostle acting as a "political" agitator, rebuking an Emperor or criticizing an imperial policy, as "empire-critical" interpreters are often thought (usually unfairly) to do. Rather, the Pauline mission required that residents of a Roman city "make an exclusive commitment to the god of Israel and, thus, to renounce their own gods," and this constituted a fundamental break of the divine-human bond that everyone understood was the basis of civilization.[19] I see no reason to avoid describing the threat so conceived as "political," since the perceived order of the *polis* was at stake. Others might insist the issue it was "religious" or "theological"—but to polarize these categories as opposites is fatally to miss Professor Fredriksen's point.

I don't mean to lay on either Professor Fredriksen or Professor Sanders the responsibility for the directions in which I (or any of the empire-critical cohort) has wandered. It is a matter of fact that the empire-critical approach

---

17. Fredriksen, *From Jesus to Christ*, esp. 165–70.
18. Fredriksen, *From Jesus to Christ*, 154.
19. Fredriksen, *Paul the Pagans' Apostle*, 167–74.

appeared after their works. I submit that the thoroughgoing search for a political dimension to Paul's theology was made possible, first, by Sanders sweeping away the standard theological expositions of his thought, and then, by Fredriksen drawing a compelling, if not inevitable, historical conclusion and insisting that theologians take its implications with utmost seriousness.[20]

Suffice it to say that the earthquake of 1977 has been followed by decades of intense new construction, according to a wide variety of standards, tastes, and interests. To adapt a Pauline theme, time will tell what endures (1 Cor 3:10–15).

---

20. I refer to the last two paragraphs of *From Jesus to Christ*, which should be recited regularly by Christian seminarians, pastors, and professors.

3

The Anti-Imperial Message of the Cross

"When I first came to you, brothers and sisters," Paul wrote to the Christians in the Roman colony of Corinth, "I resolved to know nothing among you except Jesus Christ, and him crucified."

It is impossible to exaggerate the importance of the cross of Jesus Christ to Paul. Not only did his encounter with Jesus as the crucified generate the revolution in his conviction and action that we customarily call his "conversion," it energized his entire apostolic endeavor. His proclamation in the cities of the Roman Empire consisted in the "public portrayal of Jesus Christ crucified" (Gal 3:1). The entrance rite of baptism was in his eyes nothing less than co-crucifixion with Christ (Rom 6:1–5); the common sacred meal, the "Lord's supper," a solemn and public proclamation of the Lord's death (1 Cor 11:26). The atmosphere of the congregation was to be charged with constant regard for the brother or sister "for whom Christ died" (Rom 14:15; 1 Cor 8:11).

As soon as we recognize the centrality of the cross of Christ for Paul, the common view that Paul was uninterested in political realities should leave us perplexed. The crucifixion of Jesus is, after all, one of the most unequivocally political events recorded in the New Testament. Behind the early theological interpretations of Jesus' crucifixion as a death "for us," and behind centuries of piety that have encrusted the crucifixion with often grotesque sentimentality, stands the "most nonreligious and horrendous feature of the gospel,"[1] the brutal fact of the cross as an instrument of imperial terror. If in his theologizing Paul muted or suppressed the politically

---

1. Beker, *Paul the Apostle*, 207.

engineered horror of the cross, then we would have to conclude that Paul himself mystified the death of Jesus, accommodating his "word of the cross" to the interests of the very regime that had brought about that death.

Martin Hengel's study of crucifixion in the Roman world highlights its political significance.[2] As a means of capital punishment for heinous crimes, crucifixion was the "supreme Roman penalty," yet "almost always inflicted only on the lower class (*humiliores*); the upper class (*honestiores*) could reckon with more 'humane' punishment" (such as decapitation). Crucifixion was "the typical punishment for slaves," practiced "above all as a deterrent against trouble," the most spectacular example being the crucifixion of six thousand followers of the slave rebel Spartacus in 71 BCE. A special location was reserved on the Campus Esquilinus in Rome for the public crucifixion of slaves: Hengel compares it to Golgotha, outside Jerusalem.[3] The Roman lawyer Gaius Cassius explained this use of crucifixion as he pressed in court, in the face of mass protest by people from the lower classes, for the execution of four hundred slaves after their master, the prefect of Rome, was murdered by one of them: "You will never restrain that scum but by terror" (Tacitus, *Annals* 14.42–45).[4]

Only those Roman citizens who by acts of treason "had forfeited the protection of citizenship" might be crucified, but this happened only very rarely. Much more commonly, crucifixion served as "a means of waging war and securing peace, of wearing down rebellious cities under siege, of breaking the will of conquered peoples and of bringing mutinous troops or unruly provinces under control." First among these "unruly provinces," of course, was Judea, where the Romans crucified tens of thousands of Jews. The Roman general Varus put down a rebellion there in 4 BCE, crucifying two thousand suspected rebels at once (Josephus, *War* 2.66-79). The Roman procurator Felix, confronted by widespread resistance and sporadic guerrilla action in the 50s of the common era, won the hatred of his subjects by indiscriminate mass crucifixions, putting to death "a number of robbers [*lēstai*] impossible to calculate" (*War* 2.252-253: Josephus uses the pejorative term preferred by Rome for its most ungrateful subjects). His successor, Florus, provoked full-scale rebellion first by plundering the Temple treasury, then by suppressing the ensuing (nonviolent) protest with mass crucifixions even of Jews who held equestrian rank as citizens of Rome (*War* 2.293-300). During the subsequent siege of Jerusalem, the Roman general

---

2. Hengel, *Crucifixion*, reprinted with *The Son of God* and *The Atonement* in *The Cross of the Son of God*. Citations are from the reprint edition.

3. Hengel, *Crucifixion*, 125–37.

4. Cited by de Ste. Croix, *Class Struggle*, 409.

Titus crucified as many as five hundred refugees from the city per day, until "there was not enough room for the crosses" outside the city walls (*War* 5.446–451).[5]

In the Roman practice, "whipping, torture, the burning out of the eyes, and maiming often preceded the actual hanging."[6] Josephus reported that Titus's troops captured poorer Jews escaping from Jerusalem to seek food outside the walls, and tortured, scourged, and crucified them in the sight of the city's defenders. In one instance they hacked off the hands of torture victims and drove them back, mutilated, into the city to coerce its inhabitants into surrender (*War* 5.553–561).

As Hengel summarizes the point with regard to crucifixion, the chief reason for its use was "its allegedly supreme efficacy as a deterrent." The Romans practiced crucifixion above all on "groups whose development had to be suppressed by all possible means to safeguard law and order in the state."

The brutality of crucifixion was not exceptional in the order established by Rome. The so-called Pax Romana, the cessation of "hot" wars of expansion and competition among military rivals, was celebrated in rhetoric and ritual as a new golden age, the gift of the gods; but it was a "peace" won through military conquest, as Roman iconography clearly shows. The "altar of the peace of Augustus" was placed on the Hill of Mars, god of war. Coins struck under Augustus link the armed and armored First Citizen with Pax, goddess of peace, trampling on the weapons of subdued enemies, and Victoria, goddess of conquest, treading upon the globe itself.[7]

Most of our literary sources for this period, coming from the hands of the upper classes, who benefited from the "sheer rapacity" of an empire that "plundered the provinces on a vast scale,"[8] speak of the arrangement in the most admiring terms. "Not surprisingly, the imperial regime was hardly legitimate in the eyes of the conquered."[9] The last point bears emphasis. In a speech put on the lips of a Briton by the Roman historian Tacitus:[10]

> Harriers of the world, now that earth fails their all devastating
> hands they probe even the sea; if their enemy has wealth, they

---

5. De Ste. Croix, *Class Struggle*, 138–42.

6. Beker, *Paul the Apostle*, 206 (citing Josephus, *War* 5.44.9).

7. A less enchanted view of the Pax Romana comes from the Marxist historian de Ste. Croix. The cessation of war was "made inevitable by the exhaustion of Italian manpower . . . too many Italians had been fighting for too long" (*Class Struggle in the Ancient Greek World*, 358).

8. De Ste. Croix, *Class Struggle*, 355.

9. Horsley, *Jesus and the Spiral of Violence*, 20–29; he cites Dom Hélder Câmara, *Spiral of Violence*, 29–31.

10. Wengst, *Pax Romana and the Peace of Jesus Christ*, 52–53.

have greed; if he is poor, they are ambitious; East and West have glutted them; alone of mankind they behold with the same passion of concupiscence waste alike and want. To plunder, butcher, steal, these things they misname empire; they make a desolation and call it peace. Children and kin are by the law of nature each man's dearest possessions: they are swept away from us by conscription to be slaves in other lands; our wives and sisters, even when they escape a soldier's lust, are debauched by self-styled friends and guests: our goods and chattels go for tribute; our lands and harvests in requisitions of grain; life and limb Themselves are used up in levelling marsh and forest to the accompaniment of gibes and blows. Slaves born to slavery are sold once for all and are fed by their masters free of cost; but Britain pays a daily price for her own enslavement, and feeds the slavers. (*Histories* 4:17:2)

And again, a Judean voice, the seer of 4 Ezra describing a vision in which a lion (the messiah) addresses the Roman eagle:

> Are you not the one that remains of the four beasts which I had made to reign in my world, so that the end of my times might come through them? You, the fourth that has come, have conquered all the beasts that have gone before: and you have held sway over the world with much terror, and over all the earth with grievous oppression; and for so long you have dwelt on the earth with deceit. And you have judged the earth, but not with truth; for you have afflicted the meek and injured the peaceable: you have hated those who tell the truth, and have loved liars; you have destroyed the dwellings of those who brought forth fruit, and have laid low the walls of those who did you no harm. And your insolence has come up before the Most High, and your pride to the Mighty One. And the Most High has looked upon his times, and behold, they are ended, and his ages are completed! Therefore you will surely disappear, you eagle . . . so that the whole earth, freed from your violence, may be refreshed and relieved, and may hope for the judgment and mercy of him who made it. (4 Ezra 11:39–46)

The "peace" that Rome secured through terror was maintained through terror,[11] through slavery, fed by conquest and scrupulously maintained through constant intimidation, abuse, and violence;[12] through the ritualized

---

11. Horsley, *Jesus and the Spiral of Violence*, 29.

12. See Bradley, *Slaves and Masters in the Roman Empire*; Patterson, *Slavery and Social Death*.

terror of gladiatorial games, where the human refuse of empire—captives of war, condemned criminals, slaves bought for the arena—were killed in stylized rehearsals of conquest, their fate decided by the whim of the empire's representatives;[13] through the pomp of military processions, which often culminated in the execution of vanquished captives;[14] and on the ideological plane, through imperial cult and ceremonial, the rhetoric of the courts (where the torture of slaves was a routine procedure for gathering evidence), and an educational system that rehearsed the "naturalness" of Rome's global hegemony.[15] It was within this civilization of terror that crucifixion played its indispensable role. Among the massive applications of force were the enslavement of 150,000 Epirots in 167 BCE and the destruction of Corinth in 146 BCE, to which we should add the best documented case, the suppression of Judea in 66–73 CE.[16] Acts of exemplary violence such as crucifixion make large-scale social control possible.

THE POLITICAL CHARACTER OF JESUS' DEATH

Paul's letters show little interest in recounting the words or deeds of Jesus. Of course, since these letters are written to already established congregations, we should not assume that they reproduce either the content of Paul's initial proclamation, the "teaching" or "traditions" he has handed on, or the extent of his knowledge of the Jesus tradition (with which he may be more familiar than his few explicit citations would suggest).[17] We should nevertheless take seriously Paul's declaration that he sought to know "only Jesus and him crucified" among the Corinthians (1 Cor 2:2).

In his letters Paul does not rehearse the historical course that led Jesus to the cross. But that does not mean that he was unaware of, or uninterested in, the historical causes of Jesus' death. Comparing Paul and the Gospels on this point can be misleading. Paul may be less interested than the Evangelists in recounting the words and deeds of Jesus because he does not share

13. The standard reference is Robert, *Les gladiateurs dans L'Orient grec.*

14. See P. B. Duff, "Apostolic Suffering and the Language of Processions," 469–93.

15. See de Ste. Croix's discussion of "Class Struggle on the Ideological Plane," in *Class Struggle*, chap. 7; on the emperor cult, Fishwick, "The Development of Provincial Ruler Worship."

16. De Ste. Croix, *Class Struggle*, 344.

17. Paul refers rather frequently to the "teaching" he expects Christians to remember and hold fast to: *tēn didachēn*, Rom 16:17; *typon didachēs*, Rom 6:17; *tas paradoseis*, 1 Cor 11:2; *ton logon akoēs tou theou*, 1 Thess 2:13). For a concise discussion of Paul's contact with the Jesus tradition, see Fitzmyer, *Paul and His Theology*, 32–34, and the bibliography there.

their need, in the wake of the Judean war, to provide Jesus with a dramatically messianic past.[18] He is, rather, concerned constantly to stir up among his congregations a fervent expectancy of the Messiah's future (see Rom 8:18–25; 1 Cor 15:59–58; 1 Thess 5:1–11).

In contrast to the Gospels, Paul is content to say no more about Jesus than that he was "obedient," and that this obedience was the cause of his death, which Paul specifies was by crucifixion (Phil. 2:6–8). The obedience of the one equal to God (2:6) consists not simply in becoming human, but in taking a particular place within humanity, as a slave (2:7); not simply in taking on mortality, but in being so humbled as to accept the most humiliating of deaths, the form of execution reserved for slaves under Roman rule, crucifixion (2:8).[19] That very emphasis on the manner of Jesus' death, shameful and horrific, yes, but also unavoidably political in its connotations, stands in sharp tension with the view that Paul sought to obscure or mystify Jesus' death. The cross was for Paul the signature in history of the forces that killed Jesus.

Nevertheless, "Paul appears totally uninterested in tracking down and identifying the villains responsible for Jesus' crucifixion, nor does he offer any historical reasons why they did it."[20] There are only two possible exceptions to this statement: 1 Thess 2:15–16, where "the Jews" are blamed for killing "the Lord Jesus," a passage rightly regarded as an interpolation made by a Christian scribe in the wake of the Judean war, and 1 Cor 2:8, where Paul writes that "the rulers [*archontes*] of this age" crucified "the Lord of glory." Since this latter passage might be the only place in Paul's letters where he alludes to the human actors in Jesus' death, it clearly merits our attention.

Just what does Paul mean by the phrase "the rulers of this age"? Unfortunately, this is one of many places where the apostle's style is abrupt and elliptical. To make matters more complicated, he uses a term, *archōn*, that can have a range of meanings in classical and koine Greek. Although elsewhere in the New Testament *archontes* refers straightforwardly to human rulers,[21] the word could also refer to superhuman beings (e.g., the angelic "princes" behind the Persian and Greek empires in Dan 10:13, 20).

It is evident from the immediate context, however, that Paul is not interested in examining political tensions in Judea or the vicissitudes of Pilate's career some two decades earlier. The context of his interpretation of Jesus'

---

18. Fredriksen, *From Jesus to Christ*, chaps. 3, 9.

19. Käsemann, "The Saving Significance of Jesus' Death in Paul," 36; see now the discussion in Wright, *The Climax of the Covenant*, chap. 4.

20. Cousar, *A Theology of the Cross*, 26.

21. Luke 23:13, 35; 24:20; Acts 4:8–10, 26; 13:27–28; John 7:26. See Wink, *Naming the Powers*, 40.

crucifixion is the mythic symbolism of the Jewish apocalypses. In the cross of Jesus, the Wisdom of God decreed "before the ages" (2:7) has confounded the rulers of this age who are being destroyed (*katargoumenon*, 2:6). The terms used here are echoed in the prophecy at the end of 1 Corinthians: At the end, Christ will "deliver the kingdom to God the Father after destroying every rule and authority and power" (15:24). The parallelism, including both the verb "destroy" (*katargoumenon*, 2:6; *katargēsē*, 15:24) and the related nouns "rulers" (*archontes*, 2:8), "rule" (*archē*), "authority" (*exousia*), "power" (*dynamis*, 15:24), suggests that "the rulers of this age" in 2:8 should be taken to include potentially "every rule and authority and power" that remains hostile to God (as Death is "the last enemy," 15:26). Further, the language echoes the apocalyptic vocabulary of the book of Daniel, where we are told that God disposes "rule" (*archē*), "sovereignty" (*basileia*), "power" (*ichthys*), "honor" (*timē*), and "glory" (*doxa*) to the rulers of earth (2:37, Septuagint), until at the end God establishes a kingdom (*basileia*) that will "shatter and bring to an end" all the other kingdoms of the earth (2:44).

Earlier scholarship, heavily influenced by the "religio-historical school," tended to find 1 Corinthians saturated with gnostic motifs; the "rulers of this age" were set within a gnostic scheme of supernatural powers through which a "redeemer" would descend to bring salvation.[22] More recent scholarship has decisively criticized this interpretation, however, pointing out that the construct of a pre-Christian gnostic redeemer myth is a retrojection into the time of Paul of a pattern that first appears in gnostic literature a century or more later, a pattern often dependent on Paul's letters.[23] Recent studies of 1 Corinthians 2 tend to set Paul's language within the conceptual world of Jewish end-time speculations, seeing "the wisdom of God as an apocalyptic power."[24] Indeed, this passage is one of the most important evidences of Paul's apocalypticism in his letters.[25]

"Apocalypticism" is, of course, another scholarly construct, and its precise definition in relation to the ancient sources continues to attract

---

22. Bultmann sees in the passage an allusion to the gnostic redeemer myth (*Theology of the New Testament* 1:175, 181). See also Conzelmann, *First Corinthians*, 61; Delling, "*archōn*," 1:488–89; Dibelius, *Die Geisterwelt im Glauben des Paulus*, 89 (cited by Wink, *Naming the Powers*, 40).

23. Colpe, *Die religionsgeschichtliche Schule*; a similar presentation in English, depending in part on Colpe's work, is Yamauchi, *Pre-Christian Gnosticism*; and now see Petrément, *A Separate God*. Birger Pearson's demonstration that Paul used terms like *pneumatikoi* and *psychikoi* differently from later Gnostics was also decisive in undermining the "Gnostic" interpretation of 1 Corinthians: see *The Pneumatikos-Psychikos Terminology*.

24. See E. Elizabeth Johnson, "The Wisdom of God as Apocalyptic Power."

25. Kovacs, "The Archons, the Spirit, and the Death of Christ."

debate.²⁶ It is sufficient for our purposes to observe the symmetrical language in 1 Corinthians 2 and 15, the characteristic apocalyptic tendency to "view reality on two levels: behind the events of human history lies the cosmic struggle of God with the forces of evil." The references to "the rulers of this age" or to "rules, authorities, powers" reveal that Paul experiences the present time as under the dominion of evil rulers. That Paul describes the rulers as "being destroyed" (*katargoumenōn*, 2:6) shows that Paul sees in the cross the beginning of the destruction of the evil powers—but only its beginning. When Paul refers at "the climax of the whole letter" to every rule and authority and power being destroyed and all things being subjected to the Messiah, it is clear that Paul looks forward to the completion of God's victory in the imminent future.²⁷

Recognizing that Paul conceives Jesus' death as the decisive event in a cosmic struggle may disappoint our sense of history. After all, other writers in Paul's age could describe Pilate's savagery in Judea in journalistic detail. For Paul, however, Pilate's individuality seems to have dissolved within the apocalyptic category of "the rulers of this age." But this hardly means that Paul has softened the political force of the crucifixion.²⁸ Two illuminating comparisons are at hand in the writings of Paul's near contemporaries, Philo of Alexandria and Flavius Josephus, both Jews. When in his *Embassy to Gaius* Philo described Pontius Pilate as "naturally inflexible, a blend of self-will and relentlessness," guilty of "briberies, insults, robberies, outrages and wanton injuries, executions without trial constantly repeated, ceaseless and supremely grievous cruelty" (301-302), he took care to point out that Pilate's brutality violated the intentions of Tiberius, who had instructed his procurators to "speak comfortably to the members of our nation in the different cities" and to regard Jews and their customs with respect (161). Philo reserved the greatest praise for Tiberius's predecessor, "who first received the title of Augustus for his virtue and good fortune, who disseminated peace everywhere over sea and land to the ends of the world" (310). The point of Philo's argument is that even the barbarities of a renegade officer like Pilate did not come near the horror Gaius proposed to inflict on the Jews when he ordered that his statue be erected within the Temple itself.

---

26. See Hanson, Grayson, J. J. Collins, and A. Y. Collins, "Apocalypses and Apocalypticism." For issues in recent scholarship see the essays in J. J. Collins, ed., *Apocalypse*; Hellholm, ed., *Apocalypticism*; A. Y. Collins, *Early Christian Apocalypticism*; and a judicious synthesis, J. J. Collins, *The Apocalyptic Imagination*.

27. Kovacs, "Archons, the Spirit, and the Death of Christ," 224-25.

28. Jon Sobrino discusses the tension between the "eschatologization" of Jesus' death and its historical significance as a death taking place among the poor: *Jesus in Latin America*, 39-40.

Thus Philo can contrast the depradations of Pilate, which he attributes to grave personal defects, to the benevolent policies of the preceding Caesars. His rhetoric suggests that Philo is prepared, of necessity, to make peace with the Roman order, so long as the excesses of a Pilate or a Gaius are curtailed.

In recounting Pilate's massacre of Jews protesting his expropriation of Temple funds for a building project, Flavius Josephus restricts his moral judgments to noting that Pilate's soldiers "inflicted much harder blows than Pilate had ordered" (*Ant.* 18.60-62). When he relates the crucifixion of Jesus, apparently because he is aware that "the tribe of the Christians" persists in his own day, he is satisfied to note that Pilate condemned Jesus "on the accusation of men of the highest standing among us" (18.63-64); no questions of justice disturb the account. Pilate's massacre of Samaritan villagers in Tirathana was answered by an embassy from the council of the Samaritans to Vitellius, governor of Syria, accusing Pilate of slaughtering refugees, not suppressing rebels. Vitellius sent Pilate to Rome to answer the charges, but Tiberius died before he could hear the case; Josephus shows no interest in pursuing the matter further (18.85-89). Josephus's concern in this section of the *Antiquities* is to emphasize the unscrupulous violence of Jewish agitators, motivated by personal greed, who infected Judea with perversely revolutionary sentiments and thus invited disaster throughout the decades leading up to the war (18.6-10); he is not prepared to question Roman policy in Judea.[29]

Neither writer impugns the legitimacy of Roman order as such. Paul shows no such reserve, however. The crucifixion of Jesus is not for him an instance of official misconduct, a miscarriage of Roman justice. It is an apocalyptic event. It reveals "the rulers of this age," indeed "every rule and authority and power"—procurators, kings, emperors, as well as the supernatural "powers" who stand behind them—as intractably hostile to God and as doomed to be destroyed by the Messiah at "the end." Jesus' crucifixion "is

---

29. Between his accounts of these incidents in Judea and Samaria, Josephus narrates two "scandals" in Rome that reveal a similar disposition toward Roman order. First, a senator's wife was seduced with the connivance of the staff at a temple of Isis; Tiberius crucified the temple staff and the maidservant of the seduced woman but banished the seducer (who was after all a Roman citizen). "Such," Josephus concludes, "were the insolent acts of the priests in the temple of Isis" (18:65-80). Again, when another senator's wife was bilked by Jewish conmen, Tiberius exiled the whole Jewish population of Rome, impressing four thousand able-bodied Jewish men into a military campaign on Sardinia—to suppress popular "brigandage," Suetonius tells us (*Tiberius* 36)—and "punishing" any who refused; this, Josephus concludes, resulted from "the wickedness of four men" (18:81-84).

the crux of God's plan for unmasking and overthrowing the powers of this world."[30]

Paul's view of the cross of Jesus is certainly informed by the symbolism of Jewish apocalyptic mythology. But it would miss the point to set this symbolic background over against the "naked facts of history," as if these were available to the impartial observer. If there were a position of neutral objectivity from which the violence of the cross might have been regarded, neither Paul nor Philo nor Josephus was apparently able to find it. Rather, we should compare Paul's apocalyptic interpretation of the cross with other interpretations of violence in Judea that acknowledge, however subtly, the legitimacy of Roman rule implicit in the mythology of empire. We should marvel, not that Paul can speak of his "word of the cross" without specifically identifying Pilate, but that his indictment goes beyond Pilate to include all the powers of heaven and earth together that stand hostile to God. Nevertheless, the reference to crucifixion prevents this symbolic interpretation of Jesus' death from losing its moorings in history and becoming a strictly otherworldly drama.

Far from "denationalizing" the cross, Paul has, so to speak, internationalized it. He insists that the Roman colonists of Corinth, thousands of miles from the troubles in Judea, must mold their lives into a constant remembrance of one particular crucifixion in Judea, because through that crucifixion God has revealed the imminent end of the Powers and has begun to bring "the scheme of this world" to an end (1 Cor 7:31).

PAUL AND "THE POWERS"

The political force of the "word of the cross" could hardly be announced more powerfully. If we are unaccustomed to perceiving this force, part of the reason may be that it has occasionally been blunted by scholarship. Interpreters have often slighted these passages from 1 Corinthians as "less central" to Paul's thought than the more "anthropological" or "existential" understanding of what Bultmann called "the powers of this age: Law, Sin, and Death," as these appear in Romans 5–8.[31]

---

30. Hamerton-Kelly, *Sacred Violence*, 82.

31. Bultmann, *Theology of the New Testament*, 1:298. Bultmann and his followers also insisted that Paul's theology of the Powers in 1 Cor 2:6–8 was both uncharacteristic of the apostle's own thought and completely separate from the "word of the cross," which represented the genius of Paul's theology in demythologizing apocalyptic and gnostic mythologies into "believing self-understanding" (*Theology of the New Testament*, 1:293).

Even when Paul's thought is construed as genuinely apocalyptic, however, interpretation may slight the global horizon of God's struggle against the Powers as we find it in 1 Corinthians 2 and 15. J. Christiaan Beker, an advocate of an "apocalyptic Paul," has distanced Paul from the mythology of the apocalypses and emphasized his "transformation" of Jewish apocalyptic. Beker observes, first, that Paul "does not engage in apocalyptic timetables, descriptions of the architecture of heaven, or accounts of demons and angels; nor does he take delight in the rewards of the blessed and the torture of the wicked." Second, he asserts that even when "traditional apocalyptic terminology" does appear (in Rom 8:38–39, 1 Cor 2:6–8, and 15:24–28), Paul uses these motifs only "sparingly" and interprets them "anthropologically." Thus "the major apocalyptic forces are, for him, those ontological powers that determine the human situation," that is, "the 'field' of death, sin, the law, and the flesh" that figure in Romans 6–7. Beker finds Paul's own apocalyptic interpretation of the cross more in the latter texts than the former, and consequently writes that "the death of Christ now marks the defeat of the apocalyptic power alliance."[32]

But Paul never declares that the existential powers of sin, death, or the Law have been defeated. He says rather that those who are "in Christ" are no longer to let sin rule as lord over them, not because sin has ceased to exist as a power, but because Christians have "died to sin" (Rom 6:2, 6). Similarly, Christians are "free from the Law," not because the Law has ceased to be valid (to the contrary, as Paul insists in Rom 3:31; 7:12, 22, 25!), but because Christians have "died with regard to the law" (Rom 7:1, 4).[33] Further, Paul clearly affirms that the cosmic power of death remains unconquered (1 Cor 15:26). If for Paul the field of cosmic powers opposed to God "operates as an interrelated whole . . . no power can be viewed in isolation from the others," the powers continue as active and insubordinate to God, although (with the exception of death) they no longer have any dominion over the Christian.

Moreover, even when Paul does use more "traditionally apocalyptic" language, he clearly insists that the Powers remain unconquered (1 Cor 15:24). This insistence plays an important role in Paul's argument in 1 Corinthians.[34] It is not clear, therefore, why the apocalyptic conception so important in one letter (1 Corinthians) should be subordinated to the so-called anthropological categories of another (Romans). Indeed, it appears arbitrary to declare that the Powers as understood in 1 Corinthians

---

32. Beker, *Paul the Apostle*, 189–90.

33. On the translation of the dative (*tō nomō*), see Elliott, *The Rhetoric of Romans*, 243–45.

34. Beker, *Paul the Apostle*, 168.

have in fact been "reinterpreted" as the Powers of Romans, and on this basis to conclude—contrary to the intention of 1 Corinthians 15—that Paul understands the Powers to have been decisively defeated; how much more arbitrary to support this judgment with texts from the pseudo-Pauline Colossians and Ephesians![35]

It may be to the point here to observe that what Beker describes as "traditional apocalyptic elements" do in fact appear in Paul's letters, although they are not emphasized. The "word of the Lord" in 1 Thessalonians 4 is a rudimentary "apocalyptic timetable," complete with archangel's trumpet. The "architecture of heaven" can hardly have been unknown to someone who had been caught up to "the third heaven" (2 Cor 12:2), who refrains from describing "visions and revelations" only because their content is unutterable (12:5).[36] Finally, Paul is evidently comfortable with judgment according to works (Rom 2:6-11) and divine recompense for the wicked (Rom 2:5; 12:19-20).[37] The net result of these observations is to situate Paul's thinking even more within the apocalyptic tradition. There is no good reason to marginalize the clearly apocalyptic viewpoint of 1 Corinthians 2 and 15 within Paul's thinking.[38]

Our unfamiliarity with "God's war of liberation" as a Pauline theme may also result from the way Colossians and Ephesians have shaped our perception of Paul's theology of the Powers. The pseudo-Pauline letters already began to modify Paul to serve the churches' agenda in the postapostolic period, and to an extent to accommodate the word of the cross to the interests of empire. In the ears of the Roman dynasts of ancient Corinth, talk of Christ's having already defeated the powers would have seemed "a pleasantly harmless" myth; one can almost hear their collective sigh of relief at the Christian reassurance that "our struggle is not against human beings."[39]

This is not Paul's theology of the Powers as it appears in 1 Corinthians. I want to stress the following differences between Paul's theology of the Powers as it appears in 1 Corinthians and that of the pseudo-Paulines:

1. Paul himself is not concerned to speculate on the origins of "the powers." It is not important for him to affirm that they are "created" (a point made in Col 1:16). Paul was presumably familiar with the myths of God apportioning the nations to the "sons of God," that is, the "angels

---

35. Beker declares that "the author of Colossians interprets Paul correctly on this point," citing Col 2:15 and Eph 1:20-22 (*Paul the Apostle*, 190).

36. On Paul's visionary experience see Tabor, *Things Unutterable*; Segal, *Paul the Convert*, chap. 2.

37. Snodgrass, "Justification by Grace—to the Doers."

38. Kovacs, "Archons, the Spirit, and the Death of Christ," 224–25.

39. De Ste. Croix, *Class Struggle*, 432 (on the language of the Magnificat).

The Anti-Imperial Message of the Cross 65

of the nations" (Deut 32:8-9) and of the "fallen angels."[40] But he says no more than that "death entered by one man" (1 Cor 15:21; Rom 5:12, 18), that "God subjected the creation to futility [*mataiotēs*]" and that creation is consequently in "bondage to corruption" or "decay [*phthora*]" (Rom 8:20-21). He seems simply to assume, with the apocalyptists, a worldview in which spiritual forces stand behind political powers on earth.

2. Nor does Paul speak of the rehabilitation of the Powers; he speaks rather of their "destruction" (RSV) or "neutralization," their *katargēsis* (1 Cor 2:6; 15:24). The language echoes the apocalypses, where God will give dominion to the saints of the Most High (Dan 7:22, 27) and will "shatter these other kingdoms and make an end of them" (2:44). Further, Paul locates this divine triumph "at the end," not in the cross of Christ (vs. Col 2:15).

3. Paul does not hesitate to describe the Powers as continuing in hostility against God. Death is "the last enemy to be destroyed" (1 Cor 15:26). Similarly, the apparent intention of the "angels, principalities, things present, things to come, powers" is to "separate us from the love of God which is in Christ Jesus" (Rom 8:38).

4. In Paul's own letters, the work of "heavenly" Powers opposed to God ("angels, principalities") is clearly described as being carried out through very human instruments: "oppression, distress, persecution, starvation, destitution, peril, sword" (Rom 8:35-39). Paul here lists "the sanctions of primarily human powers," things that "the evil will of human beings can concoct."[41] These earthly sanctions cannot separate us from the love of God, Paul says. It is hardly incidental that this rhetorically powerful passage in Romans 8 gives way immediately to Paul's appeal for his audience's sympathy with the people Israel (Romans 9-11),[42] an appeal motivated not only by recent imperial legislation harshly restricting Jewish rights in the city of Rome, but perhaps also by the savagery in Roman Palestine during these same years.[43]

---

40. On the mythic background of "powers" language, see Wink, *Naming the Powers*, 13-35.

41. Romans 8:35 "refers not simply to hardships, such as 'famine' (RSV) but to things done to us by 'someone' (*tis*) who wants to 'separate us from the love of Christ'" (Wink, *Naming the Powers*, 48).

42. On the rhetorical connection between Romans 8 and 9, usually not recognized by commentators, see Elliott, *Rhetoric of Romans*, 253-70.

43. See Wiefel, "The Jewish Community in Ancient Rome"; see my discussion in *Rhetoric of Romans*, 43-59. On Palestine under "The Roman Procurators A.D. 44-66," see the "new Schürer," *The History of the Jewish People*, 1:455-70.

5. Corresponding to the view that the Powers continue to wreak violence and misery on earth, Paul understands "living in the Spirit" not as a turning away from earthly misery toward the contemplation of "things heavenly" (compare Col 3:2), but rather as an agonized groaning in sympathy with an oppressed creation. The Spirit draws Christians into the trauma of a cosmic childbirth, as those who live in the Spirit await not only their own corporeal emancipation from the thrall of the Powers, but the liberation of the whole of creation itself (Rom 8:22-23). This experience of the Spirit issues directly, for Paul and, he hopes, for his readers, in "great sorrow and unceasing anguish" for his own people, Israel, as they await the liberation of the messianic age which is their birthright (Rom 9:1-5).

6. In contrast to the statement in Colossians that God "disarmed the principalities and powers and made a public example of them, triumphing over them" in Christ (Col 2:15), Paul uses the metaphor of the triumphal procession more sparingly, and only to refer to his own physical abuse at the hands of very real earthly authorities. After his "affliction" (*thlipsis*) in Asia, when "we were so utterly, unbearably crushed that we despaired of life itself" and "felt that we had received the sentence of death" (2 Cor 2:8-9), he describes himself as being "led about" by Christ in a triumphal procession, giving off the "stench of death" to those who see only the victim of Roman punishment (2 Cor 2:14-16; compare 4:7-12).[44]

I conclude that, in contrast to Colossians and Ephesians, which have been allowed to play so dominant a role in scholarship on "the Powers," Paul's apocalyptic language about the Powers resists transposing the significance of Jesus' death from the earthly to the heavenly plane. It is precisely Paul's own insistence that the Powers remain unconquered until "the end," when they meet their decisive defeat at God's hands, that resists any narrowly spiritual interpretation of the Powers. Paul interprets Jesus' death as the beginning of God's final "war of liberation" against all the Powers that hold creation in thrall through the instruments of earthly oppression. The death of Jesus unmasks the rulers of this age as intractably opposed to the wisdom of God, but they are not yet overcome.

Further, Paul speaks eloquently about his own freedom from the persistently lethal threats of the Powers: "We are afflicted in every way, but not crushed; perplexed, but not driven to despair; persecuted, but not forsaken; struck down, but not destroyed" (2 Cor 4:8-9). This freedom marks his own identification with the crucifixion of Jesus: "We are always carrying about in the body the death of Jesus" (4:10). Paul is sustained in that freedom by a

---

44. On the metaphor of triumphal procession, see P. B. Duff, "Apostolic Suffering"; P. B. Duff, "Metaphor, Motif, and Meaning."

very traditionally apocalyptic hope in the resurrection of the dead, though to be sure this hope is confirmed for him by Jesus' resurrection.

Yes, the cross robs the Powers of Death of their "final sanction," exposing the Powers "as unable to make Jesus become what they wanted him to be, or to stop being who he was." "On the Cross these stupid powers displayed for all to see the one secret that they had to keep if they were to retain their power, the secret of founding violence."[45] But this is an insight possible for Paul only in light of the resurrection, for the crucifixion alone would only rehearse, not expose, the logic of founding violence. It is the resurrection of Christ the crucified that reveals the imminent defeat of the Powers, pointing forward to the final triumph of God. "The death and resurrection of Christ in their apocalyptic setting constitute the coherent core of Paul's thought."[46]

The mythological language with which Paul discusses the death of Jesus serves clear rhetorical purposes in 1 Corinthians, effectively extending the significance of Jesus' death at the hands of "the rulers" so as to determine how citizens of a flourishing Roman colony, hundreds of miles distant from dusty Judea, ought to conduct themselves toward the "scheme of this age, which is passing away" (7:31), on the one hand, and toward the "have-nots" in their own community (11:22) and in Judea itself (16:1–4), on the other. Given the profound distaste for the subject of crucifixion that Hengel documents for the Roman upper class, Paul's insistence on talking about the cross of Jesus, his insistence that this event has begun the dissolution of the Roman order, and his insistence that wealthy and prestigious Corinthians within the Christian congregation must now relate to the poor in a new way because of that crucifixion can scarcely be described as "minimizing the political aspects" of the cross!

THE CROSS AND THE JUSTICE OF GOD

Paul's perspective on the death of Jesus is thoroughly and profoundly apocalyptic. Paul thus participates in a broad current in Second Temple Judaism through which Jews sought to "make sense of and to respond to concrete historical situations of oppression and even persecution." Apocalypticism empowered people to "remain steadfast in their traditions and to resist systematic attempts to suppress them."[47]

In the cross, God has annulled the wisdom of this age and of the rulers of this age. Further, since the one whom the rulers crucified has been raised

---

45. Hamerton-Kelly, *Sacred Violence*, 85.
46. Beker, *Paul the Apostle*, 194–98, 205–8.
47. Horsley, *Jesus and the Spiral of Violence*, 139.

from the dead, the rulers have clearly marked themselves out as doomed to destruction (1 Cor 2:6–8; 15:51–58). The immediate consequence is that the Christian is no longer obligated to the scheme of this world, which is passing away (1 Cor 7:31), but is called to obey the God who has chosen the weak, those "without rank or standing in the world, mere nothings, to overthrow the existing order" (1:28, Revised English Version).

This apocalyptic theology centers on the vindication of God's ancient purposes for the covenant people, and through them for the liberation of all creation. The questions at the heart of Paul's theology do not center on how the conscience-stricken individual may be saved, or on how a movement that includes Gentiles as well as Jews may be legitimized. His questions are the questions of his fellow apocalyptists: How shall God's justice be realized in a world dominated by evil powers?[48] For Paul, as for his pious contemporaries, the justice of God stood or fell with God's covenant faithfulness,[49] for the "plight" Paul conceived was dramatically focused in Israel's oppression, a "real, indubitable fact of first-century life. As long as Herod or Pilate ruled over her, Israel was still under the curse of 'exile.'" In this sense "nothing less than the framework of covenant theology will do justice" to Paul's thought.[50]

Paul's doctrine of the cross is thus a doctrine of God's justice and God's partiality toward the oppressed. In the crucifixion of the Messiah at the hands of the Roman oppressors, God has recapitulated the history of Israel's exile and brought it to a decisive climax; indeed, in a slave's death on a cross (Phil. 2:8) the enslavement of the whole creation is embodied (Rom 8:20–22).

Paul has not obscured the nature of the cross as historical and political oppression; rather he has focused it through the lens of Jewish apocalypticism. Only a Gentile church unaccustomed to that perspective, and more familiar with the sacrificial logic of the blood cults, could have transformed Paul's message into a cult of atonement in Christ's blood (the letter to the Hebrews) and a charter of Israel's disfranchisement (the Letter of Barnabas).

---

48. On the phrase "the righteousness of God," see Manfred Brauch's appendix in recent scholarship in Sanders, *Paul and Palestinian Judaism*, 523–42. Käsemann showed that the phrase has its background in Jewish apocalypticism and refers to God's "salvation-creating power" ("The Righteousness of God in Paul"); Hays finds the same background already in the Bible ("Psalm 143 and the Logic of Romans 3"). Against Käsemann, I doubt Paul's use of the phrase is directed against Jewish covenant theology (see Wright, *The Climax of the Covenant*, 234).

49. See Beker, "The Faithfulness of God."

50. Wright, *The Climax of the Covenant*, 261.

Paul's own letters show that he recognized these tendencies within the gentile church of his own day, and opposed them.

4

Paul and the Politics of Empire: Problems and Prospects

THE RELEVANCE OF EMPIRE

"WE ARE AT A point in our work when we can no longer ignore empires and the imperial context in our studies." In his postcolonial manifesto, *Culture and Imperialism*, Edward Said has called interpreters to recognize, within the cultural texts they study, the importance of the attitudes and concepts by which empire finds legitimacy, the "notions that certain territories and people require and beseech domination." A prominent critic of U.S. policy in the Middle East, Said insists the interpreter's task be nothing less than an "intervention" in the production and transmission of imperialist culture. There can be no position of neutrality: "The world today does not exist as a spectacle about which we can be either pessimistic or optimistic, about which our 'texts' can be either ingenious or boring. All such attitudes involve the deployment of power and interests." We must choose between "the projection, or the refusal, of the wish to dominate, the capacity to damn, or the energy to comprehend and engage with other societies, traditions, histories." In contrast to what he calls the "astonishing sense of weightlessness" in Western academia "with regard to the gravity of history," Said notes that for interpreters in postcolonial nations, it has proven "impossible to write of liberation and nationalism . . . without also declaring oneself for or against them"; given the totalizing tendency of imperialism, "one either was on the side of empire or against it."[1]

1. Said, *Culture and Imperialism*, xx, 6, 279, 303; see also Said, *Orientalism*; and

Taking empire seriously has revolutionized recent study of the historical Jesus. In "a serious departure from much previous biblical scholarship," Richard Horsley began his book *Jesus and the Spiral of Violence* (1987) with chapters discussing "The Imperial Situation" and forms of popular Jewish resistance in Roman Palestine. He went on to argue that Jesus "directly and sharply opposed the oppression of the ruling groups" in Judea, and even "engaged more fundamentally in a revolt against the powers controlling the imperial situation in Palestine." Similarly, John Dominic Crossan began his study of *The Historical Jesus* (1991) with four chapters on "Brokered Empire"; anthropological studies of imperialist societies, by Gerhard Lenski and John Kautsky, played an important part in his method. Crossan concluded at length that Jesus' practice of "free healing and common eating" expressed "a religious and economic egalitarianism that negated alike and at once the hierarchical and patronal normalcies of Jewish religion and Roman power."[2] Debate will continue over Crossan's characterization of "Jewish religion,"[3] but it is clear that Roman imperialism is now firmly established as a relevant context for historical Jesus study.

The question of empire has begun to touch on our interpretation of the apostle Paul as well. New Testament interpreters are responding, in part, to recent advances in classical studies, which have moved beyond traditional themes of dynastic politics, military conquest, and law as seen from the perspective of the Roman aristocracy. Simon R. F. Price and Paul Zanker have described the production and dissemination of imperial ideology through images and ritual, a production of culture in which provincial elites were only too happy to participate.[4] G. E. M. de Ste. Croix, P. D. A. Garnsey, and Richard Saller, among others, have analyzed perceptively the fundamentally exploitive, "parasitic" nature of economic globalization under the

---

Said, *Covering Islam*.

2. Horsley, *Jesus and the Spiral of Violence*, 156; Crossan, *The Historical Jesus*, 422. Both scholars make good use of sociological and anthropological studies of imperial and colonial societies, for example, Lenski, *Power and Privilege*; and Kautsky, *The Politics of Aristocratic Empires*.

3. In an important critique of one aspect of recent Jesus scholarship, including Crossan's, Paula Fredriksen remarks that "E. P. Sanders' 1977 book *Paul and Palestinian Judaism* finally removed the Pharisees from the cross-hairs of Christian historical fantasy. But the replacement target of choice now seems to be the Temple and the biblically mandated laws of purity." Thus "the old polemical opposition 'law versus grace' has simply been replaced by an even more self-congratulatory antithesis, purity versus compassion." See Fredriksen, "What You See Is What You Get"; also Fredriksen, "Did Jesus Oppose the Purity Laws?"

4. Price, *Rituals and Power*; Zanker, *The Power of Images*; see also Gordon, "The Veil of Power." The preceding are helpfully excerpted in Horsley, ed., *Paul and Empire*. See also Galinsky, *Augustan Culture*.

Roman "world system."[5] As a consequence, Justin Meggitt has been able to cast considerable doubt on the now-conventional wisdom that the Pauline churches were populated by lower-middle-class artisans and entrepreneurs, suffering perhaps from "status inconsistency," but not from real poverty. Given the nature of the Roman economy, Meggitt demonstrates that "poverty was an absolute and not relative phenomenon."[6]

It may not be obvious, however, what specific implications current studies of Roman imperial culture and ideology have for the interpretation of Paul and his letters. One may well ask what Rome has to do with Jerusalem, or Tarsus.

GAPS IN THE "NEW PERSPECTIVE"

Pauline studies have seen undeniable progress—some scholars speak, with good reason, of a "paradigm shift"—as an older interpretive agenda, driven by Christian dogmatics, opposing Paul's doctrine of justification by faith to a spurious scheme of Jewish "works-righteousness," has collapsed beneath the weight of historical improbability. Krister Stendahl's significant contribution to that development is widely recognized, and justly honored, along with roughly contemporary work by Rosemary Radford Ruether and E. P. Sanders.[7] One can argue, nevertheless, that the so-called "new perspective on Paul," now in the ascendancy, has not yet gone beyond the fundamental assumption that Paul must be interpreted over against Judaism.

Scholarship remains preoccupied with the contrast between "particularistic" or "ethnocentric" Judaism and the "universalism" of Paul's theology. Those categories remain problematic, however, for several reasons. First, they derive from the nineteenth-century idealist historiography of Ferdinand Christian Baur, and as Calvin Roetzel has shown, their use in current studies is all too often contaminated by now-defunct racial theory.[8]

---

5. De Ste. Croix, *Class Struggle*; Garnsey and Saller, *The Roman Empire*; on the colonization of Greece, Alcock, *Graecia Capta*; on world-systems theory and Romanization, Woolf, "World-Systems Analysis and the Roman Empire"; see also Woolf, "Becoming Roman, Staying Greek," and Woolf, "Beyond Romans and Natives."

6. Meggitt, *Paul, Poverty and Survival*. On "status inconsistency," see Meeks, *The First Urban Christians*, 51–73.

7. Stendahl, *Paul among Jews and Gentiles*; Ruether, *Faith and Fratricide*; Sanders, *Paul and Palestinian Judaism*.

8. Baur, *Paul: His Life and Works*, vol. 1, chap. 3. On the "new perspective," see Sanders, *Paul and Palestinian Judaism*; Dunn, "The New Perspective on Paul." For critiques, see Deidun, "James Dunn and John Ziesler on Romans in New Perspective"; and Roetzel, "No 'Race of Israel' in Paul's Letters."

Furthermore, despite its initial promise to reverse centuries of theological anti-Judaism, the "new perspective" offers a Pauline "universalism" that leaves little room for the Torah-observant Jew. Jewish scholar Daniel Boyarin draws the ultimate conclusion from this reading of the apostle: Paul's "is a bitter gospel not a sweet one, because it is conditioned precisely on abandoning that to which we hold so dearly, our separate cultural, religious identity, our own fleshy and historical practice, our existence according to the flesh, our Law, our difference. Paul has simply allegorized our difference quite out of existence."[9] Finally, what is taken in this common reading for Paul's "universalism" is usually informed by, even identified with, the "universalism" of Gentile Christianity as expressed in Ephesians. But there are good reasons to doubt that this is the theology of Romans, or of Paul himself.[10]

A preoccupation with Paul's supposed critique of Judaism, or Jewish ethnocentrism, prejudices the weight we give to social and ethical aspects of Paul's theology. Elaine Pagels perceives a "double standard" in conventional treatments of Paul's social thought:

> To continue observing kosher laws is to deny "the freedom for which Christ died," but to continue observing social, political and marital laws and conventions remains acceptable, even commendable. Although the "new humanity" has transformed the entire relationship between Jews and Gentiles, Paul does not allow it to challenge the whole structure of the believers' social, sexual, and political relationships.[11]

Halvor Moxnes perceives a similar "double standard" in the language of honor and shame in Romans. While Paul "broke down the barriers between Jews and non-Jews" in Romans 1–4, in such a way as to establish for Paul's communities "a separate identity vis-a-vis the synagogue," the exhortation in Rom 13:1–7 served rather to "strengthen an integration of Christians into the Hellenistic symbolic universe," reinforcing the social stratification experienced in public life. Thus Paul seems to have "accepted the system of honor operating on the public world of Greco-Roman society," encouraging Christians "to live within the given power structures and to conform to the civic virtues of honor and praise."[12]

---

9. Boyarin, *A Radical Jew*, 203, 152.

10. For a response to Boyarin see Elliott, "Figure and Ground." On the theology of Israel in Romans, see Campbell, *Paul's Gospel in an Intercultural Context*; and Nanos, *The Mystery of Romans*.

11. Pagels, "Paul and Women"; see also Elliott, *Liberating Paul*, chap. 6.

12. Moxnes, "Honor, Shame, and the Outside World in Romans"; Moxnes, "Honor

It is fair to say that much of the debate over Paul's social and ethical thought revolves around the question of this apparent "double standard." Is Paul more concerned in his letters to maintain a social and symbolic boundary against the public world of Hellenistic virtues and imperial ideology, or against the values of a more intimate social space, the diaspora synagogue? Moxnes shows that this question coheres with the interpretation of Romans, for there we find, almost side by side, the exhortation to "be subject to the governing authorities" (13:1–7), which appears to encourage civic conformity, and the exhortation "not to be conformed to this world" (12:2). Moxnes concludes that Paul "accepted the system of honor operating on the public world of Graeco-Roman society but rejected this society as shameful in the area of 'private life,' gender roles and sexuality." Paul's greater concern was to "ease the transition from the synagogue to the Christian groups and strengthen their independence"; thus "it is the particular boasting of the Jew" which Paul attacks.[13]

The same "double standard" regarding Paul reappears in John M. G. Barclay's sweeping study, *Jews in the Mediterranean Diaspora*. The question of culture and imperialism is central here, as Barclay seeks to explore "the varied modes of accommodation or resistance" which diaspora Jews like Philo, Josephus, or the author of 4 Maccabees adopted with regard to their Greco-Roman environment. Barclay appeals to modern studies of colonialism showing that colonized people make "variant uses of the colonizers' culture—in some cases to modify or even obliterate their native cultural traditions, in others to equip them to resist the colonizers' cultural imperialism." Barclay finds the same range of responses among Jews of the Roman diaspora. Sensitive to "contemporary concerns in multicultural politics," he also hears in recent debate over Paul "echoes of the contemporary rejection of colonialism and the current concern with 'the politics of difference.'"[14]

Ironically, however, given that Hellenistic and Roman imperialism is in view through the rest of Barclay's work, it is primarily against Jewish "nationalistic presuppositions" or "ethnic restrictions" that he sees Paul to be struggling. True, Paul's apocalyptic perspective still regards the non-Jewish world as "a cess-pit of godlessness and vice (Rom 1:18–32; Phil. 2:15)." But in Barclay's view, although Paul did "try to lay down some limits to [his converts'] assimilation to Graeco-Roman society," his "tactical abandonment of key Jewish practices . . . made him dangerously assimilated in the eyes

---

and Righteousness in Romans."

13. Moxnes, "Honor and Righteousness in Romans," 71.

14. Barclay, *Jews in the Mediterranean Diaspora*, 9–10, 97–98; Barclay, "'Neither Jew nor Greek,'" 205.

Paul and the Politics of Empire: Problems and Prospects   75

of many" of his Jewish contemporaries. Barclay has gone so far as to refer to *"Jewish* 'cultural imperialism'" as the horizon against which Paul's letters must be read.¹⁵

These examples suffice to show that even when questions of culture and imperialism have been raised in Pauline studies, it is more often Judaism, construed as an "imposition" on others, rather than Roman imperialism, that continues to occupy center stage.¹⁶ Even within a so-called "new perspective," the abiding preoccupation with Paul's supposed debate with Judaism continues to eclipse any critical interaction on his part with the ideology of empire. Richard Horsley's summary of our predicament is apt: "In the theologically determined metanarrative of the field, the replacement of the overly political and particularistic religion 'Judaism' by the purely spiritual and universal religion 'Christianity' . . . rendered virtually irrelevant the overall imperial situation and particular colonial relations in response to which those movements and writings emerged."¹⁷ The consequence, as Robert Jewett declares, is that Pauline interpretation in the United States remains "a cultural colony of Europe" in its preoccupation with a theological agenda inherited from the Reformation.¹⁸

ELEMENTS OF A PARADIGM SHIFT

Some recent studies nevertheless point us toward areas of investigation where the question of Paul and empire is being addressed.

The Politics of Paul's "Conversion"

Reconstructions of the social and political context in which Jesus moved have relied heavily on our knowledge of the character of Pontius Pilate's

---

15. Barclay, *Jews in the Mediterranean Diaspora*, 104; Barclay, "Neither Jew nor Greek," 205–6, emphasis added. Barclay cites Dunn, *The Theology of Paul's Letter to the Galatians*, and his own *Obeying the Truth*, 250–51.

16. Even as he argues in *The Mystery of Romans* that Romans is "not directed toward Jews, or Jewish exclusivism, except paradigmatically," i.e., to correct misguided views "among the *gentile* believers in Rome" (10), Mark Nanos occasionally refers (without argument) to "ethnocentric insistence [among *Jews*] that gentiles must become Jews" (9–10, 37–39). Similarly, though recognizing that in Galatians "Paul's opponents are not actually Jewish Christians," Daniel Boyarin refers to "Jewish-Christian opponents" in Galatia (*A Radical Jew*, 116–17); he declares, though without argument, that Romans 2 is an "attack" on Jews (87).

17. Horsley, "Submerged Biblical Histories," 154.

18. Jewett, *Paul the Apostle to America*, 19.

years as procurator. Strangely, although the Pharisee Paul's persecution of the Judean churches almost certainly began during these same years, similar attention to possible political motives for his activity has been absent until recently. Paula Fredriksen has explained that activity in terms of the imperial situation. She writes,

> News of an impending Messianic kingdom, originating from Palestine, might trickle out via the ekklesia's Gentiles to the larger urban population. It was this (by far) larger, unaffiliated group that posed a real and serious threat. Armed with such a report, they might readily seek to alienate the local Roman colonial government, upon which Jewish urban populations often depended for support and protection against hostile Gentile neighbors. The open dissemination of a Messianic message, in other words, put the entire Jewish community at risk.[19]

Along similar lines, Richard Horsley and Neil Silberman have contended that the *Ioudaismos* in which Paul says he had advanced (Gal 1:14) was "not merely a matter of religious observance but a movement of political activism and autonomy by diaspora Jews." Thus Saul's "zeal" was directed toward "the end of ensuring community solidarity and security in Damascus" against "the specific political threat" posed to the larger Jewish community by the Jesus movement.[20]

A political explanation of Saul's persecuting activity suggests a political interpretation of Paul's "conversion" as well. In *Liberating Paul*, I argued that the sort of visionary experiences Alan Segal discussed so helpfully in *Paul the Convert* would have functioned, in first-century Judea, to provide self-authorizing scripts for differing policies of accommodation or resistance to Rome. It must suffice here to observe that on his own account, Josephus's surrender to Vespasian after the siege of Jotapata was motivated by his own expert knowledge of apocalyptic traditions, which revealed to him that "fortune has passed over to the Romans" (*War* 3.336–408). He speaks condescendingly of the common people of Jerusalem who failed to grasp the same import of heavenly prodigies just before that city was destroyed (*War* 6.312–313). Surely another apocalyptically minded Jew, also identifying himself as a Pharisee well versed in the ancestral traditions of his people, could have recognized direct political implications in the

---

19. Fredriksen, "Judaism, the Circumcision of Gentiles, and Apocalyptic Hope," 556; Fredriksen, *From Jesus to Christ*, 154.

20. Horsley and Silberman, *The Message and the Kingdom*, 121; see also Elliott, *Liberating Paul*, 143–49.

apokalypsis that the crucified Jesus now stood vindicated at the right hand of God in heaven.[21]

Political Aspects of Paul's Theology and Praxis

But what of Paul's activity as an apostle of Christ? Although we are repeatedly told that Paul's gospel was fundamentally apolitical,[22] social and expressly political explanations have surfaced recently for various aspects of Paul's work and thought.

Years ago Frederick Danker argued that "public documents" like Paul's letters were best interpreted in the light of the public language of inscriptions; in particular, he showed that Paul's conception of God had been shaped by the ubiquitous Greco-Roman symbolization of the *Benefactor*.[23] More recently, important studies of social stratification, depending on the pioneering work of Gerd Theissen, and of the steep social "pyramid of power and patronage" in the empire have reshaped our understanding of 1 and 2 Corinthians, where "Gnosticism" was once the explanatory category of choice.[24] Anthony Saldarini's work on the social location of Pharisees compares Paul with the class of "retainers" within the imperial system;[25] similarly, Antoinette Clark Wire provides a compelling profile of Paul's situation as a freeborn Jewish male who, like many of his compatriots, had watched "their independence disintegrate under Roman rule," and had learned to "seek dignity in Stoic self-denial."[26] The ritualization of patronage in the imperial cult has also informed Holland Hendrix's study of 1 Thessalonians.[27] Aspects of Paul's theology echo the poetry and propaganda of the Augustan and Neronian eras. Paul calls his message *to euangelion*, borrowing "a

21. Segal, *Paul the Convert*, chap. 2; Elliott, *Liberating Paul*, 149-67. Similarly Horsley and Silberman argue that ancient Jewish apocalypticism best informs our understanding of Paul's reversal, not so much a "conversion" as a personal, visionary confirmation of ancient promises to Israel (*Message and the Kingdom*, 121-24).

22. Paul's theology "denationalizes Christ," "praises a reality that is utterly spiritual," and thus "shrinks the significance of contemporary politics" (Fredriksen, *From Jesus to Christ*, 173). "Apocalyptic turns his gaze continually to the future and it no longer matters to Paul if his churches are vindicated in the historical and political realm" (Barclay, *Jews in the Mediterranean Diaspora*, 393).

23. Danker, *Benefactor*.

24. Theissen, *The Social Setting of Pauline Christianity*; L. M. White, ed., *Social Networks in the Early Christian Environment*; de Ste. Croix, *Class Struggle*, 364-72; Chow, *Patronage and Power*; Marshall, *Enmity in Corinth*.

25. Saldarini, *Pharisees, Scribes, and Sadducees*, 139.

26. Wire, *Corinthian Women Prophets*, 66-67.

27. Hendrix, "Thessalonians Honor Romans."

technical term for 'news of victory'" from the Hellenistic and Roman vocabulary of international diplomacy.[28] By specifying that he proclaims Jesus as the "son of God," Dieter Georgi suggests, Paul implicitly parodies the theological claims made on behalf of the Julio-Claudian dynasty; such language must have been calculated to be politically provocative.[29] Similarly, Paul's references to the *parousia* of Christ (1 Thess 2:19; 3:13) played on diplomatic language for the arrival of a king or general at the gates of a city, with all the potential for threat or promise that such an advent implied.[30] His warning of doom when others proclaim "peace and security" (1 Thess 5:3) is widely regarded as a not-so-cryptic critique of imperial propaganda, for "peace and security" was the motto of the Roman world after the establishment of the Principate.[31]

Indeed, Paul's proclamation of Jesus as *kyrios*, the "lord of God's empire," relied heavily on Roman political concepts,[32] and "could easily be understood as violating the 'decrees of Caesar' in the most blatant manner."[33] As Calvin Roetzel and John L. White have shown, the very breadth of his eschatological vision—of an *oikoumenē* of nations, united in faithful obedience to a single lord—relies upon Hellenistic, and most especially Roman, political ideology.[34]

The imperial context provides more than a conceptual background for Paul's theology, however. The ritual medium for the dissemination of imperial values, so thoroughly described by Simon Price, allows us to recognize the performative character of Paul's apostolic presence and proclamation.[35] Just as members of the provincial elites "drew on religious symbols to negotiate various power relationships in the Roman Empire,"[36] so Paul understood his apostolic praxis as the manifestation of divine power on the public landscape. Indeed, his repeated play on metaphor and imagery drawn from

28. Georgi, *Theocracy*, 83; Friedrich, "εὐαγγελίζεσθαι."

29. Georgi, *Theocracy*, 52–58; compare Wright, "Gospel and Theology in Galatians," 228.

30. Georgi, *Theocracy*, 16–17; compare Donfried, "The Cults of Thessalonica," excerpted in Horsley, ed., *Paul and Empire*, 217.

31. Georgi, *Theocracy*, 28–29; Koester, "Imperial Ideology," 158.

32. J. L. White, *The Apostle of God*, 173–205.

33. Donfried's suggestion ("Cults of Thessalonica," 217), referring to oaths of allegiance offered to the emperor in various provinces.

34. Roetzel, "*Oikoumene*"; Roetzel, *Paul: The Man and the Myth*, 16–19; J. L. White, *The Apostle of God*, 93–138.

35. On what might be called the "apodeictic" character of Paul's rhetoric (compare 1 Cor 2:2, 4) see Pickett, *The Cross in Corinth*, 9–36.

36. Edwards, *Religion and Power*, 7; see also Price, *Rituals and Power*, passim.

imperial ceremonial—being "led in triumph" by God (2 Cor 2:14–16; 5:14); being made a spectacle in the arena (1 Cor 4:9–13); "carrying about" the dying of Jesus in the persecution he shared with his coworkers (2 Cor 4:10; 6:4–10)—is more than irony. Paul opposes the apostolic manifestation of God's power to its inevitable rival in the city square, the imperial ritualization of power.[37]

Re-examination of the "Pauline Legacy" of Social Conservatism

Over the last thirty years, significant challenges have been raised to the conventional view of Paul's "social conservatism," i.e., his perceived acceptance of social inequities and unjust social structures while proclaiming an "inner" or "spiritual" equality "in Christ." Close readings by S. Scott Bartchy and Norman Peterson of Paul's references to slavery overturned older interpretations that assimilated Paul's message to the pseudo-Pauline *Haustafeln*. Feminist readers highlighted the differences between references to women, especially in leadership positions, in the unquestioned letters of Paul and in the Pauline pseudepigrapha, including the suspected interpolation at 1 Cor 14:33–35.[38]

These studies lead inevitably to the suspicion that the historical effect, and probable purpose, of the pseudo-Pauline writings has been to misdirect our interpretation of "the Pauline legacy." Indeed, I argued in *Liberating Paul* that interpretive strategies that assimilate Paul to the pseudo-Paulines, under the guise of describing a "Pauline school" or "Pauline churches," misconstrue literary resemblances, an effect of pseudepigraphy, as historical continuity. Given the pseudepigraphic intention to manage, or hijack, the authority of Paul's legacy, I suggested applying to the Pauline literature a "criterion of dissimilarity" similar to that used in historical Jesus research. That is, unless clearly required by evidence from the genuine letters of Paul, we should practice a healthy skepticism toward any interpretation that serves to assimilate Paul's thought and praxis to the recognized purposes of the pseudo-Paulines.[39] At the same time, due weight must be given to the functional resemblances of subordinationist language in Paul's genuine letters to codes of subordination in the wider Roman culture. Here critical

---

37. I explored this theme at length in a paper presented to the Birmingham Colloquium on Ideology and Interpretation in August 1997, chapter 6 in the present volume.

38. Bartchy, *Mallon Chrēsai*; Peterson, *Rediscovering Paul*; Scroggs, "Paul and the Eschatological Woman"; Pagels, "Paul and Women"; Elliott, *Liberating Paul*, 32–48.

39. Elliott, *Liberating Paul*, 25–86.

works by Elisabeth Schüssler Fiorenza, Cynthia Briggs Kittredge, and Elizabeth Castelli have proven invaluable.[40]

While all of these studies suggest the contours and context of a dramatically new picture of the apostle Paul, several other areas in which that picture could have equally dramatic implications remain largely unexplored. I turn next to these challenges.

PROSPECTS FOR FURTHER RESEARCH

Contextualizing Paul's Rhetoric within Empire

Since Hans Dieter Betz's landmark 1973 essay and subsequent commentary on *Galatians*, rhetorical criticism has found a secure home in Pauline studies.[41] With some notable exceptions, most of the explosion of recent rhetorical-critical studies have sought to align tracts of Paul's argument, and especially whole letters, with the categories of genre and partition used in ancient Greek and Roman rhetorical handbooks. While such studies have brought occasional insights into Paul's argumentation, sometimes they have also simply "repackaged" standard historical and theological interpretations by means of a new technical vocabulary.[42] We have not yet seen a full-length exploration of Paul's rhetoric in the wider contexts of imperial or colonial *rhetorics*, that is, the discourses shaped by the social dynamics of imperialism and colonialism, what James C. Scott has called the "great" and "little" traditions," or "public" and "hidden transcripts."[43]

This is surprising and dismaying, for several reasons. Roman authors themselves offer ample evidence that the traditional categories of rhetoric reflected the privileged view of a narrow, but vastly powerful social elite. Judicial rhetoric was exercised by Roman lawyers serving "the interests of the class to which they themselves and their clients belonged"; in practice, "there was one law for the rich and another for the poor."[44] The public as-

---

40. Schüssler Fiorenza, "Rhetorical Situation and Historical Reconstruction"; Castelli, *Imitating Paul*; Kittredge, *Community and Authority*.

41. Betz, "Literary Composition"; Betz, *Galatians*.

42. For discussions of the problem see Classen, "St. Paul's Epistles and Ancient Greek and Roman Rhetoric"; Reed, "Using Ancient Rhetorical Categories"; Porter, "Theoretical Justification"; Porter, "Ancient Rhetorical Analysis."

43. Scott, "Protest and Profanation"; Scott, *Domination and the Arts of Resistance*. Important beginnings at applying Scott's work to Pauline studies have been made by Horsley, "Rhetoric and Empire—and 1 Corinthians"; West, *The Academy of the Poor*; West, "Disguising Defiance in Ritualisms of Subordination."

44. De Ste. Croix, *Class Struggle*, 330; Jones, *The Later Roman Empire*, 1:517.

sembly, the proper domain of deliberative rhetoric, was also the political arena of the aristocratic classes, well insulated from the peasantry;[45] thoroughly anti-democratic sentiments were quite at home there.[46]

The third classical genre, ceremonial or epideictic rhetoric, concerned the values of "praise and glory and disgrace and dishonor." But Cicero made it very clear in his *De re publica* that the "best men" in society may hope to promote such values through rhetoric only among their peers, who are motivated by the real possibility of winning honor from one another. Others, however—slaves, most notably—are more naturally motivated by terror, and for them, force is more effective than rhetoric (3:41). Thus shame and fear operate as twin mechanisms of public control (5:6).[47] Closer to Paul's day, the historian Velleius Paterculus and the philosopher Plutarch similarly contrasted rhetorical persuasion with coercive force.[48] Modern rhetoricians Chaim Perelman and L. Olbrechts-Tyteca confirm that epideictic rhetoric will be practiced "by those who, in a society, defend the

---

Aristotle himself had regarded the "art of rhetoric" to apply when more customary means of arriving at the truth, such as the torture of slaves, was not available (*Rhetoric* 1.1376). Centuries later, the handbook *Ad Herennium* discussed a variety of reasons to doubt testimony given under torture, yet considers such testimony reliable in most cases because "men are compelled by violent pain to tell all they know" (2.6.10). Clearly more was at stake in judicial torture than the dubious enterprise of arriving at truth; see the illuminating study by DuBois, *Torture and Truth*.

45. Aristocrats "could never dream of permitting peasants as peasants to vote or participate in their councils" (Kautsky, *The Politics of Aristocratic Empires*, 274).

46. In Xenophon's *Memorabilia*, Pericles is challenged by Socrates' student to admit that "whatever the assembled majority, through using its power over the owners of property, enacts without persuasion is not law but force" (*Memorabilia* 1.2.40–46). De Ste. Croix declares this passage "one of the best anti-democratic arguments produced in antiquity" (*Class Struggle*, 414–15).

47. Cicero, whose political speeches are "of prime value" for purposes of the study of Roman propaganda (Brunt, "*Laus Imperii*," 160), repeatedly expressed his contempt for the limited democracy practiced in the Greek assemblies, whose dominant feature was "irresponsibility" (*pro Flacco* 14–16). Indeed, as one of the dialogue partners in Cicero's *De re publica* puts it, "there can be nothing more horrible than that monster which falsely assumes the name and appearance of a people"; in contrast, "nothing could be more advantageous for a state than to be ruled by a select number of good men" (3:45). Dictatorship was clearly preferable.

48. Under Tiberius, "justice, equity, and industry, long buried in oblivion, have been restored to the state. Rioting in the theater has been suppressed; all citizens have either been impressed with the wish to do right, or have been forced to do so by necessity" (Velleius Paterculus, *History of Rome* 2.126). Later, Plutarch considers it significant that the Romans have numerous altars to Fortune, the god who has delivered countless military triumphs into their hands, but "they have no shrine of Wisdom or Prudence," or Mind or Reason, as do peoples who place value on persuasion (*The Fortune of the Romans* 318).

traditional and accepted values," and will be encouraged, even as a matter of compulsion, by the powerful.[49]

I conclude from these brief examples that to continue seeking analogues to Paul's letters in the classical rhetorical handbooks, without giving sustained attention to the publicly acknowledged relationship between rhetorical patterns of persuasion and the coercive force inhering in slavery and empire, would be profoundly inattentive to the sources themselves.

Indeed, members of the Roman aristocracy spoke candidly enough among themselves regarding the clear, absolute, and necessary difference between those destined to rule and to be ruled.[50] In his discussion of "class struggle" in the Greco-Roman world "on the ideological plane," classical historian G. E. M. de Ste. Croix refers to the simplest form of psychological propaganda, which merely teaches the governed that they have no real option anyway but to submit; this tends to be intellectually uninteresting, however effective it may have been in practice, and consists merely of the threat of force. It was particularly common, of course, in its application to slaves.

Far more interesting to the historian was "the attempt of the dominant classes to persuade those they exploited to accept their oppressed condition without protest, if possible even to rejoice in it."[51] "In some cases," writes John H. Kautsky, "the exploitative relationship between aristocrat and peasant may be a brutally frank one . . . However, that relationship can also be ideologically concealed by some concept of reciprocity," which functions to make the exploitation more acceptable to the peasantry and "to justify the aristocracy's rule in its own eyes."[52]

---

49. Perelman and Olbrechts-Tyteca, *The New Rhetoric*, 55 (on "Argumentation and Violence").

50. Already Aristotle had found in the intimate coercion of slavery an apt metaphor for the political domination of empire: "Authority and subordination are conditions not only inevitable but also expedient; in some cases things are marked out from the moment of birth to rule or to be ruled" (*to archein kai archesthai, Politics* 1254a 22–24). Said observes that imperialism and colonialism "are supported and perhaps even impelled by impressive ideological formations that include notions that certain territories and people require and beseech domination": "notions about bringing civilization to primitive or barbaric peoples, the disturbingly familiar ideas about flogging or death or extended punishment being required when 'they' misbehaved or became rebellious, because 'they' mainly understood force or violence best; 'they' were not like 'us,' and for that reason deserved to be ruled" (*Culture and Imperialism*, 8–9; xi). Noam Chomsky finds such sentiments regarding other peoples to be "the common coin of modern political and intellectual discourse" in the U.S. (*Deterring Democracy*, 361).

51. De Ste. Croix, *Class Struggle*, 409.

52. Kautsky, *The Politics of Aristocratic Empires*, 110–11.

De Ste. Croix has shown that "the most common form" of imperialist propaganda was already well established in the ancient Greek world, namely, "that which seeks to persuade the poor that they are not really fitted to rule and that this is much better left to their 'betters.'" Plato had argued in the *Republic* that "ruling should be the prerogative of those who have the right kind of intellectual equipment and have received a proper philosophical education. In practice, needless to say, virtually all such men would be members of the propertied class."[53] A Roman imperialist like Cicero merely inherited the theme: "Do we not observe that dominion has been granted by Nature to everything that is best, to the great advantage of what is weak?" (*De re publica* 3.37). Romans like Cicero "did not concede that their subjects or dependents had any right to be free of Roman rule. Liberty was the privilege of the imperial people," and Jews and Syrians could be dismissed as "peoples born for slavery." During the Principate Virgil could similarly divide humanity "into two categories, those too insolent to accept [Rome's] god-given dominion, and those who submitted to it."[54] That applied to the Roman plebs as well, regarded by Nero's chief advisor as "this vast throng—discordant, factious, and unruly, ready to run riot alike for the destruction of itself and others" if it should break the yoke of empire (Seneca, *De Clementia* 1.1). "The rhetoric of power all too easily produces an illusion of benevolence when deployed in an imperial setting," Said remarks.[55] The symbolism of benefaction in particular can function as an ideological concealment for the true exploitative nature prevailing between the aristocracy and the peasantry.[56] Cicero, for example, could declare that Roman taxation was primarily directed toward the benefit of the provincial population. To the frankly acknowledged combination of force and fortune that had brought Rome to the status of an imperial power, the Romans were eager to add a third factor, their own virtue. It was one of Cicero's favorite themes that Roman hegemony "was ordained by the gods, whose favor Rome had

---

53. De Ste. Croix, *Class Struggle*, 411.

54. Cicero, *De Provinciis consularibus* 10; see also book 3 of *De re publica*; Brunt, "Laus Imperii," 183–84. See the full discussion of this *topos* in Balch, *Let Wives Be Submissive*.

55. Said, *Culture and Imperialism*, xvii.

56. "The aristocrat's claim to provide benefits to the peasant probably serves the function of making the peasant's exploitation more acceptable to him so that he will pay his dues and perform his labor services more willingly and cause less trouble for his lord." But the relationship is not really reciprocal: "Even if the peasant does benefit from it, the provision of protection in return for his labor or taxes does not really involve a reciprocal relationship. Whereas the aristocrat is free to take or not to take the peasant's taxes, the peasant is not free to accept or reject the aristocrat's protection" (Kautsky, *The Politics of Aristocratic Empires*, 111–14).

deserved by piety and justice"; the gods had implanted in the Roman people "a love of peace and tranquility which enable justice and good faith most easily to flourish." "Fortune and Virtue" had brought world hegemony to Rome, so that "it was by our scrupulous attention to religion and by our wise grasp of a single truth, that all things are ruled and directed by the will of the gods, that we have overcome all peoples and nations."[57]

Of course, successful colonization includes cultivating the acceptance of the colonial relationship among the colonized. De Ste. Croix observes that "Rome made sure that Greece was kept 'quiet' and friendly to her by ensuring that the cities were controlled by the wealthy class, which now had mainly given up any idea of resistance to Roman rule and in fact seems to have welcomed it for the most part, as an insurance against popular movements from below."[58] In essays in *Imperialism in the Ancient World* (1976), M. H. Crawford described the common interest shared by Greek and Roman aristocracies; he was hardly surprised to find the intellectual class in the provinces waxing eloquent on the inevitability of Roman rule.[59] And V. Nutton described a widespread "Beneficial Ideology," perpetuated by intellectuals in the provinces, hailing the "peace" and "security" Rome had established through military force. Provincials like Plutarch could revel in "the true freedom of the inhabitants of the Roman Empire, for an essential difference between it and other ancient empires is that the Romans govern free men, not slaves" (*Moralia* 814F). In another place Plutarch pretended to debate whether Virtue or Fortune had been more responsible for the Romans' sovereignty; the right answer, of course, was "both." Despite the evidence of Roman brutality ("the multitude of corpses and spoils"), Plutarch saw in Rome's dominion the sublime work of the gods: "For such a welding together of dominion and power," evidently Virtue and Fortune had "joined forces" and thus "cooperated in completing this most beautiful of human works" (*The Fortune of the Romans* 316, 323). As Nutton points out, through civic ritual and rhetoric, subject cities directed their energies "to preventing local disorder or at least restraining it lest the Romans be led to intervene"; the "concord" (*harmonia*) celebrated in the city square served "apotropaically to announce to the governor and the emperor that police action [was] unnecessary."[60]

57. Brunt, "*Laus Imperii*," 187; 165.
58. De Ste. Croix, *Class Struggle*, 344.
59. Crawford, "Greek Intellectuals and the Roman Aristocracy."
60. Nutton, "The Beneficial Ideology," 212. On "harmony," or *homonoia*, speeches as background for 1 Corinthians see Mitchell, *Paul and the Rhetoric of Reconciliation*; and Martin, *The Corinthian Body*.

The Romans secured their interests through an aristocracy in Judea as well, as Martin Goodman and Peter Richardson have recently made clear.[61] We should hardly be surprised, then, to find Roman benefaction echoing in some Jewish sources from the period, as in the aphorism attributed to the first-century Rabbi Hanina, "Pray for the welfare of the state, for were it not for the fear of it, we should have swallowed each other up alive" (m. Avot 3:2). Josephus's *War* is merely the best example of the pattern, "the most forthright expression of Jewish-Roman political accommodation known to us."[62] He is at pains at once to exonerate the Romans for the destruction of Judea and to describe Jerusalem as a hotbed of misguided insurrection on the part of Jews inadequately educated in their own traditions. The more authentic expression of Judaism, according to Josephus, involved recognizing that God had given the sovereignty of the world over to Rome, as the climactic speech from Herod Agrippa makes clear (*War* 2.345–404). Josephus even allows Agrippa to call his fellow Jews "those to whom thralldom is hereditary" (2.357). Echoing themes from Roman aristocrats and other provincial enthusiasts, Josephus could frankly declare that "the might of the Romans was irresistible," yet preferred to couch his counsel of submission in terms of "an established law" in the cosmos: "'Yield to the stronger,' and 'The mastery is for those pre-eminent in arms.'" God was manifestly on the side of the Romans. But more, the Romans had proved, by their "reverence for the holy places of their enemies," to be more deserving of God's approval than the Jewish rebels occupying the Temple (*War* 5.363–368).

The Talmud preserves from the time of the Second Jewish Revolt a debate over the "benefits" of the Romans:

> "How splendid are the works of this people," declared Rabbi Judah; "they have built marketplaces, baths and bridges." . . . But Rabbi Simeon bar Yohai answered, "Everything they have made they have made only for themselves—marketplaces, for whores; baths, to wallow in; bridges, to levy tolls." (b. Shabbat 33b)

To be sure, as N. R. M. de Lange observes, the picture of empire in Jewish sources "is a complex one." But "between the two extremes of militant zealotry and fawning appeasement we must imagine a whole gamut of attitudes to Roman rule. Probably the majority of Jews grumblingly accepted the status quo. Belief in messianic redemption was not inherently incompatible with acceptance of Roman rule and even appreciation of its benefits."[63]

---

61. Goodman, *The Ruling Class in Judaea*; Richardson, *Herod*.
62. Barclay, *Jews in the Mediterranean Diaspora*, 356.
63. De Lange, "Jewish Attitudes to the Roman Empire," 262.

Such nuanced, "strategic" discourse is perhaps best illustrated in Philo, whose *Embassy to Gaius* both hails the benefits at first felt by the whole world after the emperor's accession (8–13), then goes on to detail the depredations of the "iron-hearted and utterly ruthless" tyrant. According to E. R. Goodenough, Philo provides, in his treatise *On Dreams*, "one of the most vital passages from ancient literature," one of the finest examples of what James C. Scott would later call a "hidden transcript." There Philo describes the caution and circumspection normally accorded the rulers who in other ways, Philo implies, appear as brutish as pack animals.[64]

Goodenough's work suggests we may find more evidence of "hidden transcripts" in Philo's work than previously imagined.[65] The point of this extended discussion, of course, is that achieving a thicker description of Jewish thought under Roman colonial pressures will allow us to appreciate similar nuances, either of accommodation or resistance, to those pressures in Paul's rhetoric as well. De Lange's remarks, quoted above, and Goodenough's observations regarding Philo of Alexandria suggest that we need not expect to find in Paul, or any other first-century Jew, a clear, consistent, univocal "pro-Roman" or "anti-Roman" posture,[66] but should look for more tenuous, situationally determined traces of his response to the pressures of Romanization. When we compare Paul with his contemporaries on these terms, we may find striking examples of antagonism not only to Hellenistic culture[67] but also to the propaganda and pretense of the Roman Empire itself.

Which "Imperialism": Roman or Jewish?

Once we recognize the relevance of empire for reading Paul, how do these political aspects of his thought relate to the themes that have predominated

---

64. Goodenough, *An Introduction to Philo Judaeus*, 55–57. See my essay, "Romans 13:1–7 in the Context of Imperial Propaganda," now chapter 7 in Elliott, *Paul against the Nations*."

65. Goodenough's assessment is by no means universal; Frank H. Colson regarded *De Somniis* 2 as characterized by "a poverty of thought which makes it the weakest of the whole series" (*Philo*, vol. 5, 433).

66. Literary traces of outright anti-Roman sedition may be few indeed; Josephus only allows faint echoes of "pompous panegyrics on liberty" as his pro-Roman protagonists set about to offer rebuttals (*War* 2.348, passim). We are most confident we are dealing with anti-Roman rhetoric in texts where "Rome" and "Romans" are not mentioned, except in properly biblical code—"Kittim," "Babylon," "Esau."

67. Barclay, *Jews in the Mediterranean Diaspora*, 381–95.

in scholarship for so many centuries, Paul's theology of the Torah and of Israel?

In different ways, N. T. Wright and Robert Jewett have argued that Paul's theology addressed the covenant understanding of Israel's destiny under Roman imperialism. According to Wright, at the heart of Paul's theology is the apocalyptic question, "How shall God's justice be realized in a world dominated by evil powers?"[68] Paul's answer had everything to do with Israel's survival despite the hegemony of Rome. Jewett argues that, although Paul's hope for Israel's redemption (Rom 11:26) was "not precisely fulfilled," nevertheless "some of the features of his program in Romans"—an "ethic of individual responsibility for the transformation of the secular world," for example—were embodied in the Jewish restoration after the catastrophic war of 66–70.[69]

In most Paul scholarship, however, the theological convention of reading Paul's theology as a critique of Jewish identity and practice remains almost overpowering. Wright, for example, persists in describing Paul's struggle against Israel's "meta-sin, the attempt to confine grace to race," to "treat the Torah as a charter of automatic national privilege."[70] In different ways, John Barclay and Daniel Boyarin regard Paul as an "anomalous" Jew, uniquely obsessed with the problem of a distinctive Jewish identity while his fellow Jews struggled to maintain that identity against Hellenizing and Romanizing pressures.[71] Decades ago Gunther Bornkamm put this perspective in the starkest terms in his discussion of Romans: "Paul's opponent is not this or that section in a particular church, but the Jews and their understanding of salvation."[72]

F. C. Baur's dialectical reading of early Christian history posited a monolithic Jewish, and Jewish-Christian, front, including the Jerusalem apostles and Jewish Christians in Antioch and Galatia, against which Paul struggled throughout his apostolic career. That polarized reading, based on Paul's references to *Ioudaismos* and the "traditions of the fathers" in Galatians 2, persists today, despite numerous efforts to correct it by pointing out the Gentile identity of Paul's addressees and the broad agreement regarding circumcision that Paul shared with the Jerusalem apostles.[73]

68. Wright, *The Climax of the Covenant*, 140–41.

69. Jewett, *Paul the Apostle to America*, 43.

70. Wright, *The Climax of the Covenant*, 240–43, 248–51; for critiques see Fredriksen, "What You See Is What You Get," and Roetzel, "No 'Race of Israel' in Paul's Letters."

71. Barclay, *Jews in the Mediterranean Diaspora*, 381–95; Boyarin, *A Radical Jew*.

72. Bornkamm, *Paul*, 95.

73. Johannes Munck's effort to concentrate attention on the Gentile recipients of Galatians (*Paul and the Salvation of Mankind*, 69–133) has been revived by Lloyd

S. R. F. Price and others have shown that first-century Asia Minor was characterized by an enthusiastic cultivation of emperor worship among the provincial elite. Romanization remained primarily an urban phenomenon, however, only beginning to penetrate into the countryside in Paul's day. Surely we can imagine that colonizing pressures would be experienced as a threat to native identity among non-elite residents of Asian cities and smaller towns. One likely response on the part of hard-pressed natives might be to want to affiliate, as quickly as possible, with an alternative ethnic identity that already enjoyed acceptance and considerable prestige in the empire, namely, Judaism. We should expect on this hypothesis precisely the sorts of behaviors that are reflected in Galatians: a rush on the part of former pagans (4:8) to be circumcised, for its value as a marker of ethnic identity (3:3; 5:2), and thus to avoid persecution (6:12; cf. 5:11); along with a reluctance to accept the full obedience to the Torah that any Jew would know circumcision required (5:3; 6:13). On these terms we could understand the Galatian controversy as the result of colonizing pressures and nativist counter-pressures, rather than perpetuate a caricature of an aggressive and hypocritical Jewish proselytizing campaign as the necessary background to the letter.[74]

A NEW READING OF ROMANS

As stated earlier, the scholarly preoccupation with Paul's supposed debate with Judaism tends to eclipse aspects of a more egalitarian social ethic, not least because of the perceived social conservatism in Romans, especially in 13:1–7. The view that Romans represents a summary of Paul's theology, and that his theology is developed there in fundamental contrast to Jewish thought, persists, for example, in James D. G. Dunn's magisterial volume *The Theology of Paul the Apostle*:

> In the movement and dialogue of Paul's theologizing, his letter to the Romans is a relatively . . . fixed feature . . . It was written under probably the most congenial circumstances of his mission, with time for careful reflection and composition. And, above all, it was clearly intended to set out and defend his own mature understanding of the gospel (1:16–17) . . . Romans is still far removed from a dogmatic or systematic treatise on theology,

---

Gaston (*Paul and the Torah*), but has won only limited acceptance. Baur's dialectical schema is given new life in a social-scientific commentary by Esler, *Galatians*.

74. Gaston similarly attributes the Galatian legalism to "uncertainty" on the part of Gentiles (*Paul and the Torah*, 25).

but it nevertheless is the most sustained and reflective statement of Paul's own theology by Paul himself.[75]

We have seen important alternative readings, however. In *A Rereading of Romans*, Stanley Stowers questioned the nearly ubiquitous tendency to import Jews or Jewish-Christian opponents into the interpretation of Paul's argument. The heart of the letter is Paul's appeal to the Romans to recognize his gospel as a means to achieve the goal of self-mastery that dominated first-century thinking in the Augustan age. Gerald Downing offered a similar reading of Romans as evidence for Paul's thorough acquaintance with and advocacy of Stoic and Cynic-like ethics.[76]

William S. Campbell, Mark Nanos, and Mark Reasoner have offered readings of the letter as Paul's confrontation with a Gentile-Christian ideology of supersession that denies the value of Jewish identity, an ideology linked to prevalent Roman views of the Jews as a subject people.[77] Although this context is widely recognized for Romans 11, the far more common interpretation today still reads the rest of the letter as Paul's defense of his law-free mission among Gentiles, over against Jewish "ethnocentrism" or "boasting" or "national righteousness." I have argued, as have others, that Gentile-Christian supersessionism is Paul's principal target in Romans.[78] Here it must suffice to offer a few exegetical observations suggesting that Paul's target is more closely connected with Roman imperialism than with any supposed Jewish "cultural imperialism."

First, Paul's declaration in 1:16, "I am not ashamed of the gospel: for it is the power of God unto salvation," is often read as the "thesis" of the letter, rather as if we were beginning an essay in dogmatics. But the declaration of shamelessness is a formal feature of the apology the faithful make before their impious accusers. We find it already in Socrates' defense before his fellow Athenians;[79] it sounds repeatedly from the lips of Jewish martyrs in this

---

75. Dunn, *The Theology of Paul the Apostle*, 25.

76. Stowers, *A Rereading of Romans*, 21-33; Downing, *Cynics, Paul, and the Pauline Churches*, 274-82.

77. Campbell, *Paul's Gospel in an Intercultural Context*; Nanos, *The Mystery of Romans*, 99-101; Reasoner, *"Strong" and "Weak."*

78. Elliott, *The Rhetoric of Romans*; Elliott, *Liberating Paul*, 73-75, 181-89, 214-26.

79. Meletus's accusations are "disgraceful" (*aischron*, *Apology* 24A); Socrates challenges an Athenian, "are you not ashamed" (*ouk aischynei*) to be careless regarding philosophy? (29D). He refuses to act disgracefully by pleading for his life (35A); at length, he declares he has been convicted on account of "lack of shamelessness" (*anaischyntias*, 38D).

period.⁸⁰ The protest of innocence, of having nothing to put one to shame, is as frequent in Christian martyrologies.⁸¹

The contrast at the beginning of the letter is not between two ways of being righteous before God—through "faith" or through "works" (that contrast is not made until 3:20!)—but between the justice of God (*diakaiosynē tou theou*, 1:17) and the utter injustice and impiety of human society (*adikia kai asebeia*, 1:18–32). Theologians of liberation have rightly seen that for Paul, as for Israel's prophets before him, social injustice, the desire to impose "dehumanized relations" on others, is the root of idolatry. Paul's concern is "the justice which the world and peoples and society . . . have been awaiting."⁸² As we have seen, Georgi and Stowers argued that the most appropriate background for the indictment of wholesale human wickedness in Romans 1 is the vaunt of divine justice made by or on behalf of the Roman emperor. The poet propagandists of the Augustan principate hailed a "golden age," the banishing of War, the return of Faith and Justice to rule over the earth, the flourishing of Law and Right, a flood of piety—all embodied in the person of the Augustus, the *Sebastos* himself.⁸³ The theme of moral "self-mastery" which Stowers traces throughout Romans was a cornerstone of the Augustan reform—but note that it is also the philosophical theme of that script for resistance to empire, 4 Maccabees.⁸⁴

Stowers notes that "Paul wrote Romans early in Nero's reign, when golden age ideology and hopes may have reached their highest peak since Augustus." No less than in Augustus's day, the "gospel" of the emperor's accession proclaimed the restoration of a "golden age," not only for the Roman people but for all peoples fortunate enough to be brought beneath the benevolent wings of empire. "Kindly Justice returns to the earth," hymns Calpurnius Siculus: "Peace in her fullness shall come"; the gods have brought "holy rites instead of war."⁸⁵ But as Stowers also shows, Roman propagandists were as concerned as any Jewish apocalyptist to lament the sinfulness of the age. "Full of sin, our age has defiled first the marriage bed, our offspring,

---

80. When, in 4 Maccabees, the aged Eleazar defies Antiochus Epiphanes, he refuses to let his people or the Torah be put to shame (5:34–38); he renounces the "shamefulness" of submitting to the king (6:20). The youths whose martyrdoms follow refuse to put their ancestors to shame (9:23); the shame falls rather on the Greek king (12:11).

81. See Schottroff, "'Give to Caesar What Belongs to Caesar.'"

82. Miranda, *Marx and the Bible*, 160–79; Segundo, *The Humanistic Christology of Paul*, 28–29.

83. Georgi, *Theocracy*; Stowers, *A Rereading of Romans*, 52–58.

84. Stowers, *A Rereading of Romans*, 124.

85. Calpurnius Siculus, *Bucolica*; and the *Einsiedeln Eclogues*, in *Minor Latin Poets*, trans. J. W. Duff and A. M. Duff.

and our homes," cried Horace, citing the new dances teenage girls are trying out as evidence that "the stream of disaster has overflowed both people and nation" (Third Ode). Even Virgil's buoyant Fourth Eclogue admits that although the final traces of Roman guilt shall vanish in the Augustan age, "some traces of ancient sin shall still survive" elsewhere, calling Romans forth to occasional wars of pacification. Paul's focus on sexually abusive behavior in Rom 1:24-27 calls to mind the anxieties of Roman propagandists over the sexual machinations of women in the imperial household.[86]

These brief observations suffice to show that from its first chapter, the letter Paul directed to Rome is not a theological brief. It is a defiant indictment of the rampant injustice and impiety of the Roman "golden age." We know other similar repudiations of the empire's empty self-aggrandizement from Jewish and pagan sources.[87] The whole letter is structured around the contrast between the shameful deeds of the present dark age (1:18-32; 13:11-14), deeds of which Paul's readers are "now ashamed" (6:20-23), and the holiness and sobriety that is now possible "in the Spirit" (6:15-19; 8:4-17; 12:1-2). Victor Paul Furnish showed decades ago that the contrast between former shameful living and the new life in Christ, the "once-but now scheme" of early Christian preaching, gives the letter its underlying structure. His case is strengthened by Halvor Moxnes's observation that the contrast of honor and shame language is more pervasive than "justification" language in structuring the letter.[88]

I suggest that we have here the key to the coherence of Paul's argument in Romans: He seeks to move his Gentile Christian readers away from a theological "boast" over a vanquished Israel (11:13-32) to the "sober judgment" (*sophrosynē*, 12:3) that governs chapters 12-15. Within these chapters lies the notorious passage 13:1-7, which threatens to shipwreck

---

86. Velleius Paterculus, *History of Rome* 2:99 (Julia); Tacitus, *Annals*, passim.

87. The bankruptcy of Rome's claims is a theme in other Jewish literature in the period, though usually expressed in code. In the *Commentary on Habakkuk* from Qumran, it is the "Kittim" who "march across the plain, smiting and plundering the cities of the earth"; they "inspire all the nations with fear. All their evil plotting is done with intention and they deal with all the nations in cunning and guile" (1QpHab 3; Vermes, *The Dead Sea Scrolls in English*, 3rd ed., 284; *Complete* ed., 479). Genesis Rabbah declares, "Just as a pig lies down and sticks out its hoofs as though to say 'I am clean,' so the evil empire robs and oppresses, while pretending to execute justice" (65:1); see de Lange, "Jewish Attitudes."

The theme is also expressed in "pagan" literature. The Roman historian Tacitus provides a compelling anti-Roman speech on the lips of the Briton chieftain Calgacus: "to plunder, butcher, steal, these things [the Romans] misname empire; they make a desolation and call it peace" (*Histories* 4.17.2).

88. Furnish, *Theology and Ethics in Paul*, 105-6; Moxnes, "Honor and Righteousness"; Moxnes, "Honor, Shame."

any but a politically conservative reading of the letter, and indeed of Paul's theology. These verses cannot be excised as an interpolation,[89] although as several scholars observed decades ago, tensions here resist harmonization with Paul's theology more broadly, and preclude generalization as Paul's "theology of the state."[90] When we recall Roman and provincial discussions, so prevalent in Paul's day, regarding public control through consent and coercion,[91] it must seem significant that Paul both describes ruling authorities as "God's ministers" and "servants" (13:4, 6), in no way a "terror to good conduct" (13:3), and warns the Roman Christians to "submit" to them (13:2), not to oppose them, invoking the threat of the not-so-idle sword (13:4). To "conscience" Paul adds the fear of "wrath" as a motive for obedience; both honor and "fear" are due the authorities. These tensions suggest that Rom 13:1-7 may be another example of the sort of cautious "hidden transcript" that we observed in Philo as well.[92]

The "boast" Paul opposes within Roman Gentile Christianity is not a narrowly theological phenomenon; it coincides with more widespread

---

89. Leander E. Keck offers an important warning to interpreters of 13:1-7: "What Makes Romans Tick?"

90. Käsemann, "Principles on the Interpretation of Romans 13," 212-13; Kallas, "Romans XIII.1-7: An Interpolation"; O'Neill, *Paul's Letter to the Romans*, 209ff.

91. Perelman and Olbrechts-Tyteca observe that "the use of argumentation implies that one has renounced resorting to force alone," and that "recourse to argumentation assumes the establishment of a community of minds which, while it lasts, excludes the use of violence" (*The New Rhetoric*, 55). As the previously discussed extracts from Cicero show, however, within the context of imperialism, persuasive speech remains the prerogative of the ruling class, alongside other forms of political coercion, including overt violence. (See also Noam Chomsky's discussion of "Force and Opinion" in his analysis of modern (U.S.) imperialism: *Deterring Democracy*, chap. 12.)

Jewish provincials could observe the relationship between persuasion and coercive force, but only in order to contrast them. Thus the Jewish heroes of 4 Maccabees repeatedly defy the coercive "appeals" of the Greek tyrant, while confessing their being "persuaded" by Torah. Both Philo and Josephus mark the difference between the Jewish *politeuma* of persuasion and government by force: thus, Philo contends, Moses resisted the temptation of "issuing orders without words of exhortation, as though to slaves instead of free men," which "savored of tyranny and despotism." Therefore "in his commands and prohibitions he suggests and admonishes rather than commands," with laws written "in order to exhort rather than to enforce" (*De Vita Mosis* 2.49-51). The same theme appears in Josephus's apology *Against Apion*: Moses, rather than creating a monarchy or an oligarchy, created a theocracy based upon persuasion, setting in supreme position the priests, "pre-eminently gifted with persuasive eloquence and discretion." The result is that each Jew is "firmly persuaded" personally to be willing "to brave all manner of suffering rather than to utter a single word against the Law" (2.164-167, 186-187, 218-219).

92. I have pursued this suggestion further in "Romans 13:1-7 in the Context of Imperial Ideology," now chap. 13 in Elliott, *Paul against the Nations*.

currents of anti-Jewish prejudice in Rome, prejudice fueled by riots and disturbances in Alexandria, Palestine, and Rome itself.[93] It is no mere flourish when Paul construes the rhetorical situation as the opposition of two forms of worship: the shameful idolatry of the Roman world (1:18-32), which is at its root the surrender of one's body to the power of sin and injustice (6:12-20), and the "rational worship" *logikē latreia* (12:1) practiced by Christians as they present their bodies for God's justice (6:19). Paul presents himself in Romans in sacerdotal terms: he introduces himself (in 1:9) as one who performs sacred service to God (*latreuō*); at last (15:14-16) he sums up his "bold" exhortation to the Romans as his "priestly service of the gospel of God," the "offering up" of holy persons (*hierourgeia*; *prosphora*). As William Cavanaugh has pointed out in a profound discussion of Paul's "body of Christ" language in the context of the modern torture state, Paul's language demobilizes Christians from the worship of Roman gods (the much-vaunted *eusebeia* of imperial rhetoric, *asebeia* to Paul) and enlists them in the spiritual worship of the God who raised Jesus from the dead.[94] The letter to the Romans is nothing less than a direct challenge to the ritual and ceremony of empire.

These remarks hardly exhaust the significance of imperialism for the study of ancient rhetoric. They may point us toward a program, however, in which "taking empire seriously" includes setting Paul's letters in the context of imperial propaganda and panegyric, and the voices of demurral and submission, or discontent and resistance, raised against it by Paul's Jewish contemporaries. The result may be a dramatically new appreciation of Paul.[95]

---

93. Gager, *The Origins of Anti-Semitism*, 63-88; Nanos, *The Mystery of Romans*, 99-101; Elliott, *Liberating Paul*, 215-16.

94. See Cavanaugh, *Torture and Eucharist*.

95. I am grateful for the comments of fellow scholars at a session of the Pauline Epistles Section at the 1996 annual meeting of the Society of Biblical Literature, at which an earlier form of this essay was read. I am particularly grateful to Robert Jewett, Allen Callahan, and Elisabeth Schüssler Fiorenza, my fellow panelists at this session, and to Richard A. Horsley, who conceived and organized it.

5

The "Patience of the Jews"
Strategies of Resistance and Accommodation to Imperial Cultures

PREFACING HIS DISCUSSION OF the Judean war, Tacitus comments that under Claudius, "the Jews patiently endured their fate until Gessius Florus became governor. During his term of office war broke out" (*Histories* 5.10). Such a curious reference to the "patient endurance" of the Jews would puzzle any modern attempt to explain the revolt in terms of long-standing Jewish resentment of Roman occupation. Of course, Tacitus has much more to say—all hostile—about the "superstition" of the "servile" Jews; but little to say about their grievances against Rome.

Tacitus represents a characteristically Roman viewpoint on subject peoples in general, and the Jews in particular.[1] Most of the time, to the extent that they attracted the notice of the Roman imagination at all, subject peoples appeared "patient" and compliant, accepting their divinely ordained role within the Roman political economy. In the case of the Jews, this meant, for Tacitus, accepting "discipline" as they were "brought to heel," like domesticated animals. On the other hand, when—sporadically and spontaneously—the ungrateful rose up in rebellion, it could only be attributed to their character as a barbaric people. So Mary Smallwood has observed that the Jews appeared in Roman histories primarily "when they gave serious trouble."[2] Dixon Slingerland's fine analysis of Claudian policy toward the

---

1. Schäfer, *Judeophobia*, 31–33.
2. Smallwood, *Jews under Roman Rule*, 233–34.

Jews has shown that Romans like Suetonius had little interest in exploring possible motives for Jewish resentment or rebellion. It was easier to rely on stereotyped references to "rabble-rousing Jews and their plots against well intended imperial order."[3]

There are other perceptions of Jewish "patience," however. The author of 4 Maccabees speaks at length of "patient endurance," but means the courageous defiance of tyranny that liberates the individual and, eventually, redeems the nation. The treatise provides no explicit call to revolutionary violence, but we readily detect the carefully sanitized language of a disciplined *intifadeh* against Roman rule.

Our scholarly literature abounds with characterizations of early Judaic apocalypticism as an "ideology of resistance." We are often reminded that "happy people don't write apocalypses,"[4] and that the Zealots of the late first century CE were inspired by a generally apocalyptic ideology.[5] Such generalized linking of apocalypticism with rebellion begs some questions, however. In addition to the abiding puzzles of definition—what exactly constitutes an apocalypse, or apocalypticism?—we may with reason ask how an apocalyptic perspective *functions*. Is it necessarily an ideology of revolt, or can it also provide symbolic compensation for a group experiencing perceived deprivation?[6] Can't apocalyptic language also function to encourage a policy of "quietism," as in the book of Daniel?[7] Just how "revolutionary" *is* apocalypticism? If "happy people" don't have the *motive* to write apocalypses, surely it is equally true that the desperately poor do not have the *opportunity*, and that populist or rebel leaders could usually not depend on literary production to rally a successful social movement. We find no direct links between the constant ferment in the Galilee and the writing of particular apocalypses, for example.

We have usually construed first-century Judaism within a stark polarity between "resistance," cast in the militant revolutionary violence of the Zealot desperados, and "accommodation," which evokes for us the whole-hearted collaboration of a Tiberius Alexander or a Herod. No one in the current generation of New Testament scholars has done more to alert us all to the dangers of facile polarizations (e.g., "Judaism vs. Hellenism") than Calvin J. Roetzel, nor has anyone pressed more consistently

---

3. Slingerland, *Claudian Policymaking*, 166, 231.
4. Fredriksen, *From Jesus to Christ*, 82.
5. Hengel, *Die Zeloten*.
6. Gager, *Kingdom and Community*.
7. Lebram, "Piety of the Jewish Apocalypticists."

for taking serious and nuanced account of political and cultural realities.[8] Especially with regard to the interpretation of the apostle Paul—so often overshadowed by a Christian imagination that pits him against "the Jew" and "Judaism"—Cal has steadfastly reminded us that Judah was a "satellite" of Hellenistic and Roman imperial cultures, and that first-century Judaism presented a series of responses to imperial pressures.[9] It follows that Paul never responded to Judaism in a vacuum, but always to a field of cultural forces shaped by imperial pressure.[10] I hope to express my professional and personal gratitude to Cal by pursuing these insights further in these pages, along a path opened up by analysts of colonial cultures.

ATTENDING TO THE "VOICE UNDER DOMINATION"

James C. Scott reminds us that throughout human history, outright revolutionary violence has been the marked exception, and that (especially in agrarian societies) much quieter forms of peasant non-cooperation have been the norm.[11] Further, postcolonial theorists like Frantz Fanon and Albert Memmi have had much to say, not only about the complex and chaotic social configurations appearing in "the colonial situation," but about the delicate mental and emotional equilibrium which the colonized struggle to maintain against the overwhelming pressure of colonizing culture.[12] Their observations alert us all to the temptation to adopt the colonial power's perspective. How readily do we assume, when faced with a relative abundance of literary evidence from a colonizing elite, that so long as the natives have not picked up mattocks or machetes, they must have been content with their situation? In just such language Tacitus seems to refer to the "patience" of the Jews. Postcolonial theorists suggest, to the contrary, that we imagine "resistance" and "accommodation" as possibilities along a continuum of responses to a colonial situation. John Barclay helpfully proposes that we discuss Jews in the Mediterranean Diaspora using several analytical categories: (1) cultural *assimilation*—the extent to which Diaspora Jews "were integrated into, or socially aloof from, their social environments"; (2) *acculturation*—the extent to which Jews "acquired [the] common discourse of cultural ideals and recognized virtues of Hellenistic society; and (3) *accommodation*, or the use to which Jews put their familiarity with "the colonizers'

---

8. Roetzel, *World That Shaped the New Testament*, 1.
9. Roetzel, *World That Shaped the New Testament*, 24–53.
10. Roetzel, *Letters of Paul*.
11. Scott, *Weapons of the Weak*.
12. Fanon, *Wretched of the Earth*; Memmi, *The Colonizer and the Colonized*.

culture," either "to modify or even obliterate their native cultural traditions," or else "to equip them to resist the colonizers' cultural imperialism."[13] Philo of Alexandria, for example, can be shown to be "Jewish to the core and Hellenized to the same core"; thoroughly acculturated without becoming completely assimilated to the Roman-Egyptian movement.[14]

That does not mean that Jewish literary sources serve as unambiguous evidence of the level of assimilation or accommodation of their authors, even if they indicate a level of acculturation to the Greek language. Much of Second Temple Jewish literature, and especially the apologetic writings of Roman-era Jews like Philo or Josephus, present "public transcripts." Scott reminds us that whenever there is a "disparity in power between dominant and subordinate . . . the public performance of the subordinate will, out of prudence, fear, and the desire to curry favor, be shaped to appeal to the expectations of the powerful."[15] The public transcript is therefore "an indifferent guide to the opinion of subordinates."[16] To discern what subordinate peoples really think, we must attend to what Scott calls the "hidden transcript," those "offstage speeches, gestures, and practices that confirm, contradict, or inflect what appears in the public transcript."[17]

We have access to transcripts that are by nature "hidden," disguised or completely concealed from the public realm only indirectly, Scott argues—and only when the subordinate feel enough freedom in a relatively protected space to offer glimpses of what must be a fuller transcript off-stage. Scott gives an example from the antebellum US South: Aggy, a "normally taciturn and deferential black cook," watches in silence as her master beats her daughter because of a false accusation of some minor theft. After the master leaves the kitchen, Aggy turns to a white governess whom she apparently perceives as sympathetic and declares,

> Thar's a day a-comin'! Thar's a day a-comin'! . . . I hear the rumblin ob de chariots! I see de flashin ob de guns! White folks blood is a runnin on the ground like a ribber, an de dead's heaped up dat high! . . . Oh Lor! Hasten de day when de blows, an de bruises, an de aches an de pains, shall come to de white folks, an de buzzards shall eat dem as dey's dead in de streets. Oh Lor! Roll on de chariots, an gib the black people rest and peace. Oh Lor! Gib me de pleasure ob livin' till that day, when I shall see

13. Barclay, *Jews in the Mediterranean Diaspora*, 88–98.
14. Barclay, *Jews in the Mediterranean Diaspora*, 91.
15. Scott, *Domination and the Arts of Resistance*, 2–3.
16. Scott, *Domination and the Arts of Resistance*, 3.
17. Scott, *Domination and the Arts of Resistance*, 4–5.

white folks shot down like de wolves when dey come hungry out
o' de woods.[18]

Scott observes that this is not "an inchoate scream of rage." Rather it gives a glimpse into "a finely drawn and highly visual image of an apocalypse," a glimpse that could "lead us directly to the offstage culture of the slave quarters and slave religion."[19]

Note that we would *not* have this insight into the "hidden transcript" if we relied only on what slaves like Aggy were willing to say in the presence of their masters day by day. Social science in general is, Scott argues, "focused resolutely on the *official* or *formal* relations between the powerful and weak," but such a focus "hardly exhausts what we might wish to know about power."[20] The same might be said about the social-scientific exploration of ancient texts. I conclude that we cannot take the relative absence of direct protest or resistance in early Jewish writings to indicate the absence of resentment, or the perception that the situation of subordination really wasn't important to an author.

It will not be easy to recover smoldering anti-Roman resentment just beneath the surface of our texts. Indeed, as Scott observes, "the hidden transcript of many historically important subordinate groups is irrecoverable for all practical purposes."[21] Neither may we simply *presume* that such transcripts "must have" existed—for example, that Jews in general "must have" resented Roman colonialism—although this presumption is no more objectionable than the opposite presumption, that Jews in general "must have" been content with their lot in the Roman Diaspora.

Since "most of the political life of subordinate groups" is lived "neither in overt collective defiance of powerholders nor in complete hegemonic compliance," we must develop what Scott calls "an elaborate theory of *voice under domination*," attending the "the arts of political disguise." Much of the political action of subordinate groups "requires interpretation precisely because it is intended to be cryptic and opaque"; "nothing is entirely straightforward here."[22] Scott distinguishes various strategies of indirection, but his most basic distinction—and the one on which I will concentrate in what follows—is between those techniques that "disguise the *message* and those that disguise the *messenger*."[23]

18. Scott, *Domination and the Arts of Resistance*, 5.
19. Scott, *Domination and the Arts of Resistance*, 6.
20. Scott, *Domination and the Arts of Resistance*, 13.
21. Scott, *Domination and the Arts of Resistance*, 138.
22. Scott, *Domination and the Arts of Resistance*, 136–37.
23. Scott, *Domination and the Arts of Resistance*, 139.

POLITICAL DISGUISE IN ROMAN-ERA JEWISH WRITINGS

A first example: We find both maneuvers—disguise of the message, and of the messenger—combined in the commentary (or *pesher*) on Habakkuk from Qumran (1QpHab). While many apocalypses achieved anonymity by concealing the author's identity under the name of an ancient worthy, the *Habakkuk pesher* constructs the implied author as simply an innocent, though authoritative, interpreter of scripture. The repeated statement *pishro*—"its interpretation is . . ."—presents an anonymous, yet authoritative interpretation of the text of Habakkuk. In this way the author of the *pesher* is as concealed as the apocalyptic writers who wrote pseudonymously—using the names of ancient worthies (Enoch, Ezra, etc.). The burden of responsibility for the message is thus placed on the shoulders of the biblical prophet.

The *pesher* also disguises the message, most notably through a system of coded terms—"wicked priest," "man of lies," "teacher of righteousness." These terms are presumably meaningful to the *pesher's* intended audience, but opaque enough to outsiders to keep modern Qumran scholars in business for years to come. Most interpreters agree that the *pesher's* rendering of the biblical term "Chaldeans" by the archaic term *Kittim* is a coded reference to the Romans. The use of this term, immediately meaningful to the initiate, allows the author to condemn the Romans as "swift and powerful in battle," "destroying and pillaging cities," "cunning and treacherous," "more savage than wolves at night," "resorting to force," "insatiable" in their destructiveness. The term's opacity to outsiders might have been intended to disguise the message sufficiently to avert retaliation.[24]

In fact the *pesher* is an excellent example of what Scott calls the hidden transcript—literally hidden away for centuries of course, probably to conceal it (and other scrolls) from the scrutiny of Roman eyes. But the *pesher* is also *symbolically* a hidden transcript. Within the safe company of the initiate, it constructs an extensive alternative transcript (for a select "public") that reads the present situation as an exact fulfillment of biblical prophecy. The *pesher hides* this transcript from others, however, under the guise of esoteric biblical interpretation. We might say, it provides the initiate "plausible deniability" of any content that might imperil them in a wider social situation.

I have already mentioned a second example: 4 Maccabees, an anonymous writing that presents itself as a "most philosophical" meditation on "self-control." The treatise combines tropes of the wisdom tradition—the ostensible appeal to "everyone who is seeking knowledge" and virtue (1:2),

---

24. See Scott, *Domination and the Arts of Resistance*, 152.

attention to the source of wisdom itself (1:15-18)—with concepts we are more accustomed to associating with the apocalyptic tradition: the redemptive value of the martyr's death (1:11), the resurrection of the righteous dead. This text creates a social space in which the "voice under domination" can be heard by focusing the reader's studious attention on events of an earlier time (that of the Seleucid Antiochus IV). Further, the author speaks of "rational judgment," "control over the passions," and "social harmony," favorite themes of Roman imperial culture.[25] These techniques of disguise allow the author to dwell on the brutality of repression by describing gruesome, yet *safely past* tortures and executions; and to put ringing calls for defiance of the tyrant, even to the point of death, onto the lips of heroic martyrs who are being memorialized as models not of fiery rebellion but of virtue and "self-control." To the extent the rhetoric of the martyrs' speeches surpasses the philosophical categories in which the treatise is cast, that rhetoric allows glimpses into a much fuller, "offstage" transcript of apocalyptic defiance and a longing for the "purification" of Judea.[26]

A third example appears in Philo's treatise *On Dreams*, which provides another excellent opportunity to examine the interaction of "public" and "hidden" transcripts. This thoroughly Hellenized Jew—whose *Embassy to Gaius* shows that he knew well how to offer praise to an emperor in terms dictated by Roman panegyric—has also given a glimpse into another, offstage transcript among Jews in Roman Egypt. Philo never attempts to disguise himself or speak anonymously. Rather, the *message* is disguised enough (in the guise of esoteric allegorical interpretation of Genesis) to be invisible even to some modern readers, who find here only "a poverty of thought" which makes this treatise "the weakest" of Philo's allegorical treatments.[27]

Decades ago E. R. Goodenough drew attention to an intriguing section in Book 2, where Philo's theme is "caution." Ostensibly treating Joseph's dream of sheaves of grain bowing down to him, Philo takes the occasion to describe the "votaries of vainglory" who "set themselves up above everything, above cities and laws and ancestral customs and the affairs of the several citizens," proceeding so far as to impose "dictatorship over the people," bringing "into subjection even souls whose spirit is naturally free and unenslaved" (*On Dreams* 2.78-79).

We may catch oblique glimpses of a fuller, otherwise *hidden* transcript when power relations are described in ways significantly different from the

---

25. Martin, *Corinthian Body*.
26. See Elliott, *Liberating Paul*, 154-56.
27. Colson and Whitaker, trans., *Philo*, vol. 5, 433.

"official" schema of the wider public transcript. Here, Philo has described an *unnatural* imposition of dictatorship upon those who are *naturally* free. Immediately, however, he retreats: "surely that is *natural*," for

> the man of worth who surveys, not only human life but all the phenomena of the world, knows how mightily blow the winds of necessity, fortune, opportunity, force, violence and princedom, and how many are the projects, how great the good fortunes which soar to heaven without pausing in their flight and then are shaken about and brought crashing to the ground by these blasts. And therefore he must needs take caution to shield him ... for caution is to the individual man what a wall is to a city. (*On Dreams* 2.81–82)

Necessity, fortune, opportunity, force, violence, and princedom are described as natural "phenomena of the world," and from the perspective of Roman elite authors like Cicero or Tacitus or Plutarch, so they are. But if these forces are fundamentally benign in imperial eyes, subject individuals—for whom the walls of a Roman city do not provide security—must daily practice "caution" to protect themselves from harm.

Caution is exercised pre-eminently by avoiding "untimely frankness." Philo knows there are "lunatics and madmen" who "dare to oppose kings and tyrants in words and deeds." Interestingly, Philo does not say they are "lunatics" because they fail to recognize the inherent benefit of subjection to the imperial order (as the official transcript would define lunacy). Rather, they are lunatics because they fail to recognize just how harmful that order is. They are unaware that

> not only like cattle are their necks under the yoke, but that the harness extends to their whole bodies and souls, their wives and children and parents, and the wide circles of friends and kinsfolk united to them by fellowship of feeling, and that the driver can with perfect ease spur, drive on or pull back, and mete out any treatment small or great just as he pleases. And therefore they are branded and scourged and mutilated and undergo a combination of all the sufferings which merciless cruelty can inflict short of death, and finally are led away to death itself. (*On Dreams* 2.83–84)

Elsewhere Philo makes it clear that he knows Roman tax gatherers have acted with just such savagery in Jewish villages (*Special Laws* 2.92–95; 3.159–163). Although he does not name Romans here, his rhetoric is brazen enough. The political subordination Philo describes is tantamount to living as brute livestock, suffering torment and indignity until finally being butchered. No reason for honoring the rulers is recognized. Resorting again to the disguise of allegorical interpretation, Philo discerns that Abraham's obedience to the sons of Cheth (Gen 23:7) was compelled by "fear," not "respect":

> for it was not out of any feeling of respect for those who by nature and race and custom were the enemies of reason . . . that he brought himself to do obeisance. Rather it was just because he feared their power at the time and their formidable strength and cared to give no provocation . . . (*On Dreams* 2.90)

"To give no provocation" is the mark of true prudence under domination. Just as a wise pilot will "wait" until storms pass over before setting sail—just as a traveler encountering a bear or a lion or a wild boar on the road will seek to soothe and calm the beast—so the wise citizen will manifest patience and deference to rulers (2.86–87).

All this is said obliquely, in the most general of terms, and while the comparisons are hardly flattering to rulers, neither are they specific or openly defiant enough to spark offense. At just one point does Philo allow the pretense that all this is abstract and general to slip:

> Again, do we too, when we are spending time in the marketplace, make a practice of standing out of the path of our rulers and also of beasts of carriage, though our motive in the two cases is entirely different? With the rulers it is done to show them honor, with the animals from fear and to save us from suffering serious injury from them. (*On Dreams* 2.91)

Of course these qualifications come a moment too late. The distinction between rulers and brute animals is explicit—but is undermined by everything else Philo has said about the brutality of rulers. His insistence that "honor" is shown to rulers is belied by his preceding comment that fear, not honor, compels the outward deference of the subordinate.

"The sarcasm at the end is obvious," Goodenough writes—though not obvious enough to resolve the careful ambiguity of the whole passage:

> Philo has compared harsh rulers to savage and deadly animals throughout. When he mentions how in the marketplace the Jews have to make place for their rulers and the pack animals alike, it is part of the very caution he is counseling that he should distinguish between the two, once the rulers in Alexandria have been distinctly referred to, and say that one gives way out of honor to the rulers, but out of fear to the beasts . . .

thus maintaining the pretended deference to the legitimacy of Roman rule that is essential to the public transcript: "But [Philo's] Jewish readers would quite well have understood that the reason Philo gave way to each was the same, because he knew that if he did not he would be crushed."[28] That is, Jewish readers would have immediately picked up hints that seem merely incongruous in the treatise, but that make perfect sense within another, "offstage" transcript.

This passage from Philo is most valuable for my exploration because Philo explicitly distinguishes the two transcripts—the "public" transcript of deference to the imperial order, and the "offstage" transcript of defiance—under the categories of "speaking most freely," or "boldness of speech," and speaking with "untimely frankness" (*On Dreams* 2.83). "When the times are right"—when a social space is opened in which the "offstage" transcript can come onstage, the hidden transcript of defiance become public—then "it is good to set ourselves against the violence of our enemies and subdue it; but when the circumstances do not present themselves, the safe course is to stay quiet" (2.92).

DISCERNING THE "ARTS OF RESISTANCE"

The "caution" Philo describes was a constant requirement, the only defense the subordinate had in negotiating the perils of the Roman city. Courageous and defiant "endurance" in the face of threatened torture and death is the call at the heart of the martyrs' admonitions in 4 Maccabees. For the true measure of anger and anguish in the colonized heart we more profitably turn to Fanon and other modern postcolonial writers than to Tacitus's offhand references to the "patient endurance" of the Jews. At once architect and artifact of the Roman "public transcript," Tacitus was constitutionally incapable of fathoming the rebellion of the spirit that smolders beneath both these ostensibly "philosophical" texts.

Unfortunately, the modern study of this period has more usually relied on the likes of Tacitus, and on a relatively unnuanced reading of the likes of Philo. Scott's methodological attention to the "voice under domination" provides valuable direction and tools for our study of power relations between Jews and Roman imperial culture. If this brief examination of a few texts provokes further exploration of the interplay between public and hidden transcripts, we may come closer to a nuanced understanding of the "world that shaped the New Testament."

---

28. Goodenough, *An Introduction to Philo Judaeus*, 57.

6

The Apostle Paul's Self-Presentation as Anti-Imperial Performance

ROMAN IMPERIAL RITUAL AND propaganda filled the environment in which the apostle Paul worked.[1] In convergent ways, recent studies of the imperial cult, on the one hand, *and* of Paul's "theology," on the other, are moving away from the individualistic, cognitivist concerns of classical Christian theology and toward an understanding of the meaning of symbols and the function of rituals in representing relationships of power. I argue here that *both* imperial imagery and cult, *and* the performance of Paul's apostolic *parousia* (presence), constituted ritual representations of power.

Further, the evidence of Paul's letters tells us that, despite the vaunted "religious tolerance" of the Empire,[2] these two ritual strategies did not coexist peacefully. That is, they did not keep to neatly segregated "political" and "religious," or public and private, spheres (as citizens of modern Western

---

1. Dieter Georgi and Stanley K. Stowers regard Roman imperial ideology as a more relevant context for understanding the letter to the Romans than a presumed debate with Judaism: see Georgi, *Theocracy*; and Stowers, *A Rereading of Romans*. Holland Lee Hendrix ("Archaeology and Eschatology at Thessalonica") has used archaeological and numismatic evidence in a systematic reconstruction of the imperial context for 1 Thessalonians. See also the important collection of essays in Horsley, ed., *Paul and Empire*.

2. Richard Gordon notes that one ideological function of religion in the early Principate "was to insulate Rome from the cultural consequence of her own imperialism: the religion of Rome became a guarantee not merely of her supremacy but also of her freedom from contamination by her subjects . . . Rome was different from her Empire and her religion was an emblem of that difference. The so-called tolerance of the indigenous religions of the provinces is rather to be understood as a consequence of this colonial attitude" (Gordon, "Veil of Power," 207).

democracies are too prone to imagine, on the analogy of our division between "church and state"). Instead, Paul's apostolic performance constituted a rival representation of power, even if that representation was realized on the public landscape of the Roman city only rarely (and in paradoxical ways, as we shall see below).[3] Informed by the covenantal and apocalyptic traditions of Israel, and by the *apokalypsis* of Jesus Christ (Gal 1:15–16), Paul understands his *parousia* to actualize an invasive power that is at odds—indeed at war!—with the imperial power of "the rulers of this age" (1 Cor 2:8).

RITUAL REPRESENTATIONS OF POWER IN THE ROMAN CIVIC LANDSCAPE

Recent studies bring valuable light to bear on the symbolic representations of power in Hellenistic-Roman society. Especially important in this regard is S. R. F. Price's work on power and ritual. Price demonstrates that in Paul's day, imperial ritual had saturated public life throughout the provinces, including long-standing local festivals, which took on new imperial aspects, as well as new celebrations and games, festivals, and sacrifices offered to, or on behalf of, the imperial family. Those rituals were not irregular and passing events, but cults institutionalized on a regular basis. Further, they were not simply occasional accommodations imposed on an indifferent population by imperial fiat. Usually, rituals celebrating Roman power were "created and organized by the subjects of a great empire" themselves—in the absence of the emperor or even his representative—"in order to represent to themselves the ruling power."[4]

Price argues that "Christianizing" assumptions still hinder an adequate understanding of the imperial cult. These misapprehensions include, first, privileging the individual's feeling at the expense of ritual action. "With the imperial cult, the processions and the sacrifices, the temples and the images fill our sources. They are the crucially important collective constructs to which the individual reacted. Ritual is what there was."[5] Another Christianizing bias is the "theological" focus on the question of how widespread and how sincere was belief in the Emperor's divinity, a question abstracted from the social matrix of the Roman city in which the imperial cult took place. Price criticizes a scholarship too often preoccupied with a presumed

---

3. Compare Georgi, *Theocracy*, 83–88; and Stowers, *Rereading*, 14–15. Raymond Pickett's program in *The Cross in Corinth*, 9–36, is very similar to what I wish to accomplish here, on a smaller scale.

4. Price, *Rituals and Power*, 1.

5. Price, *Rituals and Power*, 11.

skepticism on the part of the Roman elite—a presumption that reduces imperial rituals to a cynical political manipulation of religious symbolism.

Instead, Price argues, imperial rituals constituted "a public cognitive system," a social "embodiment of thinking," an attempt on the part of the Greek cities "to represent to themselves their new masters in a traditional guise," and thus "to come to terms with a new type of power." He finds the origins of the imperial cult in public Hellenistic cults for rulers and prominent citizens. The transitions to cults of Roma—of the "Roman benefactors" in general, or of Roman individuals in particular—represent "clear-sighted perception of the new situation" of Roman hegemony, expressed in Greek idiom.[6] Taking seriously Price's attention to the *cultural* mechanisms of imperialism does not mean we should minimize the role of brute force in establishing Roman hegemony, of course. Paul's insistence that in one particular act of Roman brutality—the humiliation and crucifixion of Jesus of Nazareth—the "rulers of this age" had exposed their own fraudulence and folly (1 Cor 2:4–6) requires that we who seek to understand the apostle not divert our gaze from imperial violence, in the ancient world or in our own. Rather, Price points us to the thickly textured cultural process by which provincial elites sought to accommodate themselves to a force that would have been "otherwise unchangeable."[7]

Price's study of imperial cult in Asia Minor has found important echoes in other recent works[8] that demonstrate the aggressive, pervasive, and systematic representation of imperial power in public space. The redesign of city squares, the construction of new temples, the appropriation or transfer of existing shrines, monumental architecture, dedicatory inscriptions, and the proliferation of standardized images of the emperor all served the interests of the Roman government, clearly enough. Yet the imperial cult was enthusiastically produced and maintained by the provincial elites, who were eager to participate in the new networks of power, privilege, and prestige. The cult served as "a system of exchange," linking Greek and provincial elites to Rome; it "enhanced the dominance of local elites over the populace, of cities over other cities, and of Greek over indigenous cultures."[9]

Public rituals served as the medium through which the image of the emperor came to represent the network of military, economic, and social

---

6. Price, *Rituals and Power*, 8–9, 25–43.

7. Price, *Rituals and Power*, 52.

8. For example, Alcock, *Graecia Capta*; also worthy of note is MacMullen, *Romanization in the Time of Augustus*. On the Romanization of the Mediterranean economy, see Woolf, "Imperialism, Empire, and the Integration of the Roman Economy."

9. Price, *Rituals and Power*, 65–77, 248; Alcock, *Graecia Capta*, 215–30. See also Bowersock, "Imperial Cult"; and Ando, *Imperial Ideology and Provincial Loyalty*.

relationships of Roman hegemony. Most persons in the empire of Rome knew the emperor only through the proliferation of images throughout the provinces, and these dominated the celebration of the cult. Ceremonial processions frequently involved the carrying-about of images of the emperor; producing the image for the reverential gaze of the citizens was a sacred action. The omnipresence of imperial images, and their strategic manipulation through ritual, produced a considerable effect, providing a constant reminder of who ruled the world.[10] The ritualized maintenance of public order was in the imperial era focused increasingly on the person of the emperor himself, in Rome; and on the successful manipulation of the image, in the provinces.[11]

Several aspects of the imperial cult merit particular note. First, while the production of imperial images was a propaganda project from the center, Rome, their *manipulation and representation* in civic ritual, public ceremonial, and everyday conversation was enthusiastically carried on at the "periphery," by the Greek elites in the provinces.[12] Second, the rise of Augustus marked an abrupt end to the proliferation of cults to human benefactors and a consolidation of cults to the gods with the imperial cult, transparently a reflection of the colonial relationship.[13] Third, following his dramatic triple triumph in 29 BCE, Octavian, later called Augustus, consistently refused the Senate's offers of triumphs in his honor, and in a deliberate and unified political program, restricted the official triumphs, celebrated by others, to his own potential successors. At the same time, he actively promoted the use of the image and title of *triumphator* in other rituals (acclamations, supplications) and other media (architecture, coins, statues). The result was an effective *imperial monopoly on the imagery of triumph*.[14] The effect in Roman cities was that sacrifices by individual emperors in specific rituals increasingly became manifestations of a *generalized and distinctly Roman piety*, practiced and promoted by the emperors in the name of the Empire. Thus the emperor was able to accumulate "symbolic capital" for himself, and piety in the provinces became saturated with the symbolized presence of the emperor.[15]

10. Bowersock, "Imperial Cult," 173–74; Price, *Rituals and Power*, 170–206. Price relies explicitly (7–9, 239–40) on Geertz, *The Interpretation of Cultures*, for his understanding of ritual.

11. See Nippel, *Public Order in Ancient Rome*, 4–17 (on Republican Rome) and 85–119 (for the early Principate); and Zanker, *The Power of Images*.

12. Price, *Rituals and Power*, 172–76.

13. Price, *Rituals and Power*, 49–51, 54–56; Gordon, "Veil of Power," 206–7.

14. Hickson, "Augustus *Triumphator*."

15. Gordon, "Veil of Power," 205, 208, 219.

POWER AND RHETORIC IN PAUL

To the extent that Roman imperial power and ideology found ritualized representation on the Roman civic landscape, we should expect that Paul's apostolic work on that same landscape would engage imperial ritual, at least obliquely. Until recently, however, imperial ritual and symbolization have been curiously underappreciated in Pauline studies.[16] This is curious, since Paul does not simply speak *about* power; he intended his letters to function with a larger public, apostolic strategy that *represented* and *expressed power and power relations* in a way different from, and often subversive of, imperial symbol and ritual. An adequate rhetorical criticism will not be content to interpret Paul's letters as vehicles for conveying theological concepts: they are instruments of persuasion within a larger apostolic strategy.

Paul describes his own apostolic activity as the manifestation of divine power. I focus below on several key metaphors: the triumphal procession, the spectacle of the arena, and combat imagery, metaphors through which Paul seeks to represent the death and resurrection of Jesus as the decisive manifestation of divine power. First, however, we must attend to some aspects of the rhetorical *performance* of Paul's letters.

Though the Hellenistic world was far from a purely oral culture, it is nevertheless true that reading was *oral performance*.[17] In dictating letters to be read aloud to his communities, Paul sought to extend the presence of his apostolic authority and power, his "apostolic *parousia*," in circumstances where his personal presence, the primary medium through which he preferred to make his authority effective, was impossible. Paul's letters did more than maintain personal contact over distance. In contrast to our visual way of taking in the text of a letter, holding it quite literally "at arm's length," *oral*

---

16. Important recent efforts include Georgi, *Theocracy*, and the essays collected in Horsley, ed., *Paul and Empire*. Recent interpretation of the Corinthian correspondence has also focused on apparent competition within the *ekklēsia* over power, especially as represented in eloquence ("wise speech"), and upon social stratification and friction between classes. The relationship between imperial ideology and codes of "vertical reciprocity" in Roman patronage has been ably investigated by Peter Marshall, *Enmity in Corinth*; and Chow, *Patronage and Power*; also Horrell, *The Social Ethos of the Corinthian Correspondence*. The notion of a "new consensus" regarding the social setting of the Pauline *ekklēsiai*, depending on the work of Theissen (*Social Setting of Pauline Christianity*) and Meeks (*First Urban Christians*), has been challenged regarding its implicit functionalism and overgeneralizing from the particular situation in Corinth. See Tolbert, "Social, Sociological, and Anthropological Methods"; Horsley, "Paul's Counter-Imperial Gospel: Introduction"; Horsley, *1 Corinthians*; Meggitt, *Paul, Poverty, and Survival*; and Friesen, "Poor Paul."

17. As Paul Achtemeier declares, late antiquity knew nothing of the "silent, solitary reader" ("*Omne verbum sonat*," 16–19).

performance situates people in the midst of "a world of voices." The effect of Paul's message *performed orally* would have been to create an atmosphere of effectual energy, an orbit of power. We expect the creation of this "acoustic space" to have been the responsibility of the associate to whom Paul entrusted his letter; thus, Paul would presumably have taken care to prepare this messenger to *perform* the letter as a part of his apostolic strategy, for the letter had only done its work once it was performed.[18]

Ancient rhetorical handbooks gave specific instructions regarding the body and hand gestures most effective in oral performance. Even if Paul had no direct contact with those handbooks, we may expect that Paul's colleagues would have arrived in a city like Corinth prepared to present a vivid performance of his letters. The troubled interactions recorded in the Corinthian correspondence show the high esteem in which some in the Corinthian *ekklēsia* held polished rhetorical performance, such as that attributed to Apollos of Alexandria (Acts 18:24–28; cf. 1 Cor 1:17–18, 2:1–5). Also evident is the reaction of these same Corinthians to what they came to regard as Paul's inadequate rhetorical performance, and the consequent crisis for an apostle compelled to restore his authoritative *parousia* (his strategic presence) through an effective counterperformance by an apostolic colleague (or colleagues).[19]

If (as 2 Cor 10:10 indicates) some of the Corinthians found Paul's performance disappointing, the challenge facing him was to establish the authenticity of his own apostolic presence *without participating in the same self-commendation that he condemns in his rivals*. His strategy in both letters—heightened in the second—is to represent himself, not merely as a particularly able speaker among others, but as an agent of the "power of God," distinct from mere practitioners of rhetoric (so 1 Cor 4:19–20).[20]

---

18. See Funk, "The Apostolic *Parousia*"; Doty, *Letters in Primitive Christianity*; Holmberg, *Paul and Power*, 140–83; Stowers, *Letter Writing in Greco-Roman Antiquity*, 23; Aune, *The New Testament in Its Literary Environment*, 192; Botha, "The Verbal Art of the Pauline Letters"; J. Dewey, "Textuality in an Oral Culture"; A. J. Dewey, "A Re-Hearing of Romans 10:1–15"; Robbins, "Oral, Rhetorical, and Literary Cultures: A Response"; Ward, "Pauline Voice," 102–3.

19. Quintilian, *Institutio Oratoria* 1.11; Ward, "Pauline Voice," 99–101; Betz, *Galatians*, 131; Wire, "Performance, Politics, and Power: A Response," 129. The argument that a Corinthian disparagement of Paul's rhetoric was a key issue in the correspondence was first made by Munck, *Paul and the Salvation of Mankind*, 135–67; compare Dahl, *Studies in Paul*, 40–61; Betz, "The Problem of Rhetoric and Theology"; and Meeks, *First Urban Christians*, 117–18.

20. On the challenge and Paul's response, see Kraftchick, "Death in Us, Life in You," 166; Castelli, "Interpretations of Power in 1 Corinthians," 205–6; Wire, *The Corinthian Women Prophets*, 176–80; Schüssler Fiorenza, "Rhetorical Situation and Historical Reconstruction." In 1 Corinthians, Castelli, Wire, and Schüssler Fiorenza detect Paul's

Using terminology familiar from the rhetorical handbooks, Paul calls his own performance among the Corinthians a "demonstration [*apodeixis*] of the Spirit and of power" (1 Cor 2:4), not merely "persuasive words of wisdom" (NASB). One might say his rhetoric is *apodeictic*—"demonstrative of power"—rather than *epideictic* (rhetorical display). God's power is at work in Paul: thus Paul is not ashamed of the gospel because it is "the saving power of God" (Rom 1:16; cf. 1 Thess 1:5). Paul's "signs and wonders" are the work of Christ (Rom 15:18–19), or of the Spirit (Gal 3:3–5); they are "the signs of a true apostle" (2 Cor 12:12).[21]

Recognizing what I am calling the "apodeictic" character of Paul's rhetoric means shifting attention from the apostle's "consciousness, that is, what Paul *thought*" about a subject, to the *effects* he wished to achieve—including the work he intended his letters to perform, through divine power. Through them he means to fulfill his own calling as apostle *and* to realize the calling of his hearers as "holy ones," by securing their faithful obedience (Rom 1:5) and thus the sanctity of "the offering of the nations" (Rom 15:14–16, my translation).[22] But this means that the conventional rhetorical-critical approaches to Paul's letters must be expanded. The "rhetorical situation" addressed in any letter is more than the network of relationships and expectations that connect the apostle with his audience. The "deep exigence" of Paul's letters is nothing less than the apostolic horizon of God's coming triumph in power. This "deep exigence" necessarily impinges directly on the "near exigence" of the letter's audience, for Paul clearly wrote in anticipation of God acting in the congregation.[23]

---

effort to curtail the autonomy, authority, and power of charismatic women in the Corinthian congregation, an assessment depending heavily on the authenticity of 1 Cor 14:34–35 and its alignment with 11:2–16. I suspect the first passage is an interpolation, and regard Paul's rhetorical power-play as aimed at a different segment of the Corinthian church; see Elliott, *Liberating Paul*, 52–54, 204–14.

21. Betz, "Rhetoric and Theology," 35–37; Schüssler Fiorenza, "Rhetorical Situation," 392; Holmberg, *Paul and Power*, 74–75.

22. Quoting Martyn, "Events in Galatia," 161. Compare Pickett, *The Cross in Corinth*, 9–36; similarly Jouette M. Bassler speaks of Paul's mission as *activity*: "Paul's Theology: Whence and Whither?" See also Dahl, "Paul's Letter to the Galatians"; Dahl, *Studies in Paul*, 73; Kelber, *Oral and Written Gospel*, 145, 148–51; Elliott, *Rhetoric of Romans*, 94–104; Holmberg, *Paul and Power*, 70–74; J. L. White, "New Testament Epistolary Literature," 1745.

23. Martyn, "Events in Galatia," speaks of a "theological event" (163; 178–79) where Paul speaks of *God's action*. See also Käsemann, "The 'Righteousness of God' in Paul." On "rhetorical situation," see Bitzer, "The Rhetorical Situation"; Consigny, "Rhetoric and Its Situations." On the "deep exigence" of Paul's letter to the Romans, Elliott, *Rhetoric of Romans*, 17–21, 70–93.

We must not let our orientation to the Pauline *text* restrict the horizon of Paul's *parousia*. While we have no direct access to Paul's own oral performance, we do have the apostle's characterization of his performance. The fact that Paul repeatedly uses powerful metaphors drawn from the sphere of public ceremonial and the display of imperial power merits close examination, to which I now turn.

THE APOSTLE "LED IN TRIUMPH"

In 2 Cor 2:14-16 Paul takes up the language of the imperial triumph to describe his own apostolic presence:

> But thanks be to God, who in Christ always leads us in triumphal procession, and through us spreads in every place the fragrance that comes from knowing him. For we are the aroma of Christ to God among those who are being saved and among those who are perishing: to the one a fragrance from death to death, to the other a fragrance from life to life.

While earlier generations of translators and commentators regarded as "most unsuitable" the implication that Paul had been "conquered" by God,[24] more recently interpreters have emphasized precisely this theme as a key to Paul's rhetorical strategy in 2 Corinthians 8-9. Lexical evidence from the period indicates that *thriambeuein* plus accusative has the sense "to celebrate a victory already won" over someone, specifically, in a triumphal procession. To be led in such a procession means being subjected to humiliation and, routinely, to be led to one's death. The term could thus be used as a metaphor of shame and humiliation, and Paul relies on just that meaning as he confronts the enmity of a social elite among the Corinthians.[25]

Paul's opponents have accused him of breaching a relationship of reciprocal friendship based on faith. They may suspect him of initiating the collection for his own profit; further, they may even regard his subsequent imprisonment and mortal trial in Ephesus (2 Cor 1:8-10) as evidence of God's punishment for his attempt to "fleece" the church.[26] Paul responds that his conduct toward the Corinthians has been open and transparent, and that his own humiliation and mistreatment is in fact evidence that he

---

24. Findlay, "St. Paul's Use of *thriambeuo*," 404-5; Barrett, *A Commentary on the Second Epistle to the Corinthians*, 97-98.

25. Williamson, "Led in Triumph," 321; Breytenbach, "Paul's Proclamation and God's '*thriambos*,'" 259-62; Lambrecht, "The Defeated Paul" (with survey of interpretation); Marshall, "A Metaphor of Social Shame"; Hafemann, *Suffering and the Spirit*, 33.

26. Furnish, *II Corinthians*, 369; P. B. Duff, "Metaphor, Motif, and Meaning," 86-89.

is a genuine apostle! The triumphal metaphor allows Paul to reconfigure his apparent disgrace: even if God *had* displayed him as a figure of shame and ridicule, it redounds to God's triumph; the apostle remains the locus of God's power!

Paul relies upon the imagery of triumphal or epiphany processions elsewhere in 2 Corinthians: "The love of Christ has taken us captive" (5:14, my translation). Paul's presence is a fragrant substance such as the aroma spread in epiphany processions, to indicate the god's presence (2:14–16). Paul and his coworkers "carry about in the body the dying of Jesus, so that the life of Jesus may also be manifested in our bodies" (4:10, my translation). Paul bids the Corinthians "make way" as for a ceremonial procession (7:2). Paul Duff detects in this proliferation of ritual images a single strategic purpose:

> Paul ... "plays" with the definition of *thriambeuein*, expanding it ... Although Paul might look like he is being "led in triumph," a victim of defeat, the object of the vengeance of God, he is in fact a captive of the "love of Christ." He is a participant not in a military victory parade but in an epiphany procession. He has been captured, not as a prisoner of war, but as a devotee of the deity. ... He describes himself with an image which would be eagerly embraced by his opponents; but throughout the course of the letter fragment, he subtly redefines it, using metaphors and allusions drawn from the processions of the Greco-Roman world.[27]

This is not mere rhetorical "play," of course. While part of Paul's purpose is to address Corinthian charges that he has proved false by delaying his return to them (2 Cor 1:15–17; 1:23–2:4; 2:12), he must also revise their understanding of the "affliction" he suffered (1:8–10; see below). By taking up key images from the imperial ritualization of power (the triumph procession), Paul acknowledges that *he* has been made the object of public ridicule and shame in civic representations of Roman power (he refers obliquely to receiving "the sentence of death," 1:9). Indeed, the later Pauline tradition uses the language of triumphs and processions precisely in the context of public spectacles of torture, expulsion, or execution.[28] But Paul insists that the Corinthians must perceive in his humiliation the decisive display of *God's* power; wherever he goes, the "fragrance of the knowledge of God" is spread (2:14, my trans.; cf. 2:12). The peculiar double effect of

---

27. P. B. Duff, "Metaphor," 87, 91.

28. So the *Acts of Paul*, 3 (Thecla), 7 (Paul himself), in the Heidelberg and Hamburg Papyri: see Hennecke and Schneemelcher, *New Testament Apocrypha*, 2:244–45, 253.

this fragrance—to those perishing, "a fragrance from death to death"; to those being saved, "a fragrance from life to life"—is clearly an invitation and a challenge to the Corinthians to discern Paul's conduct from God's perspective.

PAUL'S "AFFLICTIONS"

All of 2 Corinthians 1–9 stands under the themes of "affliction" and "consolation" (1:3–7). Paul was "afflicted" in Asia (1:8), most probably at mortal risk during an Ephesian imprisonment;[29] he was subsequently "afflicted" in Macedonia, enduring "combats without and fears within" (7:5; my translation). Even his solicitude toward the Corinthians has been an "affliction" (2:4, 13)! Paul repeatedly lists his afflictions: in 4:8–12, where being "afflicted, . . . perplexed, . . . persecuted, . . . struck down, . . . always being given up to death for Jesus' sake" is characterized, in terms of the epiphany procession, as "carrying about in the body the death of Jesus so that the life of Jesus may be manifested in our bodies" (4:10, my translation). The triumph/epiphany metaphor in 2 Cor 2:14 and the allusion to the epiphany procession in 4:10 reveal a parallel structure: In both cases the afflictions of the apostolic workers are characterized as the public, ceremonial manifestation of the knowledge or power of God.[30]

Again in 6:4–10, Paul protests that his party of God's servants have conducted themselves with openness and purity in the face of "afflictions, hardships, calamities, beatings, imprisonments, riots, labors, sleepless nights, hunger"; he then appeals to the Corinthians to "make way" (*chōrēsate*) for these afflicted ministers, as for a sacred procession (7:2),[31] and thus to fulfill their sacred service (*diakonia*) to God (6:3–4). In 1 Cor 4:9–13, Paul presents another "affliction list" under a different though related metaphor, that of the ritualized spectacle of the arena:

> I think that God has exhibited us apostles as last of all, as though sentenced to death, because we have become a spectacle [*theatron*] to the world, to angels and to mortals. To the present hour we are hungry and thirsty, we are poorly clothed and beaten and homeless, and we grow weary from the work of our own hands. When reviled, we bless; when persecuted, we endure; when

---

29. Furnish, *II Corinthians*, 122–25.

30. P. B. Duff, "Metaphor," 89–90; Hafemann, *Suffering*, 73; on the affliction lists in general, Fitzgerald, *Cracks in an Earthen Vessel*.

31. P. B. Duff, "Metaphor," 87–88.

slandered, we speak kindly. We have become like the rubbish of the world, the dregs of all things, to this very day.

As in the passages from 2 Corinthians, the afflictions suffered by the apostles are here represented in ritual terms: first, the ghastly rehearsals of imperial power in the arena; then also the (often violent) public expulsions of ritual victims (*perikatharmata, peripsēma*) in apotropaic rituals.[32] While Paul's reference to fighting "wild animals at Ephesus" (1 Cor 15:32) should perhaps not be taken literally (as it was, however, by the author of the *Acts of Paul*!), neither is the phrase merely an extravagant metaphor for facing opposition.[33] In Jewish and Christian tradition, the metaphor of facing wild beasts was clearly associated with confronting ruling authorities, and with the possible prospect of martyrdom.[34] The overall effect of Paul's language is to cast himself and his apostolic colleagues as those who consistently are humiliated, ritually mistreated, and expelled in public events that represented the prevailing order of power, and distinguished citizens from subjects.[35]

PAUL "AT WAR"

We do not exhaust the significance of Paul's affliction lists by determining their tradition-historical background, either among Stoic and Cynic traditions or the prophetic and apocalyptic traditions. Nevertheless, one aspect of Paul's apocalyptic perspective is his occasional identification of the power behind his opponents as "the dominion of the god of this age." He is engaged, not merely in a controversy with rival opinions, but in a war of darkness against light.[36]

Paul's use of triumph imagery (2 Cor 2) and his use of affliction lists cohere in the fundamental understanding of his apostolic *parousia* as

---

32. The NRSV translates with "rubbish" and "dregs," but the Greek words are technical terms from apotropaic rituals; see McLean, *The Cursed Christ*, 98–99, 107. On the arena, see Auguet, *Cruelty and Civilization*.

33. Hanson, *Paradox*, 115–16, wrongly retreats from the "theatrical" connotations of Paul's language here. On the *Acts of Paul*, see Hamburg Papyrus 1–5; Hennecke and Schneemelcher, *New Testament Apocrypha*, 2:251–54.

34. Dan 6; Ignatius, *Rom.* 5.1. Hanson, *Paradox*, 119, gratuitously introduces "the strict party among Christian Jews" or even "the Pharisaic party among Jews" as the referent for the "wild animals."

35. Nippel, *Public Order*, 6: "Exemption from the humiliation of corporal punishment underlined the distinction between citizens and Roman subjects . . . as well as between citizens and slaves."

36. A point ably made by Garrett, "The God of This World," 117.

participation in warfare.³⁷ The language of combat recurs in Paul's letters: he calls upon the Romans to "demobilize" themselves from service to sin and to "surrender their members to God as weapons for right" (Rom 6:13, my translation).³⁸

Paul describes himself as "at war" in 2 Cor 10:3-6:

> We do not wage war according to human standards; for the weapons of our warfare are not merely human, but they have divine power to destroy strongholds. We destroy arguments and every proud obstacle raised up against the knowledge of God, and we take every thought captive to obey Christ. We are ready to punish every disobedience when your obedience is complete.

This language derives from Cynic and Stoic discussions of the wise person's "warfare" with the passions. Contesting a Corinthian deprecation of his humble self-presentation, Paul declares that his warfare "consists in his manner of life. Far from being abject, the Paul who is *tapeinos* [humble] is combative. In this respect he is like the Cynic who appears in humiliating circumstances and garb but is actually at war." This "humble warrior" image stands in contrast to the image of "the self-sufficient, self-confident Stoic, secure in the fortification of his reason," an image with which Paul implicitly characterizes his opponents.³⁹

All these metaphorical domains—the imagery of triumph, the afflictions of the arena or the expulsion ritual, the metaphor of combat—cohere in a common rhetorical strategy on Paul's part. He wishes, first, to call attention to his apostolic *parousia* as the public manifestation (*phanerōthēnai*) of divine power (Rom 1:16-17; 15:18-19). Second, he acknowledges that his *parousia* is normally characterized by both humility and public humiliation. In the context of the Corinthian correspondence, this is in part an acknowledgment of his unimpressive rhetorical skill, but also of his "afflictions," which may have been interpreted (by others) as divine punishment. Third, Paul insists, through use of a range of metaphors, that it is precisely through his apostolic *parousia* as humbled that God is glorified and God's power in Christ displayed. This paradoxical claim is the point of the triumphal image:

---

37. Similarly Lambrecht, "Defeated Paul," 185; Hanson, *Paradox*, 99.

38. Käsemann, *Commentary on Romans*, 177, considers a military sense "the most likely."

39. Malherbe, "Antisthenes and Odysseus," 170-71. Hanson's derivation of Paul's language from Isa 40:2 and Zech 9:12 (LXX) is doubtful (*Paradox*, 99-101), and importing "unbelieving Jews" into 2 Cor 10 is unwarranted.

"God will continue on his triumphal way though Paul appears only as a figure of shame in his procession."[40]

But how can weakness and humiliation manifest power?

REPRESENTING THE BODY OF THE CRUCIFIED

I emphasize again that Paul's metaphorical strategy is not "mere" metaphor. The affliction list in 2 Cor 11:23–27 is the most specific of these passages:

> Are they ministers of Christ? I am talking like a madman—I am a better one: with far greater labors, far more imprisonments, with countless floggings, and often near death. Five times I have received from the Jews the forty lashes minus one. Three times I was beaten with rods. Once I received a stoning. Three times I was shipwrecked; for a night and a day I was adrift at sea; on frequent journeys, in danger from rivers, danger from bandits, danger from my own people, danger from Gentiles, danger in the city, danger in the wilderness, danger at sea, danger from false brothers and sisters; in toil and hardship, through many a sleepless night, hungry and thirsty, often without food, cold and naked.

Note that first named among these very real "afflictions" are ritual punishments: the corporeal discipline of the synagogue, and the civic floggings of the Roman polis (city).[41] Indeed, Paul declares that his body has been inscribed with the marks of torture: "I carry the marks of Jesus branded on my body" (Gal 6:17).

The apostles' afflictions are one medium through which the crucified Jesus is publicly embodied. They are simultaneously manifestations of God's power. If Paul and his apostolic colleagues are put forward as a humiliated spectacle (1 Cor 4:9–13), they also thus reveal that "the kingdom of God depends not on talk but on power" (4:20). If the apostles "carry about the dying of Jesus" in their very bodies, it is "so that the life of Jesus may also be made visible in our bodies" (2 Cor 4:10, NRSV).

Similarly, Paul considers his proclamation of the gospel to be a medium through which the crucified Jesus is manifested publicly. Again and again in his letters, Paul speaks of representing the body of the crucified Jesus, and from what we have seen, Paul considers just these events to be

---

40. Marshall, *Enmity*, 316.

41. The "rods" (*rhabdoi*) with which Paul was beaten (*erabdisthēn*: 2 Cor. 11:25) were carried publicly before Roman magistrates; they were at once instruments of coercion and symbolic of Roman power (Nippel, *Public Order*, 13–16).

manifestations of power and life. When he first came to the Corinthians, he resolved to "know nothing among [them] except Jesus Christ, and him crucified"; this was "a demonstration of the Spirit and of power" (1 Cor 2:2, 4). Paul heatedly reminds the Galatians that "it was before your eyes that Jesus Christ was publicly exhibited as crucified!" (Gal 3:1); do they now really misunderstand how God supplied them with the Spirit and worked miracles among them (3:5)?

By speaking of the public exhibition of Christ crucified (Gal 3:1), Paul calls upon his Galatian audience as "eyewitnesses."[42] But, of course, they saw not the actual crucifixion of Jesus, but its representation in performance. We cannot know what this representation looked like. As indicated in the ancient rhetorical handbooks, contemporary rhetorical practice involved vivid and impressive deliveries, so that (as Quintilian recommended) listeners "imagined the matter to have happened right before their eyes. All kinds of techniques were recommended to achieve the effect, including impersonations and even holding up painted pictures" (though Quintilian frowned upon this latter practice). Giving an argument "presence" could mean bringing forward realia such as the marks of injury or torture. Minimally the evidence of Paul's letters suggests that Paul's apostolic performance included some visual representation of Christ as crucified. Further, Paul wanted others to see his apostolic presence, particularly in its weakness, affliction, and humiliation, as a representation of Christ—literally, a making-Christ-present-again—as crucified.[43]

This does not mean that, for Paul, the crucifixion may be regarded *in isolation* as the "demonstration of God's power." Statements to the effect that the proclamation of the cross *is* "the power of God" (e.g., 1 Cor 1:17-18) are elliptical. Therefore, it is potentially misleading to say that "it is precisely in the death of Jesus, represented to the world in the mortality and suffering of Christian apostles, that 'the life of Jesus' is manifested"; nor can recognizing the power of God be reduced to "perceiving the meaning of Christ's death

---

42. On the rhetorical echoes here see Betz, *Galatians*, 131-32. In Gal 3:1, as Betz points out, *prographein* can mean either "proclaim publicly" (so the *Jerusalem Bible*: "in spite of the plain explanation you have had of the crucifixion of Jesus Christ"), or "portray publicly" (RSV; NEB translates, "Jesus Christ was openly displayed upon his cross"). Betz argues effectively for the second interpretation.

43. Supposed distinctions between a "Semitic" orality and a "Greek" knowing through vision (e.g., Sawicki, *Seeing the Lord*, 80-81) are overdrawn. Neither am I prepared to subsume visual terminology in 2 Corinthians as "susceptible of explanation in terms of the oral gospel" (Kelber, *Oral and Written Gospel*, 141). The goal of Paul's visual imagery is not "interiorizing the essentially invisible" (Kelber, *Oral and Written Gospel*, 142), but the manifestation of God's power in public space.

and identifying oneself with that."⁴⁴ To the contrary, Paul never perceives weakness and suffering as meaningful in and of themselves.⁴⁵ Rather, for Paul, the cross manifests God's power *because of its inseparable connection with the resurrection of Christ. No contemplation of the cross alone would have turned its horror into blessing.* As J. Christiaan Beker observes,

> [In Paul's thought,] the cross of Christ does not permit a passion mysticism, a contemplation of the wounds of Christ, or a spiritual absorption into the sufferings of Christ (*conformitas crucis*). Paul never sanctifies or hallows death, pain, and suffering. There is no hint of a masochistic delight in suffering. *The death of Christ is efficacious only because it stands within the radius of the victory of the resurrection* . . . Although the death of Christ qualifies the resurrection of Christ as that of the Crucified One, the death of Christ does not in and by itself inaugurate the new age or in and by itself legitimize and sanctify suffering and death as the way in which God executes his lordship in an evil world, that is, as suffering love.⁴⁶

Paul proclaims, and through his *parousia* represents, the crucified Christ as the manifestation of God's power because this is the One whom God has raised. Paul's wretched apostolic presence, wafting an odor suggesting death to those who do not believe, is for believers "not the stench of death at all but the 'sweet aroma of [the resurrected!] Christ.'" Paul can know his "carrying about in the body the dying of Jesus" also manifests the life of Jesus (2 Cor 4:10–11, my translation) because he knows "that the one who raised the Lord Jesus will raise us also with Jesus, and will bring us with you into his presence" (4:14).⁴⁷ Thus carrying about the dying of Jesus is not itself the full manifestation of God's power: rather, it points to Paul and his colleagues as those who still contend in "Christ's battle."⁴⁸ Put another way, the embodied showing-forth of the crucified Jesus is an apostolic strategy for representing the risen Christ.⁴⁹

44. Against Furnish, *II Corinthians*, 189 (emphasis added to quotation).
45. Pickett, *The Cross in Corinth*, 141.
46. Beker, *Paul the Apostle*, 196, 199–200 (emphasis added).
47. Roetzel, "'As Dying, and Behold, We Live'"; Pickett, *The Cross in Corinth*, 140–41.
48. Hanson's phrase, *Paradox*, 114–15; see Kraftchick, "Death in Us, Life in You," 174–75.
49. Compare Marianne Sawicki's discussion of early Christian "strategies for recognizing the risen Lord," the "protocols of approach," which defined within the early *ekklēsiai* "what 'resurrection' itself means." As Sawicki puts it, "risen life is that mode of availability of Jesus to the church that results from the enactment or realization" of a particular protocol of praxis (*Seeing the Lord*, 1, 10, 79). I find it curious that Sawicki's

Knowing the risen Christ is, for Paul, neither remembering a past event—the resurrection—as past, as "dead" history; nor is it the present experience of ecstatic communion with the Lord. In Jürgen Moltmann's words, "'The resurrection of Christ' is a meaningful postulate only if its framework is the history which the resurrection itself throws open: the history of the liberation of human beings and nature from the power of death." The structure of this history is evident in Rom 8:11: "If the Spirit of the One who has raised Jesus from the dead dwells in you, the One who has raised Christ Jesus from the dead will give life to your mortal bodies also through the power of the Spirit which dwells in you" (my trans.). Here Paul "links the perfect tense of Christ's resurrection with the present tense of the indwelling of the Spirit, and the present tense of the Spirit with the future tense of the resurrection of the dead."[50]

The point of examining imperial rituals of power in the Roman *polis* is that these were the prevalent "strategies of knowing" elsewhere in Paul's day.

The *ekklēsia's* "proclaiming the Lord's death until he comes," and the apostles' "carrying about the dying of Jesus in the body," are alike representations of the power of God because the crucified one so shown forth is the resurrected Jesus. That is, precisely the body exhibited by the Empire as tortured and crucified has been decisively counter-exhibited by God's act in raising Jesus from the dead; and that counter-display continues to be re-presented by apostolic and ecclesial performance as the locus of God's life-giving power. "Showing forth the Lord's death" thus constitutes a ritual gesture of defiance, a refusal to allow the Empire's exhibition of a crucified corpse to be determinative of the future of Jesus, or of the creation.

HABEAS CORPUS CHRISTI: AN ECCLESIOLOGICAL POSTSCRIPT

What I have just described as the strategic intent of Paul's self-presentation has, I think, profound implications for the way we read Paul's letters today. Our own world, after all, is no stranger to imperial representations of power—representations often made in and upon the very bodies of subject peoples. Moreover, contemporary discussions of intentional counter-representations of power on the part of church groups present a provocative analogue to what I have described as Paul's apostolic performance.

Terrorism has been the focus of intense discussion, and the target of tremendous military action, since the spectacular terrorist attacks against

---

discussion ignores Paul.

50. Moltmann, "The Resurrection of Christ," 80–81.

the United States on September 11, 2001. We must nevertheless recognize that terrorism is neither new, nor does the strategy exclusively belong to avowed enemies of the United States. In the "national security states" developed and reinforced as an integral part of avowed U.S. policy since the 1980s, torture has routinely been used to dismember and disappear both human bodies and the body politic.

The development of torture as an instrument of terror, and thus of social control, at the level of military policy is one of the most salient aspects of our age. Latin American analysts speak of the creation of a "culture of fear" that isolates individuals and fragments the body politic so as to render a population passive and incapable of resistance.[51] The systematic effort of military strategists and architects of security policy to fund, train, equip, and coordinate military and paramilitary regimes over the decades since World War II is well documented, but is especially evident since the 1980s.[52]

State-sponsored terrorism is not a peculiarly Western phenomenon. Nevertheless, the increasingly steep upward gradient of Western power in the wake of the Soviet Union's collapse, and the apparently greater availability of democratic avenues of redress in Western democracies and the United States in particular, have led some Western activists to concentrate their efforts on ending Western support for terror regimes. Jack Nelson-Pallmeyer, for example, has argued eloquently that the stated Pentagon policy of low-intensity conflict constitutes nothing less than a "confessional situation" for Christians in the United States today; and his published indictment of the U.S. School of the Americas condenses a much larger protest movement in the United States.[53]

My purpose here is not to assess questions of relative blame, but to lift up the relevance of Paul's subversive theology and praxis to a modern world in which terror regimes thrive. In a theological analysis of explicitly eucharistic strategies of resistance in Agosto Pinochet's Chile, William Cavanaugh has argued that when Christian doctrine and liturgy have envisioned the church as the "*mystical* Body of Christ," somehow transcending the physical plane of public space, Christ has remained politically disembodied. In

---

51. On "fear as a cultural and political construct," see Corradi, et al., eds., *Fear at the Edge*; on the psychological effects of institutionalized terrorism, Martín-Baró, *Writings for a Liberation Psychology*.

52. On state terrorism as an integral component of U.S. policy, see Blum, *Killing Hope*; Herman, *The Real Terror Network*; Herman and O'Sullivan, *The "Terrorism" Industry*; Chomsky, *Pirates and Emperors*; George, ed. *Western State Terrorism*; Nelson-Pallmeyer, *War against the Poor*; Nelson-Pallmeyer, *School of Assassins*; Ahmad, et al., *Terrorism, Theirs and Ours*.

53. Nelson-Pallmeyer, *War against the Poor*; Nelson-Pallmeyer, *School of Assassins*.

such circumstances the body of Christ may be successfully "disappeared" by the torture regime.[54] However, his investigation of "the actual and potential impact of the Eucharist on the dictatorship" of Pinochet leads Cavanaugh to regard the Eucharist as "the Church's counterpolitics to the politics of torture."

Cavanaugh discusses the Sebastián Acevedo Movement against Torture in Chile to show "what it means for the church to perform liturgically the body of Christ in opposition to the state's liturgy of torture":

> What was so different and disruptive about the Sebastián Acevedo Movement was its sense of liturgy, the public ritual acts of solidarity and denunciation that members would perform with their bodies. Locations were chosen for their symbolic importance: places of torture, the courts, government buildings, media headquarters. Exactly at a prearranged time, members of the Movement—sometimes as many as 150—would appear out of the crowds, unfurl banners and pass out leaflets, often blocking traffic [and performing brief liturgies].
>
> This type of street liturgy precisely reverses the anti-liturgy of torture in that it irrupts into and disrupts the public places of the city which the regime has so carefully policed. New spaces are opened which resist the strategy of place which the regime has imposed . . . In an astonishing ritual transformation, clandestine torture centers are revealed to the passersby for what they are, as if a veil covering the building were abruptly taken away.[55]

Organized rituals of remembrance for the disappeared, taking place in public, and especially outside the chambers where bodies were tortured, defied the regime's disposition of human bodies. Recitals of the names of the disappeared ritually re-presented the tortured and demanded that the regime account for their bodies in a communal act of habeas corpus. The regime's covert application of terror to human bodies is brought to light, "not . . . by mere denunciation in words and song. The repressive apparatus is made visible on the very bodies of the protesters as they are beaten, tear gassed, hosed down, and dragged away to prison." That is, the demonstrators "use their bodies as ritual or theatrical instruments."[56]

As I have argued was the case for Paul, Cavanaugh writes that "the body becomes the battleground between evangelical and anti-evangelical

---

54. Cavanaugh, *Torture and Eucharist*, especially chaps. 3, 4.

55. Cavanaugh, *Torture and Eucharist*, 274–75. Cavanaugh also discusses the Vicaría de Solidaridad, on which see also Fruhling, "Resistance to Fear in Chile."

56. Cavanaugh, *Torture and Eucharist*, 276.

forces." Such public eucharistic liturgies thus work to reconstruct the dismembered body politic:

> The logic of Eucharist [is] an alternative economy of pain and the body . . . Where torture is an anti-liturgy for the realization of the state's power on the bodies of others, Eucharist is the liturgical realization of Christ's suffering and redemptive Body in the bodies of his followers. Torture creates fearful and isolated bodies, bodies docile to the purposes of the regime; the Eucharist effects the Body of Christ, a body marked by resistance to worldly power. Torture creates victims; Eucharist creates witnesses, *martyrs*. Isolation is overcome in the Eucharist by the building of a social Body which resists the state's attempts to disappear it.[57]

Cavanaugh stresses that this understanding of the Eucharist is based on Paul's theology in 1 Corinthians. In the light of my preceding discussion, I would go further to suggest that the public liturgies Cavanaugh has analyzed do not merely appropriate Pauline concepts or language for discrete political purposes. They embody an anti-imperial understanding of the future of human bodies and bodiliness that is structurally analogous to the "liturgical" aspects of Paul's apostolic praxis.

The "work" of the Pauline *ekklēsia* was to "show forth the Lord's death until he comes" (1 Cor 11:26, author), to hold before public gaze the representation of the Empire's victim as *the One whom God had vindicated bodily through resurrection*. This strategy, a *habeas corpus Christi*, refuses to surrender the body of Jesus to the disposition of the empire. Nor does it render that particular body irrelevant, however, by a spiritualization of Jesus' memory. The body *as tortured, as crucified*, must be carried about, represented, embodied in the persons of his apostles, until the deadly representations of the empire's power are brought to an end by the One to whom all powers will ultimately be subjected (1 Cor 15:24).[58] Cavanaugh sums up this understanding of apostolic and ecclesial liturgy as I have discussed it above—but he is describing the strategy of the Sebastián Acevedo Movement's public actions:

> Christ's Body reappears precisely as a suffering Body offered in sacrifice; Christ's Body is made visible in its wounds. But this Body is also marked with future glory, for Christ has suffered in order to triumph over suffering and defeat the powers of death.

---

57. Cavanaugh, *Torture and Eucharist*, 278–81.

58. As Pickett observes in *The Cross in Corinth*, 141, for Paul, the cruciform life "is the appropriate mode of existence only until the apocalyptic resurrection of the dead."

> The space it creates is therefore a space crossed by the Kingdom of God. We witness a liturgical anticipation of the end of history and the resurrection of the body.[59]

Today, no less than in the ancient Roman environment, the cruciformity of an apostolic performance like Paul's—a praxis that makes present the body of Christ on the public landscape—will inevitably subvert the ideology and ritualization of actual or aspiring empires. Those who wish not only to study Paul's apostolic praxis, but to take on a contemporary community discipline informed and shaped by it, may find themselves in the company of those already struggling to expose and contend against the imperial instrumentalities of terror in our own world.

---

59. Cavanaugh, *Torture and Eucharist*, 277.

8

Paul and Empire in Romans, 1 and 2 Corinthians

THE LETTERS OF PAUL present us with distinctive challenges. As letters, they provide only occasional, partial, and often oblique references to any larger narrative that might allow interpreters to describe a coherent "theology" of Paul. They represent the apostle's responses to particular situations for which we have little evidence beyond Paul's own construal, which we must infer from his rhetoric. We have neither any communication from the assemblies he addressed nor a reliable representation of the message Paul may have originally presented to attract adherents to his "gospel" (though different scholars have suggested that one or another passage in his letters provide summaries of that message). The task of describing Paul's "theology" is thus both complex and elusive, requiring inference and conjecture. How much more challenging, then, even precarious, is the effort to infer Paul's general attitude toward the Roman Empire from the surviving letters, where he mentions the "governing authorities" explicitly only once (in Rom 13:1–7). This essay will discuss some of the issues involved in present discussion of "Paul and Empire" and present observations that deserve consideration in the interpretation of 1 and 2 Corinthians and Romans.

ON INTERPRETING "PAUL AND EMPIRE"

Decades have passed since the late Edward Said, one of the pioneers of postcolonial criticism, issued his plea to "take empire seriously" in the interpretation of texts. The plea was all the more urgent given what Said described as "the astonishing sense of weightlessness" in Western academic life (to say nothing of popular culture) regarding "the gravity of history."[1] Recent essays[2] give some sense of the erudition now being mobilized in contemporary biblical studies to "take empire seriously" in the interpretation of early Christian texts. That scholarship has surfaced a number of questions regarding substance and method in the interpretation of Paul's letters that deserve attention here.

Attention to "Paul and empire" appears to be a relatively recent phenomenon. In fact, however, already at the beginning of the twentieth century, scholars like Adolf Deissmann and William Mitchell Ramsay recognized that the early Christian proclamation of Jesus as *kyrios* stood in sharp antithesis to the claims made in the imperial cult that *Caesar* was "lord."[3] If that contrast is sometimes presented today as a recent rediscovery, it may be because the intervening decades were marked by relative inattention to empire as such, and to the Roman Empire in particular, in Pauline studies. Through most of the twentieth century, the emphasis was on *theological* interpretation, an emphasis often attributed to the enthusiastic reception (particularly in American Protestantism) of Karl Barth's work. That emphasis has also usually meant interpreting Paul's letters as an important strand in *biblical* theology, from which it follows that the relevant contexts are, first, the scriptures of Israel, and secondarily, the currents of early Judaism up to and contemporary with Paul. On these terms, aspects of the Hellenistic environment or Roman imperial culture are, at best, "atmosphere" or "background." Indeed, it would seem even today that "theological" attention to Paul's use of Israel's scripture or his relationship with Judaism (the focus of the "New Perspective"), on the one hand, and focus on his place within Hellenistic culture in the Roman age, on the other, remain fairly exclusive alternatives, explored in different scholarly circles. Such polarization effectively excludes the notion that "political" interpretation might itself *be* theological interpretation.

Before the 1990s, it was customary for Paul's scholarly interpreters to address the Roman Empire only when it appeared as a topic in Romans 13:1–7 and, even then, to concentrate their remarks on explaining why Paul's appraisal of imperial power there appeared so benign. (The few exceptions were German-language studies in the 1980s, subsequently translated into English, that suggested that Paul's attitude to Empire might have

1. Said, *Culture and Imperialism*, xx, 303.

2. The original reference was to Winn, ed., *An Introduction to Empire in the New Testament* (2016), where this chapter first appeared.

3. Deissmann, *Licht vom Osten* (ET *Light from the Ancient East*); Ramsay, *The Cities of Paul*.

been more critical than those verses in Romans indicated.)[4] The late 1990s and 2000s saw multi-volume efforts to describe the theologies of individual letters, but *empire* as such appears only rarely in them as an object of reflection.[5] When I ventured to explore "the politics of the apostle" in *Liberating Paul* (1994), I could draw on important insights from a number of scholars, but these were generally isolated and had not been brought together with sustained attention to the question of "Paul and empire." Indeed, such work did not get underway until the SBL Paul and Politics Consultation was organized in 1995, under the indefatigable direction of Richard A. Horsley.[6]

If the "political" reading of Paul and, more specifically, attention to the relationship of "Paul and empire" are more established today, those inquiries have also evoked strong reaction and critique from other scholars. One categorical objection is that a "political" reading simply misses the point of Paul's letters, since Paul was concerned with proclaiming the gospel, which is a *theological*, not a "political" activity. On this view, those who claim to detect in Paul's letters a veiled critique of empire have simply committed the cardinal sin of projecting their own (presumably) left-wing concerns about contemporary political realities, which they decry under the banner of "imperialism," back onto Paul.[7] Another objection, arising from a different quarter, criticizes the anti-imperial reading of Paul as a dangerous attempt to render the apostle a heroic champion of a particular contemporary agenda. The attempt is dangerous precisely because the contemporary agenda that seeks to counteract the prejudice, subjection, and violence that is perpetrated today in partial dependence on the presumed authority of Paul's letters, requires demystifying and neutralizing that authority.[8]

My own previous work has regularly been named as one of the objects of these critiques, and I take them seriously as impetuses for greater precision and nuance in the discussion. My purpose here is not to advance an "anti-imperial" reading of Paul's letters or to adjudicate arguments for or

---

4. Wengst, *Pax Romana and the Peace of Jesus Christ* (1986/1987); Georgi, *Theocracy in Paul's Praxis and Theology* (1987/1991); Taubes, *The Political Theology of Paul* (1993/2004).

5. See the work of the SBL Pauline Theology Group, published by Fortress Press in *Pauline Theology*, vols. I-IV (1991-97), and the New Testament Theology series from Cambridge University Press.

6. See Horsley, ed., *Paul and Empire*; Horsley, ed., *Paul and Politics*; Horsley, ed., *Paul and the Roman Imperial Order*.

7. See Barclay, *Pauline Churches and Diaspora Jews*; McKnight and Modica, eds., *Jesus Is Lord, Caesar Is Not*.

8. See Castelli, "Interpretations of Power in 1 Corinthians"; Schüssler Fiorenza, "Rhetorical Situation and Historical Reconstruction"; and Wire, *Corinthian Women Prophets*.

against such a reading. It is, first, to offer several observations about the current state of discussion from which I believe we may draw helpful guiding principles for interpretation, and second, to describe considerations that are relevant to the interpretation of Paul's letters to the Roman and Corinthian assemblies in particular.

PRINCIPLES FOR INTERPRETING "PAUL AND EMPIRE"

I propose that scholarship to date on the question "Paul and Empire" offers the following "lessons learned."

1. It matters what we mean by "empire."

Some biblical and theological scholars use the term broadly, in what approaches a homiletical way, in order to draw parallels and analogies with aspects of contemporary reality. This can mean that conditions of social injustice, militarism, global income disparities, or even attitudes of modern consumerism can be described as aspects of "empire." This rather loose usage invites understandable skepticism. On the other hand, it is one thing to reject rhetorical sleight of hand; it is another categorically to reject the possibility of drawing analogies between ancient imperial realities and aspects of contemporary political and cultural reality. One reason to engage in history is precisely to understand our own historicity, and the work of history inevitably involves making analogies between past and present. The task is not to *avoid* analogies, but to be precise and clear about the terms of an analogy and its limits.

Other scholars take the opposite position, insisting that the language of "empire" should be used only when explicit references to the structures, offices, or policies of the Roman Empire, or of a specific emperor or other magistrates, are present in Paul's letters. Inevitably, of course, this more skeptical approach results in a much smaller set of data to be interpreted—practically limited to Paul's comments on the "governing authorities" in Rom 13:1–7, and consequently resulting in a much more muted understanding.[9]

It is important in this regard to note that historians of the Roman Empire—with no vested interest in the interpretation of New Testament writings—discuss under the topic of "empire" a rich and multi-dimensional reality including the imperial cult, its relationship to patronage in the cultivation of cooperative provincial elites, the "extractive" nature of the Roman economy and the mechanisms and consequences of integration of local economies into it, the ubiquitous use of images and inscriptions to convey

---

9. E.g., Barclay, *Pauline Churches and Diaspora Jews*.

(and "naturalize") imperial ideology, the ideological and visual representation of ethnicity and gender, and a texture of distinctive values, emphasizing honor and including religious piety as aspects of "Augustan culture." Insisting that we may speak of the Roman Empire only when Paul names specific administrative offices or policies is a remarkably narrow approach that flies in the face of current scholarship on the Roman Empire.[10]

2. Affirming the relevance of Roman imperial ideology and culture to the interpretation of Paul's letters does not depend on Paul having been a vocal critic of that Empire.

Another way to state this point is that framing the discussion in terms of "Paul *and* empire" is preferable to insisting that Paul's standpoint was thoroughly and in principle "*against* empire" or "empire-critical." True, some theologically motivated projects seek to describe the whole of the biblical legacy *as such* as "resistant" to empire, a totalizing approach that tends to beg the question by ignoring contradictory data. Since Norman Gottwald's pioneering work on the Hebrew Bible, however,[11] we have learned that especially where political values are in question, the various biblical writings (or the voices partially expressed in various parts of the biblical writings) represent very different social locations. When those writings (or parts of writings) were combined in ways that tended to harmonize, mute, or dilute one or another message, those efforts also represented particular social locations. I conclude that there is no single "biblical" attitude for, or against, empire. Nor is there a theoretically coherent way to identify an empire-critical "core" or "center" to the biblical testimony.

Further, the rise of postcolonial criticism of Paul's letters has alerted us to the very real possibilities that Paul's complex identity as a Hellenistic Jew, and (on the evidence of Acts) a Roman citizen as well, may have involved what contemporary theorists (following Homi Bhabha) call *hybridity*,[12] which means more than simply "ambivalence." Seeking to distill a pure and unambiguous pro- or anti-imperial posture from his letters appears, in this light, both misguided and quixotic. The object of our investigation need not be restricted to an index of Paul's thoughts about the Roman Empire; it is both more realistic and more responsible to explore the effects of imperial culture on Paul's communities and on his own self-presentation and rhetoric.

10. See the essays in Horsley, ed., *Paul and Politics*.
11. Gottwald, *The Tribes of Yahweh*.
12. Bhabha, *The Location of Culture*.

3. Insisting that Paul's letters are "theological" and not "political" is a mistake.

Opposing "theological" and "political" interpretation, as if these are methods appropriate to mutually exclusive sets of data or kinds of texts, not only projects onto the ancient data a categorical binary unknown to inhabitants of the Roman Empire; it also misapprehends both the theological and the political. It is a transparently artificial (and, arguably, tendentious) move to protect a domain of discourse, "the theological," from inquiry into its political contexts or consequences. When a scholar "doubles down" on such a move—insisting, for example, that Paul's message was theological, *not* political, and at the same time, that his message has political implications that only a theologian can rightly understand (e.g., Barclay; see note 9)—we rightly wonder whether the point is the interpretation of the ancient sources or some disciplinary turf war today.

4. At our present state of knowledge, arguments about implicit meanings in a text remain unfalsifiable, and thus require a measure of circumspection and modesty on the part of those proposing them.

The perception of an *implicit* "anti-imperial" message is often in the eye of the beholder. Whether phrased in terms of what Paul "must have meant" or what his readers "must have heard," such arguments are inevitably conjectural. Although N. T. Wright's succinct way of describing the anti-imperial thrust of Paul's gospel has become very popular—"If Jesus is Lord, then Caesar is not"—we may well ask whether the superficial logic of that formula was Paul's own, or is only a contemporary (and perhaps contentious) projection onto Paul.[13] In a public presentation (now published as a chapter in *Pauline Churches and Diaspora Jews*, 2011), John M. G. Barclay argued that Paul's concern was the theological proclamation of Christ's lordship, next to which the apparent power of any particular empire was *implicitly* simply insignificant. Curiously, however, Barclay compared Paul's letters with the theological character of Karl Barth's famous Barmen Declaration—curiously, because everyone recognizes in that document an implicit refusal of the claims of Nazism in general and the Deutsche Christen movement in particular, even though neither Hitler nor the National Socialist Party is ever mentioned in the document. As the comparison shows, in the first century or today, the force of an argument can sometimes be precisely an *intended* implication that is not expressly stated.

Indeed, though it is far more difficult to detect implication or innuendo in an ancient text (where we have neither access to nonverbal performative cues nor the opportunity to interrogate the speaker for clarification),

---

13. See McKnight and Modica, eds., *Jesus Is Lord, Caesar Is Not*.

contemporary interpreters *routinely* proceed to make inferences from what is presumed to be implicit in a text, and so long as the inference does not involve what we might consider "political" realities, no one raises an eyebrow. The question is not whether arguments regarding implicit meaning are to be ruled categorically out of bounds, but whether correlations with other information from the social and political context of the text can be adduced to offer a greater or lesser degree of probability. This is, after all, how discussions of "intertextuality" in Paul's letters proceed.[14] But nothing requires us to limit "intertextuality" to echoes from the Bible, as if we should imagine Paul and his audiences completely closed off from all the other forms of communication going on around them. It is now widely accepted, for example, that Paul's reference to outsiders who "say, 'there is peace and security'" (1 Thess 5:3) is an oblique reference to the slogan *pax et securitas* on Roman imperial coinage. Lexical studies and rhetorical criticism alike require us to recognize that Paul's vocabulary potentially carried political connotations that are obscured by the more purely religious translations in our Bibles: for example, *kyrios* ("lord," used of the Caesars), *ekklēsia* ("church," but in Paul's day a civic "assembly"), *dikaiosynē* (translated "righteousness" in our Bibles but "justice" everywhere else), and *euangelion* ("gospel") and *parousia* ("appearance"), which both had definite civic and imperial resonances. Any of these terms *could* have been heard by the recipients of Paul's letters as carrying political connotations—and taking that possibility seriously is simply a part of responsible exegesis. There is often no way to prove or disprove that a particular connotation was *intended*, of course, but ruling the possibility of one or another implicit meaning out of bounds in preference for a supposedly certain "biblical" meaning would constitute an exercise in theological special pleading.

In fact, we know that significant *implicit* communication of political meanings was not only as possible, it was also as important and prevalent in Paul's day as in our own. Theater audiences in Paul's day were attuned to pick up on politically charged innuendo in the pointed reading of a superficially innocuous line. We have clear examples from Paul's world of what political anthropologist James C. Scott has called "voice under domination," the strategic use of veiled or implied meaning in situations where the less powerful are not free to speak their minds—but are not rendered completely mute.[15] One oft-cited example is Philo's distinction of the "untimely frankness" of the reckless from the "caution" that the prudent more usually practice in the presence of powerful adversaries (*On Dreams* 2.92). Scott's

---

14. The pioneering work is Hays, *Echoes of Scripture in the Letters of Paul*.
15. Scott, *Domination and the Arts of Resistance*.

work has inspired a micro-discipline of investigating "hidden transcripts" in Paul's letters. The theory can of course be abused, as when perceived tensions within a passage (such as Rom 13:1–7) are taken as *proof* that a *"real,"* intended meaning has been "hidden" beneath the surface communication that appears to contradict it. The answer is not to reject the theory, however, which clearly applies to Paul's world, but to apply criteria of contextual correlation in order to establish a degree of probability for a particular reading.[16]

What might these considerations mean for our reading of the three longest of Paul's letters?

1 AND 2 CORINTHIANS

The effects of Roman imperial rule are certainly relevant to the interpretation of 1 and 2 Corinthians. After all, Roman forces had destroyed Corinth in 146 BCE, slaughtering its citizens and enslaving their wives and children, as a spectacularly violent example that facilitated the pacification of the rest of Achaia. Julius Caesar established the site century later as a colony, peopled by freedpersons from Rome, whose allegiance and gratitude were thereby assured. Roman Achaia was a showcase of Rome's civilizing power. Abundant inscriptions testify to the close integration of the Roman imperial cult with a system of patronage and benefaction in which local elites competed for prestige in civic and cultic offices (*leitourgiai*). Also evident are a clear hierarchy of peoples, with Romans manifestly superior to the peoples they had conquered, and a certain fluidity of ethnic identities. Through either adoption or manumission, however, a Greek freedperson could "become Roman," receiving the Roman name of his father or patron. Through the right expenditure of wealth in civic benefactions, an ambitious freedperson could display his generosity and piety and thus gain prestige as a member of the people destined by the gods to "rule the earth."

Such considerations offer a frame of reference different from the assumptions that were brought to the Corinthian letters in much earlier scholarship, which tended to focus on a supposed Corinthian propensity to (especially sexual) immorality, or on a presumed conflict between Paul's law-free gospel and the Jewish Christianity of the Jerusalem apostles, or a Jewish form of Gnosticism. The search for a single unified "opposition" has foundered on lack of clear evidence and the apparent arbitrariness with which select phrases must be assumed through a sort of "mirror-reading"

---

16. See Cynthia Briggs Kittredge's "Reconstructing 'Resistance' or Reading to Resist"; and James R. Harrison's discussion in *Paul and the Imperial Authorities*, 30–32.

to represent the views of Paul's putative "opponents." Instead, more recent scholarship has tended toward reading the letters inductively, asking about Paul's relationship with different sectors of the congregation itself.

In the late twentieth century, Wayne A. Meeks and Gerd Theissen showed the importance of "social stratification" and "status ambivalence" for understanding social realities in the Corinthian assembly.[17] If "not many" of the first members of the Corinthian assembly had been "wise by human standards, . . . powerful, . . . of noble birth" (1 Cor 1:26), these scholars argued that by implication, *some* were. It followed that aspects of the Corinthian correspondence could be correlated with socioeconomic inequality in the community. The difference between those who could provide their own (extensive) meals and those who could not was a source of shame at the Lord's Supper (1 Cor 11:17–34); the fact that poorer members could not afford often to purchase meat to eat at home and so encountered meat only as it was slaughtered in the context of pagan ritual meant that the differences between "weak" and "strong" surrounding "idol meat" (*eidōlothyta*) had a socioeconomic basis (1 Corinthians 8, 10). Respect for rhetorical skill, and Paul's suffering in comparison with the more erudite Apollos, pointed to the latter's greater success, after Paul had left, among the Corinthian elite (fueling Paul's discussion of wisdom in 1 Corinthians 2 and the self-defensive tone of parts of both letters). Controversy surrounding Paul's refusal of financial support and his insistence on self-support through manual labor— one cause of friction throughout the correspondence—pointed not only to Corinthian expectation that a legitimate apostle would depend on the community (cf. Matt 10:1–16, 40–42; Luke 10:1–12), but to the offense Paul gave potential patrons by refusing their support (and the obligation such support would have laid on him). With these postulates, Paul's own social location and his perception, for example, of manual labor, in contrast to perceptions among the Corinthian church, also became objects of study.

More recently, other scholars have challenged the declared "consensus" just described, criticizing the implications of a free and open market of wealth and status in which fluctuation of status and upward social mobility were the norm. Vast inequality characterized the Roman world; the majority in a city like Corinth would have lived near subsistence level.[18] The point of patronage was precisely to extend inequality, and inequality of obligation, as the structuring principle of civic, economic, and social relationships. Generalizations about the "steep pyramid" of wealth and power in Roman

---

17. Meeks, *The First Urban Christians*; Theissen, *The Social Setting of Pauline Christianity*.

18. So Meggitt, *Paul, Poverty, and Survival*.

society, with a tiny elite on top and the mass of the people living at subsistence level, can be applied in Roman Corinth as well. Augustus's "reforms" to marriage laws lubricated the circulation of property and wealth among those who already had it, making it easier (for example) for elite families to retain their wealth through marriages, divorces, and deaths; to describe these laws as "liberalizing" is to mistake their function.

More recent scholarship casts a wary eye at any modern generalization about "new opportunities" for "upward mobility" for a significant Roman "middle class." Those are the anachronistic projections into the past of late twentieth-century U.S. cultural assumptions. We must take seriously what might be called the precipitating forces of economic relationships in Roman society. We should not imagine life in Roman Corinth, or in the *ekklēsia* within it, as a sort of fluid suspension in which a variety of statuses might circulate in a random and indeterminate way. We should instead think metaphorically of fluid run through a centrifuge, so that the majority of particulates are pressed down, leaving only a small proportion "floating" on top.

Similarly, questions of social stratification are too complex to be addressed by generalizations about "the Corinthians." *Differences* among different groups, especially differences in socioeconomic status, come to the fore in conflicts there. Feminist interpreters have shattered the possibility that we mighty innocently presume that Paul's letters simply describe the objective situation in Corinth. Responsible interpretation requires that we recognize in Paul's own rhetorical efforts to persuade a respect for the opinions of those he addresses. For some feminist interpreters, the object of attention is the role played by spiritual women in the congregation who may have shared much of Paul's theology, but perceived its significance differently, in terms of their own social experience of enhanced honor and spiritual endowment. On this point, Antoinette Clark Wire's discussion of social location and its correlation with theology in *The Corinthian Women Prophets* is exemplary; its only potential weakness is her conviction that the whole of 1 Corinthians was written with the women prophets of Corinth as its "target." If that was not the case, we must ask the same questions regarding a number of social locations occupied by members of the Corinthian assemblies, including that of men who enjoyed some relative measure of power and prestige on the civic landscape.

I will not attempt here a thorough discussion of the history of Paul's relationship with the Corinthians, though that relationship is obviously an important and complex one, requiring careful reconstruction of the sequence of correspondence (including letters that have not survived, from Paul as well as from the Corinthians, and letters that have survived only fragmentarily in 2 Corinthians). I draw attention to several themes in this correspondence that bear comparison with aspects of Roman imperial culture.

The "Turn" from Idols

We may assume that part of Paul's initial teaching, at the founding of the *ekklēsia*, included the call to "turn to God from idols" (on the model of 1 Thess 1:8–10). But to what extent did eschewing "idolatry" mean avoiding the ceremonial aspects of the imperial and civic cult? These were not only the lifeblood of public life, they were the channels of advancement in Roman provincial society, and so Paul's message is not just a matter of holding the right ideas about the gods; it has eminently practical consequences. But what exactly were those to be? He repudiated the promises of an age destined to pass away (1 Cor 7:31); he warned his hearers away from "the table of demons," referring to the food offered at ceremonial banquets (1 Corinthians 10). That food, carried away to meals in private homes, apparently was a different subject, however. The idol is no real thing; unless the dinner host declares the food dedicated to a (false) god, Christians should eat what is set before them in equanimity (1 Corinthians 8). That accommodation was advised, much later, in the Mishnah (Avodah Zarah), so is hardly scandalous from the point of view of Jewish halakah. More to the point, as Theissen observed, Paul's advice regarding food in private meals would have been more congenial to the interests of higher-status members of the *ekklēsia*, who might have been invited regularly to "private" dinners—though in sacred precincts, like the excavated dining halls in the precincts of Apollo's temple in Corinth—on a regular basis. (Note that Paul actually contemplates the possibility that one member of the *ekklēsia* might observe another exercising "liberty" by "eating in the temple of an idol": 1 Cor 8:4–12.) Lower-status members would normally encounter consecrated meat only at the public ceremonies where the idolatrous connotations were unavoidable. Because social stratification was so closely intertwined with benefaction and the performance of civic cult, Paul's divergence from some in Corinth may have less to do with differences of theological belief than with the strength of theological convictions to shape, or discipline, civic involvement. In other words, some in Corinth may have understood "wisdom" as consonant with a posture of indifference to social boundaries between the civic ceremonial and the *ekklēsia*. To such individuals, Paul's strident insistence that "what pagans sacrifice, they sacrifice to demons" and that "you cannot drink the cup of the Lord and the cup of demons" (1 Cor 10:14–22, NRSV) might have seemed unnecessarily austere and provocative.

Head Coverings and Worship

If the previous point appears to involve aspects of Roman imperial cult only indirectly, another subject in 1 Corinthians may have a more direct connection. The almost inscrutable discussion of how women are to present their heads when prophesying in the assembly (1 Cor 11:2–16) has been explained in more than a dozen different ways, none of which has won the day, in part because the several arguments Paul advances about women's heads are inconsistent. But perhaps Paul's chief concern is not with *women's* heads or head coverings. In Roman cult, *men* ordinarily pulled their togas over their heads to offer sacrifice, as demonstrated in the statue of Augustus from Corinth (and elsewhere). Note that Paul begins his discussion by declaring that "the head of every man is Christ" (11:3), and draws the consequence, first, that "any man who prays or prophesies with his head covered dishonors his head [*kephalē*]," that is, Christ (11:4). Though the passage is a notorious exegetical quagmire, its rhetorical movement at least allows that Paul is relying on tropes of what is "natural" and what is "shameful" for women in order to shame as unnatural specific behaviors on the part of *men*—actions at home precisely in Roman worship. It is possible that Corinthian men are not only dining in sacred precincts but *offering worship* to Roman gods or even to the genius of Caesar. More would seem to be at stake here than Paul's challenge to idolatry; the language of "headship" suggests that we adapt Wright's famous line to read, "if Christ is the 'head,' then Caesar is not." For Paul, acting otherwise is not merely a matter of sharing honor among different gods (as the Corinthian participants might imagine, in good Roman fashion): it is a direct and shameful affront to Christ.[19]

Marriage, Divorce, and Sexual Relationships

The topic of marriage and divorce in 1 Corinthians 7, "matters about which [the Corinthians] wrote" (7:1), likely were linked to issues of social status as well. Higher-status women members of the *ekklēsia* might have been in a better position to withdraw from pagan husbands or fiancés than poorer women, who would have been more dependent on partners for their economic welfare and under more pressure, if abandoned by their pagan

---

19. See my fuller discussion in Elliott, *Liberating Paul*, 209–11.

husbands, to remarry. If higher-status members, men and women alike, had looked down on such women married to pagan husbands (or divorced by them) as lesser believers because they were not able to actualize the same level of freedom, we might understand Paul's concern both to affirm an ideal ("it is well for a man not to touch a woman," 7:1) and to reassure women in different situations. He urges that living with a pagan spouse does not disqualify the man or woman in Christ; the spouse and the children of such a "mixed" household are sanctified (7:12–16); the separating woman may remain unmarried; the single woman bound to marry does not sin by marrying (7:28). The maxim that each should "remain in the calling to which you were called," regardless of circumstance (7:17, 20, 24), is as widely misunderstood as it is generally mistranslated, as if Paul were advocating a fixity of social roles, when the contrary is evidently the case.[20] The ambivalence of Paul's advice—he would prefer that unmarried members not marry, and married members not separate, but expressly allows exceptions to these ideals—convinces some interpreters that Paul is retreating from ideals he in fact shares with some of the "spiritual women" in Corinth because he realizes the potential for social disruption their freedom would imply. (The subsequent accounts of Paul's companion Thecla in the third- or, possibly, second-century CE *Acts of Paul* show just how disruptive such actions could be: as Thecla preaches her "gospel of virginity," whole cities are "shaken" by the tumult of women's voices [*Acts of Paul* 9].) "The immorality Paul exposes," especially in chapter 6, "is male," Wire writes. "The solution he calls for is marriage," a burden to be borne especially by the women in the assembly.[21]

On this reading, Paul's sympathy with lower-status members of the *ekklēsia* has a clear limit: he is not willing to foster a situation in which marriages (and other social relationships with which they are intertwined?) are disrupted. Indeed, the differences between Paul and socially superior members of the Corinthian assembly should not be overstated. Paul himself seems to consider his own manual labor as a voluntary self-lowering, not (as the poor of Rome would perceive it) as a simple necessity of life. He identifies with "the strong" (*hoi dynatoi*) and affirms their freedoms ("All things are lawful," 10:23), though he has "become weak" in order to move among the weak (9:22). But this makes all the more meaningful his insistence that in the (original) calling of the Corinthian *ekklēsia*, God "chose what is foolish, ... weak, ... low and despised in the world, things that are not, to reduce

---

20. See Elliott, *Liberating Paul*, 32–40; and S. Scott Bartchy's splendid study, *Mallon Chrēsai: First-Century Slavery and 1 Corinthians 7:21*, first published in 1973.

21. Wire, *Corinthian Women Prophets*, 78–97.

to nothing things that are" (1 Cor 1:26–29) and his efforts, though limited in some ways, to affirm the position of the "weak" over against the "strong." If there is ambivalence in Paul's language it reflects, I contend, the ideological limitations of his age: as Dale B. Martin describes the paradox, Paul "uses assumptions about hierarchy and status to overturn the status expectations of Greco-Roman culture. And, ultimately, he claims the highest status for himself in order to convince those of high status in the Corinthian church to imitate him in accepting a position of low status."[22]

The "Rulers of This Age" Put to Shame

This distinctively Pauline version of a "preferential option for the poor" is not only a reflex of Paul's social location; it expresses his understanding of Christ crucified as "the power of God," an offense to the wise and powerful. Paul goes further: the wisdom revealed in the crucified Christ was, and remains, inscrutable to the "rulers of this age" (1 Cor 2:6, 9) who "crucified the Lord of glory." Paul does not otherwise specify who these "rulers" were, and certainly isn't concerned here or anywhere else to identify Pontius Pilate or any other specific office-holders involved in Jesus' death. The directness of this phrase is nevertheless irreducibly political: *rulers of this age*, an age that is "passing away" (7:31), crucified Christ, and by that action showed their implacable opposition to God. Paul is not interested in the personalities or policies of particular magistrates; individual culpability is irrelevant to his apocalyptic perspective. At "the end," "every ruler and every authority and power" will be destroyed by Christ as "all things" are subjected to Christ by God (15:24–28). Nowhere in Paul's letters does he elaborate on this coming subjection, but the very incidental way in which he affirms it without explanation indicates how basic it is to his beliefs. Such categorical dismissal of worldly rulers stands in dramatic contrast to the subsequent efforts of the Gospel writers to mitigate the impression that Pilate himself was responsible for Jesus' fate.[23]

Paul's Apostolic Weakness

Nor is the contrast Paul makes between his own admittedly unimpressive self-presentation as an apostle and the elite in Corinth (1 Corinthians 4),[24]

---

22. Martin, *The Corinthian Body*, 67.
23. See Elliott, *Liberating Paul*, 109–24.
24. See Elliott, "The Apostle Paul's Self-Presentation," chap. 6 in this volume.

or the prestige of his rivals (2 Corinthians 10–13), merely a matter of different social locations. Here, too, Paul grounds his argument Christologically. Paul's rhetorical construal of his own "afflictions"—physical difficulties, like hunger or shipwreck, as well as what we might call "political" afflictions: his record of arrests, imprisonments, and civil punishments ("three times … beaten with rods," 2 Cor 11:23–27; cf. 1 Cor 4:9–13)—are the embodied manifestation of Christ. By this I meant not only that Paul couches his message as the "demonstration of power" (1 Cor 2:4; cf. 2 Cor 12:12), but that the physical presence of Paul and his fellow apostles is a "carrying about in the body" of "the dying of Jesus" (1 Cor 4:10). This language of "carrying about," like the language of the apostles becoming a "spectacle" or of "displaying" the crucified Jesus (Gal 3:1), is drawn from the sacred space of civic ceremonial and procession. Paul exploits the language of *Roman* ceremonial when he declares that the public humiliation he shares with all genuine apostles—which is so scandalous to some in Corinth—is to be understood as God leading him "in triumphal procession" (2 Cor 2:14–16). Here the metaphors of military triumph (in which the vanquished were paraded ceremonially, to their deaths) and of epiphany processions seem to be mingled. It is perhaps less important to disentangle them than to recognize Paul's rhetorical strategy. He seems to accept his characterization by his opponents a humiliated, wretched figure, but uses it for his own purpose. Even if he has been displayed as a figure of shame and ridicule, it is Christ who has thus triumphed and gained glory: the apostle *remains* the locus of God's power.

The Collection for "the Saints"

A final contrast with aspects of Roman imperial ideology is evident in Paul's appeal to the Corinthians to participate in his "ministry to the saints," the collection for Jerusalem which is the burden of (two different letters? in) 2 Corinthians 8 and 9. Noteworthy here is the language in which Paul makes his appeal: "for the purpose [of the collection] is not that there [should be] relief for others and affliction for you, but rather [it should be] out of equality. In the present time, your abundance should supply their lack, in order that their abundance may supply your lack, so that there may be equality" (2 Cor 8:13–14). Paul's argument here represents a dramatic divergence from the logic of patronage in the Roman world, according to which "equality" would have meant only an approximation of "balance" (as the NRSV translates the Greek word *isotēs*) "within an unequal friendship." Paul implies that the Corinthians are *obligated* to the Jerusalem saints because they have received a *spiritual* gift from them, and because of their own material abundance. Paul promotes something radical: "the equalization of resources between persons of *different* social classes through voluntary redistribution." More, he goes so far as to suggest that the donation for Jerusalem constitutes the submission of the Achaians to Jerusalem (2 Cor 9:13).[25] The obligation is more expressly stated in Rom 15:26-27, and in Romans, Paul introduces a new term in referring to the collection: it is not only "ministry," it represents "the offering of the nations" that it is Paul's priestly service to present (Rom 15:16). The last phrase is far grander than the language of gift and obligation; it echoes the language in which the tribute of the nations *to Rome* was described in the *Aeneid* (6:113)—but this is a tribute given by the nations *to Jerusalem*.[26] Especially given the central significance of the collection to Paul's mission, Sze-Kar Wan's characterization of the collection as "anti-colonial act" seems apt.[27]

At these points it is possible to see Paul discussing specific matters, in explicit terms, that bear comparison in one or another way with aspects of Roman imperial cult or ideology. The letter to the Romans presents a different challenge to the interpreter.

ROMANS

Except for 13:1-7, Romans offers very little in the way of explicit reference to political realities, and even there the reference to "governing authorities" is quite general. Not surprisingly, for most of the history of interpretation, Romans has not been read as touching on political realities except incidentally. It has been read as a summary of Paul's gospel, involving an explanation of the need for salvation in Christ and a critique of Judaism, as well as a meditation on the fate of Israel (in chapters 9-11).

Scholars tend now to recognize those chapters as the climax of the letter. At the end of the twentieth century, the dominant assumptions of the "New Perspective" shaped a consensus that in Romans Paul was concerned to ameliorate "ethnic tensions" between Jews and Gentiles in the Roman church. The historical circumstances that occasioned those tensions were directly connected to Roman policy: according to Suetonius (*Life of Claudius* 25.4), Claudius expelled Jews from Rome, apparently including Jews known to Paul (see Acts 18:1-2). The return of some of these Jews to Rome after Claudius' death, to churches where they were now a vulnerable and, to some extent, a humiliated minority among non-Jews, might have

---

25. See Welborn, "That There May Be Equality."
26. See Elliott, *The Arrogance of Nations*, 44-47.
27. Wan, "Collection for the Saints as Anti-Colonial Act."

occasioned the disdain and contempt against which Paul warns the non-Jews in Romans 11.

In *The Arrogance of Nations*, I argued that just that warning was at the heart of the letter and governs its rhetoric from the beginning. I will not recapitulate all those arguments here (nor cite the corroborative work of other scholars on which I gratefully depend!), but name several issues that bear directly on the question of "Paul and empire."

The Cause of Tension—and Paul's Concern

The notice in Suetonius is more ambiguous than usually recognized. *Christian* missionizing was *not* the spark of Jewish agitation named by Suetonius.[28] That expulsion was simply another episode in recurring Roman crackdowns on "the usual suspects" in episodes of civil unrest. The danger of non-Jewish Christians in Rome "boasting" over Israel—the object of Paul's warning in Romans 11—need not be taken as evidence of a manifest failure on the part of Jews to accept the gospel of Jesus. Rather, it represented the infiltration into the Roman *ekklēsia* of the same contempt for Jews as a "vanquished race" that was common among elite circles from the time of Tiberius onward. The unfortunate circumstances of returning "Claudian exiles" can only have accelerated the spread of such contempt.[29]

The Status of Israel

Despite the long history of Christian interpretation in which Romans 9–11 has been read as including a sort of theological post-mortem on a "fallen" Israel, Paul's concern throughout these chapters is the warning to non-Jews. The distinction that structures these chapters—in terms of rhetorical analysis, the "dissociation of concepts"—is not a typological argument about those who are "in" and those who are "out," but between *present* appearances, which may be deceptive, and God's ultimate purposes, which will be manifest only in the future. Israel *seems* to have stumbled, but will be restored, and "all Israel shall be saved" (11:25–26).[30] This discussion, which swirls around promises in Israel's prophets that one would "rise to rule the nations" (Rom 15:12, quoting Isa 11:10), contravened the mythology, ubiquitous in Paul's day, that the gods had bestowed the destiny of world

---

28. See Slingerland, *Claudian Policymaking*.
29. See Elliott, *Arrogance of Nations*, 96–100, 107–19.
30. See Elliott, *Arrogance of Nations*, 111–19.

supremacy to *the Roman people* and that such rule was exercised by the person of the Caesar (Virgil's *Aeneid*; the *Res Gestae*). Here it is important to bear in mind our earlier discussion of *implicit* meanings. Paul never interacts explicitly with that mythology, though it is at least suggestive to compare the narrative of Aeneas—whose unwavering piety to his ancestral gods ensured the world-conquering destiny of his descendants—with what Paul says about Abraham, the "forefather" of Jews and non-Jews alike, who was justified, though *impious* (4:5—literally so, according to Josh 24:2-4, for he repudiated his ancestors' gods). Paul's insistence that Abraham was not only the ancestor of the circumcised or of descendants "through the law" but of *all* who would "inherit the world" (4:13) would have sounded like a usurpation of Roman prerogatives to any familiar with the common themes of Roman culture.[31]

No Defense from God's Justice

The early chapters of Romans seem to have nothing to do with the political thematic I've just described. To the contrary, they are usually read, on the strength of Martin Luther's interpretation, as governed by the contrast between justification by faith (which Paul proclaims) and justification by works of law (a characterization of Judaism, which Paul rejects). I contend that this single-minded focus on themes that were central for Martin Luther blinds us to other important themes sounded from the beginning of the letter: for example, the contrast between justice (*dikaiosynē*) and injustice (*adikia*), by which Paul means not to contrast alternative modes of "justification" but to drive a wedge between the claims of those who suppress the truth and those who honor God (1:15-32). This passage is profitably compared with the notions of providence abroad in Paul's day; specifically, notions of divine justice being actualized in specific instances of visible, unmistakable punishment of the notoriously wicked. Paul names no individuals, but given the similarities of vocabulary with depictions of the emperors and imperial governors in authors like Philo and Suetonius, the "spiral of depravity" described in Romans 1 would plausibly have evoked for hearers the egregious misdeeds of the spectacularly powerful. Just as other authors could point out the public downfall and destruction of the infamous, so Paul's theme throughout the letter is God's uncompromising justice and the absence of any possible impunity. Understanding the rhetoric of the letter depends, in my view, on recognizing that this emphasis on justice and refusal of any defense or excuse is connected to the climactic warning against

31. See Elliott, *The Arrogance of Nations*, 121-41.

boasting over Israel. That is, it is not necessary to imagine that Paul is trying, in a theoretical, even-handed way, to declare all human beings *equally* lost without Christ—though that reading is crucial, of course, to various forms of Christian evangelism.[32]

Justice, the Jew, and the Law

It is to strengthen the latter point that Paul, through the rhetorical device of conversation with an imaginary interlocutor, calls a Jew to bear witness. The point of this interrogation is not to "demolish Jewish privilege" or expose some imagined presumption on the part of the Jew but to elicit from the Jew—renowned for his integrity—an unswerving commitment to the principle of justice.[33] Instead of a generalized indictment of human depravity in need of salvation in Christ—the customary Christian reading of Romans 1–3—the opening chapters constitute an indirect approach to the warning in chapters 9–11. Paul takes pains to establish a fundamental distinction between (God's) justice and human injustice—even the spectacular injustice of the powerful—because he is opposing a power gradient in which different standards apply to the powerful and their beneficiaries, on one hand, and their ungrateful and undeserving inferiors. That power gradient, naturalized by Roman ideology, made disregard for the city's Jewish population appear common-sensical; Paul is working to expose it as unjust and an offense to God.

Subjection and the "Idle Sword"

The passage encouraging submission to the governing authorities (13:1–7) remains a conundrum, not least for the interpretation of Romans that I am advancing here. Scholars have long identified tensions within the passage (does the believer owe "fear," *phobos*, to the authority, or not? Where else in the Pauline corpus does God appear to need the "ministry" of the governing authority to achieve justice?—cf. 12:19–21). To these comparisons I would add the contrast between Paul's enigmatic declaration that the authority "does not bear the sword in vain" (13:4) with the theme, abundantly exemplified in literature from the imperial court (Seneca, Calpurnius Siculus, the first *Eclogue* of Calpurnius Piso), that Nero had come to power

---

32. Elliott, *The Arrogance of Nations*, 72–85.

33. I depend here on Stanley K. Stowers' invaluable work on the diatribe (*A Rereading of Romans*), though I apply it to Romans differently.

without bloodshed—evincing superiority even to his hallowed ancestor Augustus—and that peace, "knowing not the drawn sword," now reigned. The juxtaposition suggests at least the possibility that Paul seeks to deny the "harmlessness" of the imperial sword: despite his pretensions of innocence, the ruler does *not* bear the sword in vain![34] But whatever the function of this passage in the letter, it must be balanced against the clear declarations at the beginning and end of Romans that Paul's apostolic commission consists in securing "the obedience of the nations"—surely a prerogative that, according to imperial propaganda, belonged to the emperor alone.

This hardly resolves the tensions in the letter, of course, but especially with regard to this passage it is important to keep in mind the warning that the venerable Leander E. Keck offered to any interpreter who dared to skate too assuredly on "Romans pond": "Danger: Thin Ice!"[35]

PAUL AND EMPIRE

The preceding paragraphs have only scratched the surface of interpretive possibility regarding three of Paul's most significant letters (or more, depending on our understanding of the composition of 2 Corinthians). In them I have intended to make two points: first, that the realia of the Roman Empire—including the literary and ideological representations of Roman supremacy and destiny, justice and peace—are indeed relevant to our interpretation of Paul and his letters; second, that any such comparisons should not be stated in simple terms of Paul's opposition to the Roman Empire. Paul was a man of his time; his values—though thoroughly conditioned by the legacy of Jewish apocalypticism and the conviction that God's justice would ultimately triumph over and against all earthly powers—also reflected good Roman virtues of order and harmony (*homonoia*). Paul lived within the "ideological constraints" of his time—as we live in ours.[36] The ultimate responsibility for the appropriations we make of Paul lies not with him, but with us.

---

34. On this point see Elliott, *The Arrogance of Nations*, 152–59; and earlier, Elliott, "Romans 13:1–7 in the Context of Imperial Propaganda" (now chap. 13 in Elliott, *Paul against the Nations*.

35. Keck, "What Makes Romans Tick?," 16.

36. Elliott, *The Arrogance of Nations*, 157–66.

9

The Question of Politics
Paul as a Diaspora Jew under Roman Rule

THE MEASURE OF PAUL's Jewish identity remains a matter of considerable controversy in current scholarship.[1] As Pamela Eisenbaum observes, the question has provoked anxiety among some scholars, and not surprisingly, since the study of Paul "continues to be the arena of discourse where Christians (and recently some Jews) work out their religious identity."[2] It is an indication of that anxiety that today, some thirty years since the announcement of a "New Perspective on Paul,"[3] it remains profoundly difficult for many interpreters to escape the constraining categories of an older, "Christianizing" view of the apostle.[4] This may surprise us, given the increasing popularity of the "New Perspective," which was premised on moving beyond those very constraints. One consequence is that significant

---

1. In April 2009 I had the honor of engaging Alan F. Segal in public conversation about the implications of his pioneering work in ancient Judaism and, in particular, on the apostle Paul for Christian theology. The occasion was Professor Segal's visit to United Theological Seminary, one of the last such occasions before his untimely death. His wit, graciousness, and humility were as evident as his formidable intelligence. In gratitude I dedicate this essay to his memory.

2. Eisenbaum, "Paul, Polemics, and the Problem of Essentialism."

3. The phrase derives from James D. G. Dunn's landmark essay "The New Perspective on Paul."

4. On the concept of "Christianizing" interpretations of Paul or aspects of his historical context see Slingerland, *Claudian Policymaking*, chap. 1; Horsley, "Submerged Biblical Histories and Imperial Biblical Studies."

political aspects of Paul's context (and of our own) continue to be minimized or marginalized in interpretation.

According to the older, Christianizing view, we must understand Paul fundamentally as someone whose thought and experience—however these may have been formed by his background in Judaism—had been decisively *reshaped* by his encounter with the risen Christ, which Paul described as a "revelation" or "apocalypse" of God's son to him (Gal 1:11–16: *apokalypsis Iēsou Christou*). Thus, although most interpreters today acknowledge, in general terms, that various aspects of Paul's thinking derived from Jewish traditions, many hasten to qualify that acknowledgment by insisting that those aspects came to mean something very different to Paul, *something no longer compatible with Judaism*, after this "revelation" of Christ. That "event" is often described as an interruption, a "breaking in," implying that it defies explanation in terms of Paul's Jewish heritage alone.

Central to this Christianizing view are texts in Paul's letters in which he appears to look back on his own former conduct as a Jew with critical distance, regarding it as destructive "zeal" (Gal 1:12–14), or describing his Jewish heritage now as nothing but "loss" (*zēmia*) or "rubbish" (a euphemism for the Greek *skybala*) compared with "the surpassing value of knowing Christ Jesus my lord" (Phil 3:7–9). At the heart of centuries of Protestant exegesis and theology is the irreducible opposition between striving in futility for "righteousness" before God through "works of law"—phrases that in the past were usually taken as a virtual definition of Judaism—and receiving God's gracious offer of righteousness through Christ, which was taken as definitive of life in Christ. That opposition, too, is ostensibly drawn from Paul's letters (Rom 3:21–25; 9:30–10:6; Gal 2:15–21; 3:1–14; Phil 3:2–9).[5]

That older view was imperiled, however, by criticisms, which were finally given exhaustive demonstration by E. P. Sanders, that Jews in Paul's day did *not* understand themselves to be securing God's approval through "works of law."[6] If Sanders was right, then interpreters seemed to be forced onto either of only two options. Either in the passages just named, Paul had been setting his gospel in unfair contrast with a caricature of Judaism that

---

5. The literature comparing the "New Perspective" with the assumptions of an "older" or "Lutheran" perspective is already vast. Documenting its daily expansion is the daunting task first taken on by Mark M. Mattison when he launched "The Paul Page" in 1999. The "explosion of relevant online material" compelled him to seek out the corporate sponsorship of staff at Logos Bible Software, who now manage the site (http://www.thepaulpage.com/about). For an admirably coherent and accessible summary of the chief issues and schools of thought involved, see Zetterholm, *Approaches to Paul*.

6. Sanders, *Paul and Palestinian Judaism*. Sanders himself acknowledged his debt to predecessors who had made similar arguments, though in not so sustained a way, notably Montefiore (*Judaism and St. Paul*) and Moore ("Christian Writers on Judaism").

did not in fact exist, or else Paul's Protestant interpreters had misunderstood him regarding the nature of "works-righteousness." Sanders himself and Heikki Räisänen drew the first conclusion: Paul's letters were marked by a certain logical incoherence that resulted from his enthusiasm as a convert to a new religious community.[7]

The latter conclusion is the core impulse behind much of the "New Perspective," which is actually an umbrella category under which a range of interpretive proposals may be loosely and rather uneasily grouped together.[8] The most successful among these has been the proposal that by "works-righteousness" Paul meant, not the individual Jew's striving for God's approval, but the Jewish people's *collective* effort to preserve their ethnic distinctiveness among other peoples through the diligent maintenance of boundary-marking practices like circumcision, kosher diet, and the keeping of the Sabbath.[9] On this view, then, Paul's argument is not against a false Jewish understanding of how individuals may be saved, but against a supposed effort by antagonistic Jewish contemporaries to impose boundary-marking practices on Paul's largely non-Jewish congregations. That is, Paul's polemic against "works of law" springs from his desire to defend the law-free church of Gentiles and Jews.

When put in these terms, we should recognize that much of the "New Perspective" is only as "new" as the nineteenth-century Tübingen school of F. C. Baur, with which it has much in common.[10] This approach nevertheless has gained in its appeal to many contemporary interpreters, in part, I suspect, because it has the apparent advantage of absolving Paul of having misunderstood Judaism. To the contrary, on this view, Paul appears as something of a champion of modern multiculturalism and as an opponent of ethnic chauvinism or "ethnocentrism" (which was exemplified by his Jewish opponents). It is not surprising that this approach has proven popular

---

7. Sanders, *Paul and Palestinian Judaism*; Räisänen, *Paul and the Law*.

8. A third approach is to seek to refute or minimize the relevance of Sanders's arguments, an approach fairly regarded as an exercise in special pleading (see Zetterholm, *Approaches to Paul*, chap. 6: "In Defense of Protestantism"). Yet another approach implicitly refutes one aspect of Sanders's argument by postulating that the form of works-righteousness seen in 4 Ezra or 2 Baruch—later, post-70 texts that Sanders considered anomalous—were in fact representative of a much more prevalent form of Judaism in Paul's day: an argument Martinus de Boer has recently advanced ("Paul's Mythologizing Program in Romans 5–8"). Unfortunately, this argument is not falsifiable.

9. This was the core insight and distinctive contribution of Dunn's essay "New Perspective"; it remains an important element in Dunn's magisterial discussion of *The Theology of Paul*.

10. A point made by Hafemann, "Paul and His Interpreters." See Baur, *Paul the Apostle of Jesus Christ*.

in the United States and the United Kingdom, that is, in ethnically diverse, democratic societies where more liberal interpreters see a happy integration of different peoples as a paramount value.

This interpretation (and cultural appropriation) of Paul comes at a cost, however, as a number of critics have pointed out. It routinely portrays as characteristically Jewish a collective insistence on ethnic distinctiveness, sometimes in negative terms formerly used to describe the boastful, arrogant, self-justifying Jewish *individual*. As Thomas Deidun put it years ago, "New Perspective" efforts to rehabilitate Paul as an opponent of Jewish ethnocentrism allow "practically all the old Lutheran demons" of Jewish caricature "to return unabashed to the Judaism which Sanders had by all accounts meticulously swept and put in order."[11] Similar criticisms have been raised by Mark D. Nanos and Daniel Boyarin, among others.[12]

Even when Christian interpreters today are careful to stipulate that they do *not* mean to pit Paul over against Judaism itself, but only to portray him as championing a "universal" strand of the Jewish tradition over against a "narrowly ethnocentric" strand, the result is often to pose Paul as the *only* expression of the "universal" (that is, the "good") strand. The implication remains that any Jews who did *not* follow Paul into the "universalism" of Christianity were held back by the "bad" strand of Judaism, which is generally characterized by ethnic prejudice.[13]

THE CONSTRAINING POWER OF ESSENTIALIZING CATEGORIES

Pamela Eisenbaum deftly observes that there are two fundamental interpretive errors involved in much current interpretation of Paul, including aspects of the "New Perspective." One is the "essentializing" of ancient Judaism; that is, the definition of Judaism, not in terms of the self-understanding

11. Deidun, "James Dunn and John Ziesler on Romans in New Perspective."

12. Nanos, *The Mystery of Romans*, 88–95; Boyarin, *A Radical Jew*, 209–24.

13. To take but one example of a wider phenomenon, Richard B. Hays takes pains to insist that he does *not* wish to oppose Paul to Judaism (*Echoes of Scripture in the Letters of Paul*, 55, 59). But even as he repeatedly describes Paul as representing Judaism "rightly understood," over against "a narrowly ethnocentric form of Judaism," he fails to identify a single person or text *other than Paul* that might have represented the former. The inevitable impression is left that the "narrowly ethnocentric form" of Judaism is all that there was—other than Paul. This, to my eyes, is but another example of what Daniel Boyarin has criticized as the "allegorization of the Jew" in Christian scholarship (*A Radical Jew*, loc. cit.; see Elliott, *The Arrogance of Nations*, 128–32). A similar critique of N. T. Wright's description of Judaism "perfected" in Paul's gospel (*Paul and the Faithfulness of God, passim*) is a worthy task for a different venue.

expressed by actual Jews, but in pre-defined terms of its essential *otherness*, its inherent incompatibility with an (equally essentialized) understanding of Christianity.

> Put very simply, . . . Christianity is defined as devotion to Christ; Judaism is defined as devotion to Torah. . . . In the context of this discussion, essentialism exacerbates the problem of Christian-Jewish polemic in the study of Paul because Judaism and Christianity are assumed to be mutually exclusive as well as immutable categories of religious identity. Specifically, devotion to Christ necessitates repudiation of Torah, because devotion to Christ in terms of traditional Pauline theology implies a particular theology of grace that requires a negative valuation of Torah.[14]

The second error identified by Eisenbaum is bound up with the first in a vicious circular argument. Many interpreters understand Paul as being *ethnically* Jewish—feeling group affinity or loyalty for his people—but not *religiously* or *theologically* Jewish. That is, interpreters recognize that in his letters Paul occasionally identifies himself as a Jew, still in "solidarity" with other Jews, but insist that he "was so radically transformed by his experience of Christ that he moved outside the bounds of Judaism, or at least he moved so far to the margins that he ventured into something no longer recognizably Jewish." Eisenbaum describes advocates of this pattern of interpretation as "the *kata sarka* camp," understanding Paul as a Jew *only* ethnically, *only* "according to the flesh."[15]

---

14. Eisenbaum, "Paul, Polemics, and the Problem of Essentialism," 226. See the earlier discussion by Nanos, *The Mystery of Romans*, Introduction.

15. Eisenbaum, "Paul, Polemics, and the Problem of Essentialism," 227–28.

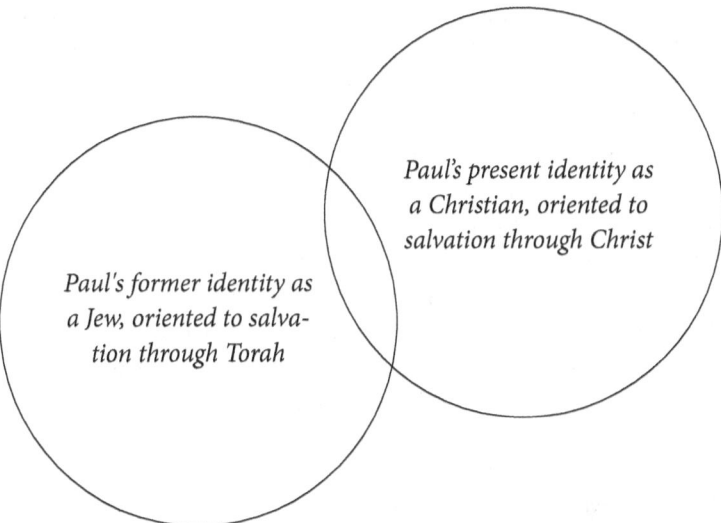

Fig. 9.1. The *kata sarka* interpretation of Paul's Judaism. The overlap between the two zones represents the vestigial aspects of Paul's merely "ethnic" identity, as a Jew "according to flesh," that continue even as Paul has come to think of himself primarily or essentially as a Christian.

Essentialism in the "Social-Science" Paul

So pervasive are the categories and habits of this "essentializing" thinking that one need not go far to find examples of its constraining power, even when scholars clearly and explicitly intend to avoid it.

One rather egregious example illustrates the problem. In their *Social-Science Commentary on the Letters of Paul*, Bruce J. Malina and John J. Pilch affirm repeatedly that "Paul was an Israelite" who "did not 'convert to Christianity' but rather continued to obey the God of Israel as he had previously done"; his work had an "exclusively Israelite nature."[16] These statements appear initially to range Malina and Pilch against the mainstream of Christian theological interpretation and on the side of some of the interpreters represented in the present volume. But Malina and Pilch go on to argue that our modern conception of Paul among "Jews and non-Jews (Gentiles)" is "completely inappropriate," and imply that under no circumstances should we think of Paul as a "Jew."

---

16. Malina and Pilch, *Social-Science Commentary on the Letters of Paul*, 10–13.

Malina and Pilch are concerned in part to "fix" the meaning of various ethnic labels in the "Mediterranean world." When Paul spoke of "Greeks," they contend, he didn't mean people from Greece, he meant "persons who were civilized," including civilized, Greek-speaking "Israelites." These, rather than "non-Israelites," were the targets of his mission as "apostle to the Gentiles" (another mistranslation, according to Malina and Pilch). They argue that "in ingroup contexts, any Israelite 'going to the other peoples' would be presumed to be going to *Israelites resident among* those other peoples."[17] The authors are aware, of course, that this claim flies in the face of the "received view," as they call it, but they insist the received view is wrong. Unfortunately, their case rests on a certain carelessness with categories,[18] and with a blunt essentialism that juxtaposes two oppositions from Paul's letters—*Hellēnoi* vs. *Ioudaioi* (Rom 1:16) and *Hellēnoi* vs. *barbaroi* (Rom 1:14)—and confuses them. That is, they at once assume that a term (like *Hellēnos*) always refers to just one thing, and that if two other terms are opposed to *Hellēnos*, those terms must be synonymous. "Greeks" (*Hellēnoi*), they consequently explain,

> referred to a status, to persons who were "civilized," indicated by the fact that they spoke Greek and adopted Hellenic values and habits in interpersonal relations. Similarly, the reference to "Jews" in poorly conceived English translations actually refers to "Judeans," people who followed the customs of one group of people living in that section of the Roman province of Syria called Palestine. The Hebrew term *yehudim* and the Greek *Ioudaioi* are simply erroneously translated in English [that is, as *Jews*] . . . To "Greeks," including Israelite "Greeks," Judeans were barbarians.[19]

---

17. Malina and Pilch, *Social-Science Commentary on the Letters of Paul*, 3–4, 7.

18. For example, Malina and Pilch tell their readers early on that "in the first-century Mediterranean there really were no 'Greeks' since there was no Greek nation nor any state called Greece" (Malina and Pilch, *Social-Science Commentary on the Letters of Paul*, 3), but proceed later to quote at length ancient authors talking about "Greeks" and "Greece" without explanation or correction. The heart of their argument, that Paul addressed Israelites rather than "Gentiles," is a single analogy, dressed up in social-science "in-group" jargon: When Israelis speak of "'going to Americans to sell U.S. tax-exempt Israeli bonds, they are presumed to be going to Jews resident in the U.S.'" (7). The analogy breaks down, of course, as soon as we imagine such an Israeli "apostle" speaking to American Jews (as Paul speaks to his congregations) and identifying them as "Americans" *rather than* as Jews. On Malina and Pilch's role in the wider discussion of ethnicity, see also Elliott, *Arrogance of Nations*, 47–52.

19. Malina and Pilch, *Social-Science Commentary on the Letters of Paul*, 5.

With this categorical infrastructure in place, Malina and Pilch are ready to interpret the whole Pauline corpus by distinguishing Paul and his fellow "Israelite Greeks," who are characterized as tolerant, even enthusiastic about the worship of other gods, from the "Judaizers" who plagued him. The latter were "Judeans" eager to impose a particularly narrow set of local Judean practices on Paul's "Israelite" communities. Chief among these peculiar practices was "infant genital mutilation," by which Malina and Pilch mean circumcision, which they assert appeared "rather late in Palestine (ca. 150 BCE), and perhaps centuries later, if at all, among Yahweh worshipers far from the region of Judea."[20] To justify these remarkable claims, they invoke Shaye J. D. Cohen's careful study of Jewish identity, but show in doing so that they have misunderstood it. Cohen observed that in the Hasmonean period, after the persecution of Judaism by Antiochus Epiphanes, an "ethic of separation" between Jews and non-Jews emerged in which certain laws and rituals, paramount among them circumcision, gained "new prominence." The Hasmoneans also granted Judean citizenship to Idumaeans and Ituraeans, who were most likely "already circumcised" (though Cohen was careful to note that the event is often misrepresented as their "forcible conversion" to Judaism).[21] But Cohen never claimed, as Malina and Pilch imply, that the practice of circumcision was a second-century innovation, or that it was localized to the environs of Jerusalem. Those claims are Malina and Pilch's inventions. Unfortunately, they seem to be of a piece with their strained effort to attribute "modern Ashkenazi Jewishness" to the ninth-century Khazars, with whom "there was no lineal development from early Israel."[22] Contemporary Western Jews are thus deprived of any historical continuity with ancient Israel, at the same time Paul is held up as the personification of the ancient Israelite (and biblical) vision. It is hard to avoid the impression that the result is a form of Christian supersession dressed up as "social science."

Paul's Almost-Jewish Identity

Another example of an "essentialist" or "Christianized" interpretation of Paul is far more sophisticated. I turn to Jörg Frey's essay on "Paul's Jewish Identity," not because it is particularly egregious example of the pattern I am describing (it is not), but simply because Frey's clearly stated intention is to understand Paul *as a Jew*. Indeed, in his survey of recent scholarship, Frey

20. Malina and Pilch, *Social-Science Commentary on the Letters of Paul*, 13–15.
21. Cohen, *The Beginnings of Jewishness*, 130–39.
22. Malina and Pilch, *Social-Science Commentary on the Letters of Paul*, 179–80.

celebrates the current dialogue between Christian and Jewish interpreters of Paul as "resulting in a mutual illumination of texts and perspectives" that he declares "the most promising progress in scholarship."[23] He decries as hopelessly one-sided and anachronistic the attempts by other scholars to deny that the apostle Paul was still a Jew; to the contrary, he insists (as we have seen Malina and Pilch do as well) that "Paul never abandoned 'Judaism' in order to join 'Christianity.'"[24] Frey also illustrates the various ways in which Paul professed solidarity with Israel, and relied upon concepts and themes (the importance of the law, the resurrection of the dead) that derived from Judaism.

Nevertheless, at several key points Frey continues to describe Paul's relationship to Judaism in essentializing ways that emphasize the distance of Paul and his "Christian" churches from Judaism, implying their fundamental incompatibility. The following review is not meant to be exhaustive, but simply to demonstrate that other scholars, including some represented in *Paul within Judaism* (ed. Nanos and Zetterholm), have proposed alternative interpretations at a number of points that allow us to understand Paul's thought and experience within the categories of ancient Judaism, *understood in the political context of Roman rule*, apart from Christian assumptions. An examination of Frey's essay thus allows us to recognize the constraining power that older, essentializing or "Christianizing" assumptions continue to exert, even when interpreters are striving for a "new perspective."

Paul's Past Persecution of the Early Assemblies

Frey regards as thoroughly "Pharisaic" the "zeal by which [Paul] had persecuted the enemies of the law," prior to the "revelation" of Christ. "Paul's activity as a persecutor," he writes, "appears as part of an inner-Jewish struggle for the recognition of the Torah against its alleged opponents" in the early churches.[25] This appears to absolve Paul of any anti-Jewish animus by explaining his persecuting activity as a struggle *among Jews* over the observance of the law. But this is simply to project an essentialist dichotomy back *behind* Paul, into the early Jesus movement. That is, it portrays the Judean *ekklēsiai* as *already* moving away from, and hostile to, the law—presumably meaning, indifferent or hostile to the law's boundary function in excluding non-Jews. These early communities, by implication, provided a proto-Christian community into which Paul could later move.

23. Frey, "Paul's Jewish Identity," 289.
24. Frey, "Paul's Jewish Identity," 291.
25. Frey, "Paul's Jewish Identity," 291.

However prevalent that assumption remains among Christian interpreters—Paula Fredriksen has described it as "an almost universal consensus"—it can hardly be judged historical, as Fredriksen has convincingly demonstrated.[26] One way Frey and other scholars portray the earliest proclamation of the messiah Jesus as being necessarily hostile to or opposed to the law is by reading Paul's aside in Gal 3:13 as evidence that *before* the "revelation" of Christ, Paul straightforwardly regarded the crucified Jesus as "cursed" by law. This means the earliest believers in Jesus would necessarily have opposed the law in order to proclaim a crucified man as messiah, and that as a Jew, Paul would have shared that judgment until God's revelation decisively reversed it.[27] But as Fredriksen points out, this supposition is undermined by "an utter lack of evidence . . . In no Jewish writing of this period, Paul included, do we find crucifixion itself taken to indicate a death cursed by God or by the Law."[28] To the contrary, archaeological evidence shows that crucified Jews were buried and memorialized honorably.[29] The notion that Paul (or any Jew) would have regarded a crucified Jew as "cursed" is historically improbable. As Fredriksen puts the question, "why, in brief, would Jews reject [another] Jew for a Roman reason?" Rhetorically, Paul's off-hand reference in Galatians 3 to a text from Deuteronomy "gets Paul where he needs to go," in a "snarled" argument addressed to non-Jews—but to load this remark with the weight of explaining Paul's "conversion," as Frey and other Christian exegetes continue to do, imposes a burden the text cannot bear.[30]

Nor would the early Jesus assemblies have been opposing the law by including non-Jews alongside Jews in their community observances. In a variety of traditions, Jewish literature gives evidence of the expectation that at the last days, non-Jews would turn from idols to recognize the true God. That did not mean that they would stop being non-Jews, however: as Fredriksen observes, "*moral conversion is not halakic conversion.* These Gentiles would not, by abandoning their idols, have the legal and religious

---

26. Fredriksen, *From Jesus to Christ*, 142–56.

27. Frey, "Paul's Jewish Identity," 318–19. In Gal 3:13 Paul declares, "Christ redeemed us from the curse of the law by becoming a curse for us—for it is written, 'Cursed is everyone who hangs on a tree'" (quoting Deut 21:22–23).

28. Fredriksen, *From Jesus to Christ*, 147–48.

29. An excavated first-century tomb northeast of Jerusalem revealed the remains of a Jew, Yehohanan, who had been crucified but nevertheless given a proper family burial next to the remains of a relative named Simon, "the builder of the Temple" (Tzaferis, "Jewish Tombs at and near Giv'at ha-Mivtar"; Zias and Sekeles, "The Crucified Man from Giv'at ha-Mitvar: A Reappraisal."

30. Fredriksen, *From Jesus to Christ*, 147.

status of converts, that is, Jews. They would remain Gentiles and *as Gentiles* would they be saved." The very fact that Jews proclaiming Jesus as messiah could find non-Jews to accept their message showed that non-Jews were welcomed in synagogues; "and the original apostles so readily accepted these Gentiles because they saw in their response, as with their leader's resurrection, yet one more sign that the Kingdom approached—indeed, its effects were already manifest."[31] Neither the presence of non-Jews in synagogues (which could have happened, Fredriksen points out, "*in Paul's own synagogue*") nor the close meal fellowship of Jews and non-Jews would have scandalized a good Pharisee, provided the meals did not involve non-kosher foods—and if they had, Fredriksen asks, how would Paul later have secured the acquiescence of those presumed monitors of Jewish observance, the Jerusalem apostles, for so long?[32]

Fredriksen concludes that the reason the Pharisee Paul persecuted the *ekklēsiai* had nothing to do with halakah. It had everything to do, she proposes, with the precarious political security of minority Jewish communities in Palestinian and Syrian cities. "The enthusiastic proclamation of a messiah executed very recently as a political insurrectionist—a *crucified messiah*—combined with a vision of the approaching End *preached also to Gentiles*—this was dangerous. If it got abroad, it could endanger the whole Jewish community."[33] In defense of what she admits is a "speculative" explanation, Fredriksen points out that her proposal has the merits of relying neither on anachronism nor the invention of otherwise unattested Jewish exegetical and halakic traditions (as "Christianizing" interpretations do); it simply "recognizes the politically precarious situation of urban Jewish communities in the Diaspora."[34] Alas, just the features that render Fredriksen's argument compelling also make it exceptional in contemporary interpretation, where the Jesus movement *even before Paul* is more usually—and more implausibly—characterized as entertaining attitudes and practices incompatible with the law.

---

31. Fredriksen, *From Jesus to Christ*, 150.
32. Fredriksen, *From Jesus to Christ*, 151–52.
33. Fredriksen, *From Jesus to Christ*, 153–54.
34. Fredriksen, *From Jesus to Christ*, 153–54. I relied upon Fredriksen's argument in my own discussion of the politics of the "apocalypse" of Christ to Paul in Elliott, *Liberating Paul*, 144–49.

The Christ-Apocalypse as Distancing Event

Although he acknowledges that "some of the convictions [Paul] held as a Pharisee remained influential for his work as an apostle," including his dedication "to the careful study of the law," Frey declares that "especially the fact that he was called" by God to be an apostle of the risen Christ, "precisely when zealously acting in defense of the law," "must have shaken his convictions fundamentally." This means especially that Paul's reflection as an apostle "on the relevance of circumcision and law"—by which Frey evidently means, their *irrelevance* to the new community gathered by Christ—"must have started quite early after his Damascus experience, when he began to preach the new message to the communities in Arabia or Syria and Cilicia," and "at the latest with the programmatic mission to pagan addressees."[35] Here, note again the equation of Paul's persecuting activity with a particular understanding of "defense of the law" as a matter of boundary observance.

Frey is certainly not alone among Christian interpreters in understanding the revelation of Christ to Paul ("his Damascus experience") as a radical *interruption* that caused a profound reversal in Paul's behavior, and in his attitude toward the law. But we should detect essentialist thinking in the assumption that the Christ-apocalypse was fundamentally incompatible with continued devotion to (the boundary-setting role of) the law. On these terms, Paul's dramatic break with his Jewish contemporaries seems inevitable, "built into" the encounter with Christ. But why? Frey offers no explanation of that inevitability, he simply asserts it. Given the frequency with which Christian discourse refers to Paul's "Damascus experience" in terms of divine revelation, perhaps Frey expects some at least of his readers to presume that the point does not need explanation. But this only renders dichotomous thinking even more impervious to criticism.

In contrast, Alan F. Segal understood Paul's visionary experience of Christ in the context of the apocalyptic-mystical tradition in early Judaism. Indeed, Segal demonstrated in *Paul the Convert* that Paul was our earliest and best (because first-person) witness to that tradition. In 2 Corinthians 12, Paul described an unnamed man's visionary journey into "the third heaven," a passage that is generally recognized to be an oblique reference to his own ecstatic experience. Segal argued that this experience was probably not an isolated event. Rather, here "Paul reveals modestly that he has had several ecstatic meetings with Christ over the previous fourteen years."[36] Participants in Jewish mysticism, "and perhaps apocalypticism as well,

---

35. Frey, "Paul's Jewish Identity," 298.
36. Segal, *Paul the Convert*, 36.

sought out visions and developed special practices to achieve them. Thus, we can assume that Paul had a number of ecstatic experiences in his life, [and] that his conversion may have been one such experience."[37] Hardly "incompatible" with Judaism in Paul's day, as language of a "rupture" or "irruption" implies, such an experience "parallels ecstatic ascents to the divine throne in other apocalyptic and merkabah mystical traditions." While those parallel sources are later than Paul, the close similarity of themes and terminology convinced Segal that Paul was indeed an early participant in a wider stream of mystical-ecstatic experience that included those later sources as well. Indeed, "Paul alone demonstrates that such traditions existed as early as the first century."[38]

Most intriguing for my purpose here are Segal's tentative comments that "it is possible, if unlikely, that 2 Corinthians 12 records Paul's original conversion experience." More likely, "Paul is describing a revelation both similar and subsequent to his conversion." Segal argued that Paul "necessarily" had several ecstatic experiences, and "that his conversion may have been one such experience."[39] This suggests—though remarkably, Segal did not pursue the possibility—that the "apocalypse" of Christ may not have been the first such visionary ascent on Paul's part. That is, in a series of ecstatic experiences in which we may suppose, on the analogy of other visionary texts prior to and contemporary with Paul, that he perceived in heaven a divine figure at the right hand of the Ancient of Days (cf. Dan 7:9–14), one such experience was the first in which that figure was perceptible to Paul *as the crucified Jesus*. Just here Segal provided us with a powerful explanation of the "apocalypse" of Christ *on fundamentally Jewish terms*.

For reasons I do not understand, Segal went on to conclude that "the meaning of these experiences" could only have been mediated to Paul "by the gentile Christian community in which he lived."[40] "We can ask," he wrote, "but we need not answer why a *Pharisee* would have a vision of *Christ*."[41] Segal himself neither tried to answer the question nor even mentioned it again in the rest of his book. Rather, he turned away from the potential explanatory power of the very Jewish visionary tradition that he had so carefully described to seek a sociological explanation of Paul's "conversion" in which the ecstatic tradition played no further part. Perhaps Segal

37. Segal, *Paul the Convert*, 37.
38. Segal, *Paul the Convert*, 37.
39. Segal, *Paul the Convert*, 26, 27.
40. Segal, *Paul the Convert*, 37, and throughout the book. On just this point, Paula Fredriksen similarly draws back, referring the reader (in a footnote!) to the concept of cognitive dissonance (*From Jesus to Christ*, 134 n. 2).
41. Segal, *Paul the Convert*, emphasis added.

assumed that a *Jewish* vision of a crucified messiah in heaven was categorically incomprehensible. Indeed, he implied that such an intense ecstatic experience would have remained completely unintelligible to Paul until, years later, some friendly non-Jews explained it to him.[42] But that implication has no logical force behind it. I propose, to the contrary, that to suppose that such a vision could only be understood on "Christian" premises is to fall into the same essentialist thinking described by Eisenbaum.[43] But such dichotomous thinking is as unnecessary as it is unfruitful.

Instead, as I have argued elsewhere, we can in fact imagine what a Pharisee would have made of a vision of a crucified messiah, and we can do so *on Jewish terms*: based, that is, on the urgent ethical and political consequences that the apocalypses drew from visions of heaven. Following Fredriksen's argument, previously discussed, we may suppose that Paul's motives for persecuting the early *ekklēsiai* had to do with concern for the political vulnerability of Jewish communities:

> We must suppose that as a Jew, as an apocalyptist, and as a Pharisee, [Paul] assumed that God's triumph over the Romans was inevitable, however indeterminate that day might be . . . If a Pharisee like Saul of Tarsus had looked upon Roman power with the eyes of the apocalyptists, he might well have concluded that God had given the sovereignty of the earth to Rome, "for a time." For that time, he might have concluded, resistance to Rome—however much he sympathized with its motives—was not only futile but impious . . . So the messianists were not only wrong about what time it was; they were dangerously wrong . . .[44]

Further, strictly on terms of comparison with contemporary Jewish texts like 4 Maccabees or the *Liber antiquitatum biblicarum*, we might suppose that Paul the Pharisee could have attributed to Jesus' death the atoning significance attributed to others executed by Rome.

> Paul would also have been taught by the apocalypses that the righteous martyred by Rome would "at the last day" be raised from the dead. We have only to suppose that this Pharisee

---

42. Segal goes on to refer to "Paul's confusion over the nature of his ecstatic journey to heaven" (*Paul the Convert*, 39), but this "confusion" has to do with whether or not Paul was "in or out of the body." Segal himself shows this was a customary, almost ritualized element of visionary reports. It hardly means that Paul could not have made sense of what he "saw" in that vision.

43. See further my critical interaction with Segal's work in Elliott, *Liberating Paul*, 141–43.

44. Elliott, *Liberating Paul*, 169.

experienced a vision of the martyr Jesus in heaven, a vision for which the Jewish apocalypses themselves provided the conceptual preparation.[45]

Once such a vision made clear to him that God had raised the martyred Jesus from the dead—again, a realization that would have been intelligible within the bounds of Jewish apocalyptic experience—the consequences would have followed a thoroughly Jewish apocalyptic logic: "The vision would have confirmed to [Paul] that what the apocalypses promised God *would* do *someday*, God had in fact begun to do *now*."[46] The consequence would have been an abrupt about-face from persecuting the assemblies, but this turn would have been motivated and remains completely explicable within categories supplied by the Jewish apocalypses.

The last point is an important one and I do not wish it to be misconstrued. I am not arguing that the Jewish apocalyptic tradition in any way "proves" that Jesus was raised from the dead; only that the claim of Jesus' being raised is, from a historical point of view, as intelligible—no more, but certainly no less—than claims made in any number of Jewish texts regarding the resurrection of the righteous or the presence in heaven of human figures as agents of the divine purpose. In contrast to essentializing thinking, I suggest that there is nothing "essentially" Christian about a Pharisee experiencing a visionary ascent to heaven and seeing the resurrected Jesus there.

Israel's Rejection of the Messiah

Frey rightly affirms that Paul's vocation as apostle to the nations ("Gentiles," in Frey's usage) is "formed by several [scriptural] passages, chiefly from the book of Isaiah."[47] This is an important recognition, especially when compared with the implication, in the work of other interpreters (as different as Heikki Räisänen and Alan Segal), that Paul "backed into" the "Gentile" church and came to adopt a gospel that included them only gradually and unreflectively.[48] For Frey, however, this priority is explained by the "principle" that he finds in Rom 1:16, "first to the Jews, then to the Greeks." This "formula" refers, Frey declares, to "Israel's priority in salvation history (cf. Rom 3:1)" and the "enduring primacy of Israel" in Paul's "missionary

---

45. Elliott, *Liberating Paul*, 171.
46. Elliott, *Liberating Paul*, 172.
47. Frey, "Paul's Jewish Identity," 300.
48. Segal, *Paul the Convert*, 58–61, 117; Räisänen, *Paul and the Law*, 258–61.

strategy." Frey explains this "principle" by reference to the narrative in Acts, where Paul is repeatedly presented preaching in synagogues to Jews and non-Jews alike: "The account of Acts, even though it may be rather schematic, generally confirms the principle mentioned in Rom 1:16: According to Acts, Paul consistently preached among the Jews (cf. Acts 9:22; 13:15ff.; 14:1; 16:13; 17:1f., 10f.; 18:4; 19:4) and only turned toward the Gentiles when facing opposition from the Jews (Acts 13:46)."[49] For Frey, Paul's apostolate to the nations was decisively "shaped by the experience of the rejection of the Gospel by many of Paul's fellow Jews."[50] Indeed, Frey finds in Rom 10:20–21 Paul's attempt "to demonstrate that the revelation to the Gentiles and the rejection of Christ by the majority of Israel are in accordance with the Scriptures."[51]

It is unfortunate that Frey has subordinated a few phrases in Romans to the narrative logic in Acts, with the result that the "primacy" of Israel in Paul's thought is thereby rendered a merely *chronological* priority: Paul preached to Jews "first," in place after place, and when they rejected his gospel, he "then" turned to non-Jews. This reads Israel's rejection of the (Pauline) gospel as a *fait accompli* in the past, a "theological fact" in the present (as Paul writes Romans). This understanding—all too common in Christianizing interpretation—fails to make sense (or in Frey's case, any mention at all) of Romans 11. Here we find Paul's clear and forceful admonition to non-Jews in the Roman *ekklēsiai* that he carries out his apostolic work among them "in order to make my own people jealous, and thus save some of them" (Rom 11:13–14). That is, Paul declares that the nations are not "primary," *even in his work with them in the present*: rather, the salvation of "all Israel" is his paramount priority, as Rom 11:25–26 makes clear.

I have argued elsewhere that the "theological fact" that Frey attributes to Paul was in fact a premise of the non-Jewish readers he addressed in Rome, but a premise, we may observe, that Paul himself explicitly rejected. Romans 9—11 have been read, since Calvin, as a defense of the honor of God in the face of the apparent lapse of Israel's covenant; but as the rhetoric of these chapters in Romans itself makes clear, the supposition that God had in any way abandoned Israel or that God's covenantal word to Israel had failed was, for Paul, unthinkable. In Frey's discussion, it would seem, the "enduring primacy of Israel" has no necessary connection to actual Jews. It remains rather a wistful theological postulate, an expression of ethnic "solidarity" that certifies Paul's bona fides as a Jew, even after the "primacy

---

49. Frey, "Paul's Jewish Identity," 301.
50. Frey, "Paul's Jewish Identity," 301.
51. Frey, "Paul's Jewish Identity," 300.

of Israel" in any material sense has been tragically contradicted by history. Paul thus comes to stand, as in much recent Christian interpretation, as a noble survivor of a vanquished race, rather like the figure of the admirably stoic Native American in the U.S. popular cultural imagination.

In contrast, the "enduring primacy of Israel" was the *horizon* of Paul's apostolate to the nations. I have argued at length elsewhere that Paul seeks, throughout this part of Romans, to disabuse some of his (non-Jewish) hearers in Rome of the very premise that Frey has attributed to Paul himself. The apostle "distinguishes a *mistaken* apprehension of the present as the fulfillment of God's purposes—that is, reading present circumstances as if they exhaust God's mercy—from a *true* apprehension of the present as a period during which God's purposes are not yet fulfilled, but are still in suspense."[52]

The "present circumstances" which Frey, and almost all Christian interpreters, read as a Jewish failure to believe in the Christian gospel are more likely to be understood, I argue (following Wolfgang Wiefel), as the actual historical circumstances of Jews in Rome, and elsewhere, at the time Paul wrote this letter.[53] Yes, Paul concedes, *some* in Israel have "stumbled," but Paul does not narrate a Jewish rejection *of his gospel* (as the Christianizing interpretation requires), nor does he suggest that the "disobedience" of some (see Romans 2 and 3) was tantamount to a failure *of Israel*. That was apparently a conclusion that was drawn in Rome, *by others*, but its basis had nothing to do with some imaginary Jewish plebiscite on the Pauline gospel (however often Christian interpreters have imagined it). The logic of "Israel's failure" aligns rather with elite Roman views of minority populations in Rome's streets. Paul insists that "the present circumstances of Israel *are God's doing*"; they are not the final consequence of Israel's failure, and they do *not* exhaust God's purposes.[54]

To repeat an important qualification: I am not examining elements in Frey's essay because it is in some way outlandish or exceptional today. Rather, I seek to point out a pattern of assumptions and premises that owe more to a received theological narrative of Christian origins than to historical consideration of Paul's letters in their Jewish context. I do not imagine that I have proved, in every part of this discussion, that Frey is wrong. It has been my goal to show that at point after point, an alternative interpretation of the data, *in terms of first-century Judaism* and without appeal to the language of "irruption" or divine revelation, is not only possible, but readily available

---

52. Elliott, *Arrogance of Nations*, 113–14.

53. Elliott, *Arrogance of Nations*, 99–100; Wiefel, "The Jewish Community in Ancient Rome."

54. Elliott, *Arrogance of Nations*, 114–19.

in the work of some contemporary scholars (including the contributors to *Paul within Judaism*).

It is also worth notice that at several of these points, attention to the Jewish context has meant attention to the social and political situation of Jews *under Roman rule*. Jews were not only participants in an ethnic or religious identity, as a neat (and essentializing) opposition between "Jews" and "Christians" presumes. Jews were also the flesh-and-blood inhabitants of a world where conquest and the ideology of Roman supremacy were daily determinants of the possible.

ESSENTIALIZING "THE POLITICAL"

The last point will appear obvious to historians of Judaism. It often proves elusive, however, to proponents of what I am here calling a Christianizing interpretation of Paul. Considerable debate swirls today around whether, or to what extent, Paul was opposed to the Roman Empire (or "Roman imperialism"). The existence of that debate is a positive development, when we consider that thirty years ago many scholars presumed that the "politics of Paul" was simply coextensive with the exhortation to "be subject to the governing authorities" in Rom 13:1–7. I have been a participant in the more recent debate, but am less interested here in continuing it than in calling attention to some of the assumptions regarding what it means to be "Jewish" (and what it would have meant for Paul to be "Jewish") that continue to be decisive in it.[55]

At the end of his richly textured discussion of *Jews in the Mediterranean Diaspora*, John M. G. Barclay affirmed that Paul should be understood as a Diaspora Jew, but an "anomalous" one. Barclay's discussion thus provides another opportunity to explore how first-century Jewish identity in general, and Paul's Jewish identity in particular, might be understood. It bears particular attention because of Barclay's express interest in the social and political components of identity, informed by recent studies of Diaspora

---

55. The debate has become a field of study in its own right. A few representative works include my own *Liberating Paul* and *Arrogance of Nations*; Horsley, ed., *Paul and Empire*; Horsley, ed., *Paul and Politics*; Horsley, ed., *Paul and the Roman Imperial Order*; Lopez, *Apostle to the Conquered*; Stanley, ed., *The Colonized Apostle*; and Harrison, *Paul and the Imperial Authorities at Thessalonica and Rome*. Surveys of the wider discussion in New Testament studies include Carter, *The Roman Empire and the New Testament*; Moore, *Empire and Apocalypse*; and Porter and Westfall, eds., *Empire in the New Testament*. Various dissenting views are available in Bryan, *Render to Caesar*; Blumenfeld, *The Political Paul*; McKnight and Modica, eds., *Jesus Is Lord, Caesar Is Not*; and Barclay, *Pauline Churches and Diaspora Jews*, esp. chaps. 1, 18, and 19.

Judaism and by the experience of colonized persons in imperial contexts, ancient and contemporary.[56] Barclay wrote deliberately with an eye to the "contemporary social scene," paramount for which was "the need to foster respect and tolerance for minority ethnic groups, in the face of the complex problems created by modern social pluralism." The Jewish Diaspora was of interest on these terms because it "has proved throughout history a 'paradigm case' of minority endurance in an alien context."[57]

Despite the impressive erudition of this study, it is hard to escape the impression that Barclay's "paradigmatic" understanding of Judaism still involves an implicit attempt to describe the "essence" of Judaism. From the very first, he takes the words of Balaam's oracle in Num. 23:9, about "a people who dwell alone, and will not be reckoned among the nations," as the defining characteristic of Judaism, "the sense of distinction which lies *at the heart* of the Jewish tradition."[58] His concern throughout the volume is with how Diaspora Jews, by definition a minority population, maintained their distinctiveness vis-à-vis "other ethnic groups."[59] Barclay is of course aware that identity is a complex matter, and thus he describes a complicated set of analytical tools to take separate measures of *accommodation, acculturation,* and *assimilation* of ethnic groups (in this case, Jews). Although these instruments are defined differently, however, they all end up in Barclay's discussion as measures of the extent to which Jews maintained their distinctive identity over against others—on the implicit assumption that being Jewish is primarily a matter of *not* being something else.[60]

Essentializing Judaism as "Other"

So, for example, Barclay relates *acculturation* to "the *linguistic, educational, and ideological* aspects of a given cultural matrix."[61] It follows that we should regard the likes of Philo or Josephus as thoroughly acculturated Jews because of their fluency in Greek language and even in the categories of Hellenistic philosophy and ethics. Barclay observes that when Josephus

---

56. Barclay, *Jews in the Mediterranean Diaspora*, 4–9, citing in particular Smallwood's "valuable conspectus of political realities" in *The Jews under Roman Rule*.

57. Barclay, *Jews in the Mediterranean Diaspora*, 14.

58. Barclay, *Jews in the Mediterranean Diaspora*, 1.

59. Barclay, *Jews in the Mediterranean Diaspora*, 2–3.

60. In a subsequent work Barclay makes much the same equation: "'Judaism,' as the ethnic tradition of the Jewish/Judean people, is a tradition socially defined by *not* being 'opened' to non-Jews" (*Pauline Churches and Diaspora Jews*, 18).

61. Barclay, *Jews in the Mediterranean Diaspora*, 92.

discusses Balaam's oracle (on Jewish distinctiveness), his "key terms, 'virtue' (ἀρετή) and 'providence' (πρόνοια), are in fact derived not from his Scriptural but from his Hellenistic education." He goes on to ask, "What sort of acculturation did he and other Diaspora Jews undergo? In what respects, and to what degree, did they merge Jewish and non-Jewish cultural traditions, and how did they employ such cultural syntheses? If, despite this acculturation, Josephus and others maintained their Jewish distinction, how did they appropriate and re-employ the Hellenism they absorbed?"[62] But Barclay's language begs the question whether Josephus (or others like him) were conscious of "merging" fundamentally different cultural repertoires; that is, did Josephus *know* that "virtue" and "providence" were unbiblical, "un-Jewish" concepts, to be "merged" with Jewish ones? Or was talking as he did simply Josephus's way of being Jewish? Is the dichotomy "Jewish vs. Hellenistic" a lively component of Josephus's thought-world, or a flawed conceptual convenience of the modern scholar of antiquity?[63]

Assimilation, Barclay goes on, refers to "*social integration* (becoming 'similar' to one's neighbors): it concerns social contacts, social interaction, and social practices"; it is a measure of "the degree to which Diaspora Jews were integrated into, or socially aloof from, their social environments."[64] Appropriately, then, one end of the spectrum (low assimilation) means that "social life [is] confined to the Jewish community." So far so good. But where one might then expect *high* assimilation to involve frequent social interaction with non-Jews, Barclay writes instead that it means the "abandonment of key Jewish social distinctives." That is, Jewish identity seems to *mean* non-assimilation: "as both Jews and non-Jews recognized, the Jewish tradition contained a number of taboos which impeded the assimilation of Jews."[65] Although Barclay recognizes that a Diaspora Jew like Philo could be, "in certain respects, Jewish to the core and Hellenized to the same core," his discussion of assimilation suggests that in social terms, this was simply a categorical impossibility. What should we make of the Jews of Alexandria who sought full citizenship alongside their non-Jewish neighbors: weren't *they* seeking to be Jewish *and* Alexandrian (or even Greek) to "the same core"? Barclay actually discusses a single Jew who petitioned for exemption from the poll tax, offering "a range of arguments . . . on the bases of

---

62. Barclay, *Jews in the Mediterranean Diaspora*, 3, discussing Josephus, *Ant.* 4.114.

63. See Engberg-Pedersen, ed., *Paul beyond the Judaism/Hellenism Divide*. To be sure, Barclay seeks to avoid just such simplistic dichotomies: "undifferentiated comments about Jewish Hellenization are of little analytical use" (*Jews in the Mediterranean Diaspora*, 91). But the analytical categories Barclay sets up seem to fail him in execution.

64. Barclay, *Jews in the Mediterranean Diaspora*, 92-93.

65. Barclay, *Jews in the Mediterranean Diaspora*, 94.

parentage, education, and age." He even notes that the papyrus petition has been corrected by a scribe: Helenos, son of Tryphon (a good Greek name for a Jew!), identified himself as an "Alexandrian," but that word was "scored out by a scribe and replaced by the words 'a Jew from Alexandria.'" Barclay also recognizes that Jews in different social classes had widely different opportunities to make claims on Alexandrian citizenship; he recognizes that elite Greek citizens opposed the granting of privileges to Jews who did not (in their view) deserve them; he knows that the actions of particular emperors insulted lower-status Jews and demonstrated "the vulnerability of the Jewish community" to shifting political alliances.[66] But these are not aspects of Jewish self-identification, they are the actions of *non-Jews*, whose perceptions of Jewish identity were bound up with conceptions of class and legal status. Such nuance is missing from Barclay's own discussion of assimilation, which risks simply fusing Jewish identity with *amixia* in such a way that social interaction *means* the "abandonment of key Jewish social distinctives."

Accommodation means, for Barclay, "the *use to which acculturation is put*, in particular the degree to which Jewish and Hellenistic cultural traditions are merged, or alternatively, polarized." This spectrum he compares with the "variant uses of the colonizers' culture" among the colonized, "in some cases to modify or even obliterate their native cultural traditions, in others to equip them to resist the colonizers' cultural imperialism." Here at last we find a recognition of the power dynamics implicit in the colonial situation which shape the possibilities available to the colonized.[67] But there is no recognition of the extent to which colonized peoples may actively organize their own lives and identities in a *hybridizing* way that defies neat dichotomies—an important theme in postcolonial literature and one that Ronald Charles has identified as particularly absent from Barclay's analysis.[68] Thus, when Barclay presents a spectrum of "accommodation," the extreme points are "antagonism to Graeco-Roman culture" (that is, a *refusal* of accommodation) on the one side, and the "submersion of Jewish cultural uniqueness" on the other. But one might have expected accommodation to mean the *identification* of Jewish cultural uniqueness *with* the values of Hellenistic culture.

---

66. Barclay, *Jews in the Mediterranean Diaspora*, 50–51.
67. Barclay, *Jews in the Mediterranean Diaspora*, 96.
68. See Bhabha, *The Location of Culture*. Ronald Charles discusses Barclay's understanding of diaspora identity in light of Bhabha's work in *Paul and the Politics of Diaspora*, esp. chap. 3. I am grateful to Dr. Charles for sharing an early draft of his manuscript with me.

The latter possibility has been raised, albeit quite briefly, by Jacob Taubes in his discussion of Paul's Hellenistic environment. "There was an aura," Taubes writes, "a general Hellenistic aura, an apotheosis of *nomos*. One could sing it to a Gentile tune, this apotheosis . . . one could sing it in Roman, and one could sing it in a Jewish way."[69] Stanley K. Stowers has made a comparable suggestion regarding a pervasive Hellenistic ethos that valued self-mastery (*enkrateia*)—an ethos cultivated among the Roman (and Romanizing) elite in the provinces, and adapted by some Jews in terms of the cultural excellence of Jewish law.[70] These proposals suggest that if part of the Roman cultural project was, in Greg Woolf's elegant phrase, to promote ways for "becoming, Roman, staying Greek,"[71] then the possibility of "accommodation" to which Barclay's analytical categories *should* point might best be described as "becoming Roman" or "becoming Greek, staying Jewish." To set Jewish identity always in opposition to Hellenistic or Roman identity, as if these were *essentially* incompatible, or as if Jewish identity was *essentially* a matter of being "not something else," would seem to be a categorical error. (The fact that Diaspora Jews read their scriptures in Greek, without, so far as we know, considering that language—for many of them, presumably, their first language—somehow a deficiency or fault, should tell us something about the artificiality of the dichotomy.) On the other hand, Barclay seems consistently to avoid an analysis in terms of political categories just where these might be most helpful.[72]

---

69. Taubes, *The Political Theology of Paul*, 23–24; see Elliott, *Arrogance of Nations*, 138–41 (on the piety of "works" in the Roman environment).

70. Stowers, *A Rereading of Romans*, esp. chap. 2.

71. Woolf, "Becoming Roman, Staying Greek"; Woolf, *Becoming Roman*.

72. Though it takes us farther afield from Paul, Barclay's discussion of 4 Maccabees highlights the inadequacy of dichotomous thinking. The writing extols obedience to the law (*nomos*) in categories known to us from Greek philosophy, yet Barclay argues that its author is not "really" Hellenistic: "his engagement with Hellenism has touched only the surface of his faith" (*Jews in the Mediterranean Diaspora*, 376). Barclay further observes that "the Gentile society which surrounds and threatens the Jewish heroes is noticeable by its absence. The martyrs are pitted against 'the tyrant' (and his human tools) but not against Gentiles or the Gentile world, and nothing is said to disparage non-Jews as such on moral or religious grounds." But this is remarkable only if one presumes that the opposition between Jewish and Hellenistic *ethnicity* and *culture* is the most adequate conception for understanding 4 Maccabees, and Diaspora Judaism more generally.

Paul the "Anomalous Jew"

The problem is exacerbated when Barclay turns at last to Paul, whom he labels an "anomalous Jew." He has already signaled that Paul's "Jewishness" was "doubted by his contemporaries," though he does not stop to explain what this means, or to offer any evidence.[73] (That Paul received synagogue discipline, 2 Cor 11:24, is taken by other scholars as evidence that Paul continued to move in Jewish contexts; it hardly suggests that other Jews considered Paul to have ceased being Jewish, as Barclay himself seems at last to concede.)[74] What Barclay regards as "anomalous" in Paul is that although he continues to express both a profound connection and loyalty to his people and a tremendous "antagonism" to "Hellenistic culture," he also claims an unparalleled distance, or "freedom," from "Jewish culture." Barclay cites several pieces of evidence for this distance. He considers Paul's claim, when addressing those outside the law, to have become "one without the law" (1 Cor 9:19-23), to be the "most revealing comment on his mission strategy"; Paul's statement regarding foods in Rom 14:14, that "nothing is unclean of itself," is a "radical principle" that other Diaspora Jews would have considered "deeply corrosive to the Jewish way of life."[75] Barclay knows that these phrases can be read as expedient or "tactical" policies, but is intent on taking them as general descriptions of Paul's attitude to "Jewish culture" as such.[76] He draws the same conclusion from Paul's activity in founding and cultivating communities of non-Jews ("Gentiles") without obligation to the Temple or to Torah. What makes Paul "anomalous" for Barclay is that he does not fit on a one-dimensional spectrum that opposes "Jewish" and "Hellenistic" identities: he did not, for example, resort to the sorts of allegorical methods that "Hellenizers" might have used to relativize the Torah's importance. To the contrary, "the main thrust of Pauline theology was inherently antipathetic" to any attempt "to find common cause with Hellenistic culture."[77]

Barclay describes Paul's theology broadly as "a sort of negative universalism" that "assaults all contemporary cultures—Jewish or Gentile" alike—with a "ferocious" antagonism. Paul thus appears to float free of any particular ethnic heritage precisely to the extent that his identity as a Jew

---

73. Barclay, *Jews in the Mediterranean Diaspora*, 91.

74. "Such punishment represents the response of a synagogue to an erring member, *not quite* the expulsion and ostracism of one judged wholly apostate" (Barclay, *Jews in the Mediterranean Diaspora*, 393-94, emphasis added).

75. Barclay, *Jews in the Mediterranean Diaspora*, 384-85.

76. Mark D. Nanos reaches very different conclusions in "Paul's Relationship to Torah in Light of His Strategy 'to Become Everything to Everyone.'"

77. Barclay, *Jews in the Mediterranean Diaspora*, 391.

has been interrupted by the appearance of Christ.[78] Remarkably, Barclay's chief basis for perceiving the apostle's "antagonism" toward Jewish culture is Romans 1—3, which Barclay reads (along with many Christian exegetes) as involving an "indictment of Jews" and as intended "to demolish the religious and cultural claims of both Jews and Gentiles."[79] But that characterization of Paul's intention is problematic. Other scholars have emphasized, as a matter of methodological principle, that all Paul's letters be read as directed to predominantly non-Jewish audiences. Barclay is familiar with the principle.[80] The consequence drawn by others, however, is that Paul's statements about the significance of the Law can be read only as describing the significance of the Law *for non-Jews*.[81]

More specifically, reading Romans, and especially Romans 1—3, in accordance with the clear signals that it is directed to a *non-Jewish* audience—and an audience tempted to its own "cultural antagonism" against Jews!—has resulted in very different interpretations of Romans, particularly of chaps. 1–3, and consequently of Paul's theology in general. I have argued elsewhere that read rhetorically, and without importing assumptions from the Christian dogmatic tradition, Romans 2 does not function as an "indictment" of Judaism.[82] Stanley K. Stowers has argued that a particular exemplar of the Jewish teacher, rather than Judaism as such, is Paul's target.[83]

Stowers further points out that the traditional reading of Romans, which works "to erase the gentile audience," does so as a "hermeneutical move that facilitates reading the letter as canonical scripture of the orthodox catholic church."[84] Barclay's reliance on a particular reading of Romans 1–3 is a case in point: it relies upon a *Christianizing* reading of Romans as an

---

78. Paul's commitment to Jewish "ancestral traditions" was evident in his persecution of the churches, but "the direction of his life was fundamentally altered by his 'call' experience in or near Damascus..." That call required that he "questioned the authority of the 'ancestral customs' which he had once vigorously defended" (Barclay, *Jews in the Mediterranean Diaspora*, 384). As we have seen above in discussing Frey, an alternative narrative of these events is possible.

79. Barclay, *Jews in the Mediterranean Diaspora*, 392.

80. Paul's letters "tell us what Paul said to his own converts but not, except by implication, how he spoke to non-Christian Jews or Gentiles" (Barclay, *Jews in the Mediterranean Diaspora*, 382).

81. See Gaston, *Paul and the Torah*; Gager, *Origins of Anti-Semitism*; Elliott, *The Rhetoric of Romans*; Stowers, *A Rereading of Romans*, esp. chap. 1.

82. Elliott, *The Rhetoric of Romans*, 127–57; Elliott, *The Arrogance of Nations*, 100–107.

83. Stowers, *The Diatribe in Paul's Letter to the Romans*; Stowers, *A Rereading of Romans*.

84. Stowers, *A Rereading of Romans*, 33.

explosion of any claim to privilege other than Paul's boast "in Christ." The result is ultimately a *kata sarka* understanding, in which Paul's identification with Israel is primarily a matter of "the anguish Paul expresses over the unbelief of fellow Jews."[85] In Barclay's view, Paul's gospel may be in its fundamental theological conceptions a "development" out of Jewish tradition, and the apostle may be "most at home among the particularistic and least accommodated segments of the Diaspora; yet in his utilization of these concepts, and in his social practice, he shatters the ethnic mould in which that ideology was formed . . . By an extraordinary transference of ideology, Paul deracinates the most culturally conservative forms of Judaism in the Diaspora and uses them in the service of his largely Gentile communities."[86] In other words, it seems, for Barclay Paul may be described as Jewish only to the extent that he is not Christian; but the call in Christ requires him to transcend his identity as a Jew.

Complicating Ethnicity Politically

As we saw in discussing Jörg Frey's essay on "Paul's Jewish Identity," here as well it must suffice simply to point to readily available alternative readings of Paul's "subversive" comments on Torah, without attempting to demonstrate their superiority. In different ways, a number of interpreters have argued that Paul's arguments regarding the Torah were motivated by "anxiety" *on the part of non-Jews* in the assemblies, rather than by some inherent aspect of Jewish identity. This anxiety fed the interest in Judaizing—that is, in the selective adoption of signal Jewish practices like circumcision—that Paul is at greatest pains to oppose.[87] Further, this "anxiety" has less to do with inherent aspects of stable ethnic identities, Jewish or "Gentile," than with the complex interaction of measures of status and privilege that were ascribed to different peoples in Paul's world. But these ascriptions were in part formed by the social and political realities of Roman Empire and the ideological representation of Roman power in terms of the superiority of the "Roman people" and of their divinely given destiny to rule the nations.

---

85. Stowers, *A Rereading of Romans*, 33.

86. Barclay, *Jews in the Mediterranean Diaspora*, 395.

87. Gaston, *Paul and the Torah*, chap. 2, followed by Gager, *Origins of Anti-Semitism*. Stowers similarly points to an interest on the part of non-Jews in the potential of the Torah as an instrument of "self-control" (*A Rereading of Romans*). Brigitte Kahl connects the interest in Judaizing among Galatian non-Jews with the Roman ideological presentation of Celtic peoples (= *Galatai*) as an inferior and conquered people (*Galatians Reimagined*).

Against the essentialist notion that ethnicity is singular and invariant—that a *Ioudaios* cannot be a *Hellēnos*—we must take seriously the existence of actual individuals, in Paul's world, who aspired to be both. The argument has often been made in fairly theoretical terms, as by the scholars just mentioned, but Lawrence L. Welborn has recently provided an intriguing example of the sort of active "Judaizing" that other scholars have posited. In the course of a very different argument, Welborn happens to discuss a Corinthian magistrate, one Gaius Julius Spartiaticus, whom Welborn identifies as "the sort of person" that the Gaius who was "host of all the assembly" in Corinth 1 Corinthians (Rom 16:23) "may have been."[88]

Spartiaticus was the grandson of a Spartan officer in Octavian's navy at Actium. After the victory, Octavian rewarded this officer with property and tremendous wealth, some of which he used to insinuate himself into Herod's court in Jerusalem, in part because he shared a current belief in an ancient kinship between Spartans and Jews (see Josephus, *Ant.* 13.164). This officer, Eurycles, persuaded Herod that his own sons had conspired against him. Herod had his sons imprisoned and killed, and Eurycles returned to Sparta with even greater wealth. He was denounced in Augustus' court, however, by a Spartan aristocrat who "no doubt resented the fact that his ancient family still lacked Roman citizenship, while an upstart, who happened to choose the winning side at Actium, dominated Sparta."[89]

Eurycles died in exile. His son Laco, who strove to ingratiate himself with Tiberius's circle, similarly fell victim to court intrigues and was compelled to settle, with his son Spartiaticus, in Corinth around 33 CE After Tiberius's death, however, Laco's fortunes were restored by Caligula, and Welborn speculates that "the [supposed] hereditary connection with Judaism may have played a role, since Caligula counted among his intimate friends the Jewish prince Herod Agrippa, grandson of Herod, the host of Eurycles."[90] Laco and Spartiaticus, father and son, both held citizenship in Corinth and "eventually attained the highest municipal offices." Spartiaticus appeared in inscriptions, around the time Paul was corresponding with the Corinthian congregations, as high priest of the house of Augustus "in perpetuity," the first Achaian to hold this, "the highest office in the province."[91]

Welborn's larger argument is that Gaius Julius Spartiaticus *might* have been the eminent "wrongdoer" of 2 Corinthians, who so vexed Paul with

---

88. See Welborn, *An End to Enmity*, 288–335; on the "spectacular" example of Spartiaticus in particular, 309–19.
89. Welborn, *An End to Enmity*, 315.
90. Welborn, *An End to Enmity*, 316.
91. Welborn, *An End to Enmity*, 311–12.

his contempt for the socially inferior apostle. My point here is simply to note that someone like Gaius—a *non-Jew* obsessed with establishing social connections through remote, or imagined, ethnic connections with Jews—existed on Paul's landscape. Here is Welborn's summation:

> Given the family history, it seems entirely plausible that Spartiaticus would have been attracted to Judaism as a God-fearer, that Spartiaticus would have formed a friendship with the respected ruler of the synagogue, Crispus, and that he would have responded with excitement to the message that the Messiah had appeared in the person of Jesus, and that, in all of this, Spartiaticus would not have sensed a conflict with his identity as an eminent Greek and Roman citizen, but would have viewed his interest in things Jewish as an act of filial piety to his great ancestor, Eurycles.[92]

So, then, if historian Greg Woolf can describe the cultural dynamics of "becoming Roman, staying Greek," and as our earlier considerations pointed us toward the possibility (*pace* Barclay) of Jews seeking to "become Greek, remaining Jewish," we should now also consider the possibility of someone like Spartiaticus being Spartan, and seeking through a perceived link to Jewish ethnicity to enhance his prestige as a Roman.

For her part, in her extensive study of the identity of Galatians (*Galatai*) and Celts (*Keltai*), Brigitte Kahl points us to the possibility that some Celts/Galatians in Paul's assemblies might have sought, if not to "become Roman," at least to gain acceptance in Roman eyes by adapting aspects of Jewish identity (and thus obscuring their identity as defeated Celts). It quickly becomes obvious from such examples that a simple polarity between "Jewish" and "Hellenistic" ethnicities is inadequate to the data, and should not be allowed to limit our efforts to understand Paul and his context. A more adequate approach will ask about practices of affiliation and constructions of identity in a wider context where these realities were shaped, in part, by the constraining force of Roman political and economic power and the ideological force of what we may call Roman ethnic reasoning.

There is no self-evident reason why such "political" considerations should not inform our understanding of Paul and his apostolate. Indeed, at various points above, I have shown that coherent and, in my view, compelling arguments have been made by a number of scholars that allow us to understand Paul *as a Jew*, responding to realities occasioned by Roman power (and the ways in which people of various ethnicities in his assemblies responded to it).

92. Welborn, *An End to Enmity*, 316–17.

INTERPRETIVE CHOICES

John Barclay has recently done interpreters a welcome service by surveying the current state of "political" interpretation of Paul, even if his goal is to question a number of its premises. The terminology is challenging; Barclay does not mean to propose that Paul's theology was "apolitical," but to challenge some of the maneuvers that have enabled what may be called the "Paul and Empire" circle of interpreters to describe Paul's gospel as posed directly in opposition to Roman imperial ideology.[93] He helpfully cautions against inferring what Paul "must have meant" or his readers "must have heard" from similarities between his expressions and the rhetoric of the imperial cult or imperial propaganda.[94] In Barclay's view, it is an error to give the Roman empire "particular significance" in Paul's thought, by which he means seeing Rome as the direct, specific, and exclusive (though covert) target of one or another expression in Paul's letters. The point is well taken, and Barclay does well to ask greater precision of those of us who set Paul's letters in comparison with expressions of Roman claims in the course of our interpretation.[95] Surely it is appropriate, *in the course of historical description*, to "beware of distortions that may arise from situating Paul's theological politics within the categories and theoretical frameworks which shape our own (post)modern understanding of 'politics.'"[96]

But Barclay himself knows there is more to the sort of interpretation that he, for one, would like to do than simple historical description. Against the identification of "politics-as-state-power," a reductionist category that (to my knowledge) plays no significant part in contemporary political interpretations, he prefers to read Paul as opposing "anti-God powers wherever and however they manifest themselves on the human stage," a category that allows him to invoke modern realities from unregulated international

---

93. Barclay, "Why the Roman Empire Was Insignificant to Paul," originally presented at a special plenary session at the Society of Biblical Literature annual meeting in November 2007; Barclay, *Pauline Churches and Diaspora Jews*, 363–87.

94. Barclay's particular target is N. T. Wright, whom he described (in the initial paper, though not in the published chapter) as the "most balanced" of the "Paul and Empire" interpreters. My own works are among those discussed peripherally in Barclay's argument, and I take many of his points as important cautions.

95. To some extent, Barclay is also arguing against a straw man, as when he insists (with N. T. Wright) that Paul "is not opposed 'entirely to everything to do with the Roman empire'" or to the Roman empire "as empire" (*Pauline Churches and Diaspora Jews*, 370–71), or interested "in the Roman empire *as Roman*" (374)—positions that are rare, if they appear at all, in the secondary literature.

96. Barclay, *Pauline Churches and Diaspora Jews*, 367.

finance to sex trafficking, from neocolonialism to domestic violence.[97] He acknowledges (in fact, insists) that the realities of the Roman Empire *were* given account in Paul's theology:

> The question is not whether Paul noticed the power of Rome—he clearly did to the extent of feeling its physical impact on his body; the question is what power he saw to be operative in such experiences . . . If Rome is not specifically named from [Paul's] angle of vision, this does not mean that Paul's theology was apolitical, only that the political is for him enmeshed in an all-encompassing power-struggle which covers every domain of life, including but not limited to the religio-political domain we call "the Roman empire," and not neatly divisible into a battle between forces "for" and "against" Roman rule.[98]

Phrased in such terms, it is hard to imagine any even among the "Paul and Empire" circle who would disagree. Who would insist that Paul's primary concern was a narrow focus on the structures and instruments of Roman state power? If anything, Barclay's wider "theo-political" reading shows the salutary effect of opening up the interpretive agenda to include the rich texture of imperial ideological and cultural expressions in Paul's day, rather than insisting (as some interpreters still do) that these are not proper topics for "Pauline theology."

This might be seen as simply a matter of Barclay's preference for theological language over overtly political categories. But there is a deeper point of contention here that requires clarification. One of Barclay's implied criticisms of the "Paul and Empire" circle is that they are motivated by other than purely historical concerns: "For some it is attractive, even ideologically necessary, to interpret Paul's polemics as directed primarily (if not solely) against an imperial power, rather than against 'Judaism'; at the very least, this offers a fresh frame for Pauline interpretation beyond both traditional and 'new' perspectives, free of any possible hint of 'supersessionism.'"[99] Whether or not it is Barclay's intention, I see this as an unnecessary polarization of interpretive choices. Barclay does not mean, I presume, to hold open a space for a sort of interpretation that *would* be governed by Christian supersessionism (though in contrast to Barclay's use of scare quotes, I regard the dreary history of such interpretation as suggesting the risk is quite real). Nor do I take him to be arguing here for the opposite, an interpretation of Paul's polemics as directed *primarily* against Judaism, *not* an imperial

---

97. Barclay, *Pauline Churches and Diaspora Jews*, 387 and n. 74.
98. Barclay, *Pauline Churches and Diaspora Jews*, 375–76.
99. Barclay, *Pauline Churches and Diaspora Jews*, 367.

power; though as we have seen, he does describe Paul's experience of the Christ event as resulting in a "ferocious" antagonism to "Jewish culture." It nevertheless seems clear that for Barclay, these are mutually exclusive alternatives between which the interpreter must choose. The risk in his eyes is that a "political" interpretation will dilute or diminish the distance between Paul and Judaism which he is at pains to emphasize. The point becomes clear in a footnote where Barclay explains his divergence from N. T. Wright: "Where Wright places Paul in ideological continuity with the biblical/Jewish tradition of monotheistic critique of paganism, I would place stronger emphasis on the new division of the cosmos created by the Christ-event (cf. Gal 1.4; 1 Cor 1.18—2.16, which strongly reshapes and reapplies the biblical categories themselves."[100] That is, in Barclay's eyes, Wright's openness to a political, empire-critical reading allows Paul to remain *too much* in continuity with the (biblical and) Jewish tradition, at just the point where Barclay seeks to pose the apostle *over against* his Jewish contemporaries precisely by virtue of a unique revelation in Christ.

In the earlier part of this essay, I sought to show that setting Paul squarely "within Judaism" means taking seriously the political situation faced by Jews under Roman rule; thus, questions about "Paul and Empire" belong within a wider discussion of Paul's place among other Diaspora Jews under Roman rule. Barclay's warnings about anachronism and imprecision in "political" interpretation should rightly direct us to closer attention precisely to the texture of ideological and cultural power relationships that conditioned the lives of Paul and other Jews. But this is not the direction Barclay himself takes. I also showed that it is possible to understand central elements in Paul's story—including his persecution of the Jesus assemblies, his vision of a crucified messiah in heaven, and the resulting apostolic work among "the nations"—in terms that render these elements intelligible and continuous with Judaism. Against these proposals, Barclay appears to illustrate a clear alternative, in which the centrality of Paul's experience of Christ (and, at least by implication, the revelatory value of that experience) requires that Paul can be described as an "anomalous" Jew, at best. If it is appropriate to describe this as a "Christianizing" interpretation, it would seem that reading Paul *within Judaism* will require of Christian interpreters a certain relinquishment of theological presumptions; but that has always been the challenge posed by historical criticism to the Christian tradition.

---

100. Barclay, *Pauline Churches and Diaspora Jews*, 384 n. 70.

10

Qui Bono?
Power Relations and the Work
"within Judaism" Language Does

WHAT BEGAN SOME YEARS ago as a minority position within scholarship on the apostle Paul, hailed early on as a "radical new perspective" on Paul (to distinguish it from the still-Protestant "new perspective" launched in the 1980s), has become a somewhat established position, institutionalized in the SBL "Paul within Judaism" Group. Some of the essays gathered in this volume represent my own contributions to this perspective on Paul.

Meanwhile, the "within Judaism" perspective has spread to the investigation of other ancient writings as well. The 2021 Annual Meeting program of the Society of Biblical Literature included sessions devoted to all four of the canonical Gospels and the Epistle to the Hebrews "within Judaism." Advocates of the "within Judaism" perspective speak of an "emerging paradigm shift" that understands "many or most" of the New Testament writings as "*expressions of* Judaism" rather than as early *Christian* writings that only interact with Judaism.[1] The phrase implies enclosure, that these writings—and the communities that produced them—may, indeed, *should* be understood as Jewish *without remainder.*

While some advocates of this new paradigm insist their motives are primarily historical, even to the exclusion of theological interests,[2] one

---

1. Hedner Zetterholm and Runesson, "The 'Within Judaism' Perspective—An Emerging Paradigm Shift"; Zetterholm, "The 'Within Judaism' Perspective—Why Does It Matter?"

2. Magnus Zetterholm calls for a "parting of the ways" between strictly historical

can observe its characteristic themes at work in scholarly and ecclesiastical settings alike. I argue in the following pages that a tension exists in "within Judaism" scholarship between historical and Christian theological motives. I do not aspire here to resolve that tension, but to argue that from a Marxist perspective, both the historical and theological poles of the discussion have not yet been pressed far enough.

OLDER QUESTIONS, NEWER WINESKINS

At one pole of the tension I seek to describe is the desire—commendable in itself—to continue Christian theology and practice free of anti-Judaism and anti-Semitism. At the other is the desire to represent history as fully and accurately as possible, whatever the consequences for Christian theology. These poles might be described as irreconcilably opposed. But by describing them as poles, as in a magnetic field, I mean to evoke a tension within a single system—such as exists in Christian biblical interpretation, in both its academic and ecclesiastical settings, today.

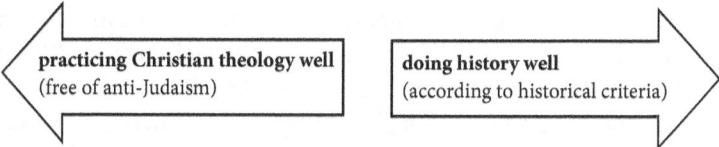

Fig. 10.1. A Tension in the "within Judaism" Perspective

Two brief anecdotes illustrate the first pole.

The preacher's text on a recent Sunday morning, from the Gospel according to John, did not obviously require a historical detour; but the preacher apparently anticipated his congregation would be uncomfortable with that Gospel's reputation as anti-Jewish. In a few sentences, he sketched the hypothesis of the Fourth Gospel's origins as developed, with variations, by Raymond E. Brown, S.S., and J. Louis Martyn.[3] The preacher mentioned neither scholar, this being an Episcopal liturgy, not an academic lecture. He was satisfied to explain that any harsh statements about "the Jews" in the Gospel were expressions of "the anger of wounded love" on the part of one Jewish subgroup which had been ostracized by another. Those expressions

---

research and the quasi-dogmatic interests of Christian theology: "The 'Within Judaism' Perspective," 14–16.

3. Brown, *The Community of the Beloved Disciple*; Martyn, *History and Theology in the Fourth Gospel*. Bart D. Ehrman presents this as the "socio-historical" approach to John in *The New Testament*, chap. 10.

were regrettable, then, but surely something that intelligent, sympathetic Episcopalians could understand.

A few weeks later, a fellow New Testament scholar posted a "public service announcement" to Facebook, warning Christian clergy approaching the texts of Holy Week to avoid negative generalizations about "the Jews" in their preaching. Her reasons were phrased as historical observations, buttressed by a short list of other scholars' names. My colleague did not engage any particular scholar's positions, this being a social media post, not an academic lecture. She was satisfied to assert that almost all the New Testament writings were composed by Jews; that negative references to *Ioudaioi* did not mean "Jews," but referred to inhabitants of *Judea*, or to some culpable subset of Jewish leaders; and that Jewish groups in the first century were a wild variety of mutually antagonistic sects, each believing their narrowly defined interpretation of halakah to be the only path acceptable to God.

In both anecdotes, the clear intent is to prevent Christians from affirming or perpetuating anti-Jewish stereotypes. In both cases, the device used is the interpreter's historical assertion that what *appears* to be supersessionist or anti-Jewish language in the New Testament is *in fact* nothing of the kind. The New Testament writings in view are, then, innocent of anti-Judaism.

There is some tension here between history and theology. Theology appears to *need* history: theological assertion alone is insufficient. But the tension is relaxed, insofar as gestures at history are employed to *serve* theology. The Gospels are absolved of anti-Judaism, and Christian liturgy may proceed.

One wouldn't know from these episodes that "within Judaism" scholarship on early Christian literature involves a cluster of *contested* questions.[4] As Magnus Zetterholm makes the point, what he calls "the Jesus movement" began within Judaism, but eventually

> ceased being Jewish although it is obvious that this was a prolonged process taking place over a long time and in different ways in various places. Some of the texts, later collected in the New Testament, may bear witness to this process, or at least to tensions within the movement that later would result in a more radical break. *The evidence is, however, inconclusive, and open to various interpretations.*[5]

---

4. As noted above, the 2021 and 2022 Annual Meeting programs of the AAR/SBL included sessions, in various Groups, on all four Gospels, the historical Jesus, Paul, and the letter to the Hebrews "within Judaism." Related questions are investigated as well by related groups like the Enoch Seminar and the Society for Post-Supersessionist Theology, and in journals like the *Journal of the Jesus Movement in Its Jewish Setting*.

5. Zetterholm, "The 'Within Judaism' Perspective," 10; emphasis added.

Zetterholm highlights as examples contrary interpretations of the Gospels of John and of Matthew and of the Letter to the Hebrews. While these arguments may continue in scholarly settings, the anecdotes I've offered present Christian interpreters representing *one* side of the argument as settled.

Nor would we know from these anecdotes that recent "within Judaism" scholarship takes place in a larger and older field of historical investigation in which theological anti-Judaism has often been traced to the New Testament writings themselves, and even identified as "the left hand of Christology."[6]

An earlier generation—one in which I was formed as a New Testament scholar—learned to regard the recognition and renunciation of Christian anti-Judaism and supersessionism as a moral imperative, and to explore and identify anti-Jewish themes and tendencies in the New Testament writings as a moral responsibility. Questions of power—specifically, of the emergence, over time, of Christian communities from the margins of ancient Judaism, and their eventual ascendancy to a licit, then the official religion of the Roman Empire, and that religion's entanglement over succeeding centuries in imperial and colonizing projects worldwide—were never to be far from our historical awareness.

I know that many of my colleagues involved in "within Judaism" scholarship today share those concerns and would endorse those commitments. But just these concerns and commitments make me wary of what seems a premature closure of the historical question. Writing to distinguish the "within Judaism" perspective from earlier scholarship, Magnus Zetterholm speaks of a shift in the burden of historical proof:

> Unlike the traditional position, which assumed a very early separation [of Christianity] from Judaism, the "within Judaism" perspective operates with the notion that *until proven otherwise texts in the New Testament should be considered Jewish texts* (regardless of the ethnic identity of the author, which in some cases may be unclear), reflecting the ideas of an apocalyptic, messianic movement in the first century CE. The starting point is that *the burden of proof lies with those who consider a certain text not to be "within Judaism" rather than the other way around.* The "within Judaism" is the normal, "outside Judaism" is the anomaly.[7]

Zetterholm's own interest is in the historical question. But because the "within Judaism" perspective as he describes it presumes that most, at least,

---

6. The classic work is Ruether, *Faith and Fratricide*.
7. Zetterholm, "The 'Within Judaism' Perspective," 15; emphasis added.

of the New Testament documents cannot be *anti*-Jewish, one apparent implication is that *theological* wariness or suspicion of the Gospels is by definition misplaced.

History is not just a matter of archaeological excavation of the past. History inevitably expresses the interests of contemporary collectives, whether scholarly or ecclesiastical or something else, as advocates of the "within Judaism" perspective assert clearly and repeatedly.[8] This has meant that historical description and assertion has often gone hand-in-hand with theological concern. We may observe that official Catholic and Protestant church statements, in the wake of World War II and the Shoah, exhorted the faithful to avoid "hatred, persecutions, displays of anti-Semitism, directed against Jews, at any time and by anyone."[9] Such statements are the hard-won result of collective self-examination on the part of Christian churches in the global North. They are a marked improvement over the blithe anti-Jewish stereotypes that prevailed in Christianity before the 1940s, and still prevail in fundamentalist and Christian nationalist collectives today.

But these exhortations also relied on quasi-historical arguments that both warned against generalized anti-Semitism and implicitly exonerated Christian scriptures. We find affirmations that Jesus and his disciples were Jews (important enough, after Nazism and the notorious project to construct an "Aryan Jesus");[10] that his opponents were "the Jewish authorities and those who followed their lead," so Jesus' death "cannot be charged against *all* the Jews, without distinction, then alive, nor against the Jews of today"; that even if "the Jews in large number" rejected the gospel of his messiahship, some did not.[11] While the intention of such comments appears salutary, the net effect of such generalizations *can* include perpetuating implicit stereotypes of Judaism.

For example, if *some* Jewish leaders *were* culpable in Jesus' death, and *they* are the real targets of Gospel references to *Ioudaioi*, then the Gospels remain authoritative enough in their depictions of Jewish perfidy; we who are Christians may continue to read them liturgically with an untroubled conscience; harder, come-to-(a Jewish)-Jesus questions about the Gospels needn't occupy us. Further, simplistic descriptions of first-century Judaism in terms of different responses to Jesus allow Christians today to appropriate the legacy of "biblical Israel," as represented by the "good Jews"

---

8. Runesson makes this his starting point in "What Does It Mean . . . ?"

9. Pope Paul VI, *Nostra Aetate*, 4.

10. Heschel, *The Aryan Jesus*.

11. Pope Paul VI's "Declaration on the Relation of the Church to non-Christian Religions"; emphasis added. Relevant Protestant statements through 1987 are gathered in World Council of Churches, *The Theology of the Churches and the Jewish People*.

who accepted him, and to explain what *seems* to be anti-Jewish language in the New Testament writings on the basis of the unfair suffering their own spiritual ancestors experienced at the hands of the *other* kind of Jews.[12] Finally, references to the prolific sectarianism of first-century Judaism[13] may distract from commitments that many Jews held in common, and play on stereotyped Jewish tendencies to hyper-scrupulosity, querulousness, and ethnic arrogance.

Space does not allow documentation of these characterizations, but fellow clergy colleagues in "liberal" churches may recognize them readily enough. They are certainly familiar concerns among Jewish scholars of the New Testament.[14]

∽

At the other pole of the tension I'm describing, scholars seek not only to investigate the past without concern to protect Christian theology, but also to demand that Christian theology accept the responsibility of historical honesty. So, Paula Fredriksen contends that historical work requires restoring the apostle Paul to his *ancient* context—meaning, to the "ethnically essentialist, god-congested, behaviorally various, culturally and socially permeable ancient Judaism(s)" of his world. In her trenchant phrase, then, placing Paul "within Judaism" also requires restoring him to a context "within paganism."[15] Such an apostle may seem inevitably foreign to us today, but a "defamiliarized Paul" should be the historian's proper goal—just as, Albert Schweitzer argued, the historical Jesus must be allowed to belong to his own time.[16]

---

12. In Paul studies, the "New Perspective" took the form of replacing earlier stereotyped oppositions—Jewish *legalism* vs. Pauline *grace* and *freedom from the law*—with supposedly more historically responsible oppositions between Jewish "ethnocentrism" and Jewish "universalism," the latter represented solely by Paul and his apostolic colleagues. See an early critique by Deidun, "James Dunn and John Ziesler on Romans in New Perspective" (the references are to Dunn, "A New Perspective on Paul"; and Ziesler, *Paul's Letter to the Romans*.

13. See, for example, the collection of John J. Collins's essays in *Scriptures and Sectarianism*.

14. See, for example, Levine, *The Misunderstood Jew*; on the Fourth Gospel, Reinhartz, *Befriending the Beloved Disciple*; and Reinhartz, *Cast Out of the Covenant*.

15. Fredriksen, "What Does It Mean to See Paul 'within Judaism'?" 374; on the peculiar challenges of the term "paganism," 362 n. 8.

16. Fredriksen, "What Does It Mean to See Paul 'within Judaism'?," 380; Schweitzer, *The Quest of the Historical Jesus*, 398–99.

Fredriksen's insistence does not allow the historian and the theologian to quietly go their own ways.[17] With regard to the Gospels, she insisted in an earlier work that Christian theology must be accountable precisely to rigorous historical work. That requires, she wrote,

> the renunciation of a simplistic reading of identity-confirming narratives, even if these are the ones offered by the gospels. Such a reading can only result in bad history. But bad history, for the church, results in bad theology, the subtle Docetism of anachronism.[18]

I submit that the tension between these poles is real. As Matthew V. Novenson observes, Karl Barth could endorse the goal of historical criticism—but sought to move *through* and *beyond* it, toward the imagined *dissolution* of historical distance from the past and the creation of *immediacy* with the "subject matter" (the *Sache*) of the biblical text.[19] Such immediacy was also an admired aspect of Martin Luther's preaching, and a goal of Ignatius of Loyola's spiritual exercises; it remains an ideal today in liturgics and homiletics courses at Christian seminaries. Barth was perhaps exceptional only in recognizing the reality of historical distance; other Christian biblical scholars have announced their easy familiarity with biblical realities as their presumed epistemic advantage.[20] For such interpreters, it would seem the yoke of historical investigation is easy, and its burden light.

Of course, the fullest possible encounter with past realities is the historian's goal. But as Marxist theorist Fredric Jameson insists, a "genuine philosophy of history" will involve "respecting the *specificity* and *radical difference* of the social and cultural past while disclosing the solidarity of its polemics and passions, its forms, structures, experiences and struggles, with those of the present day" (emphasis added). In Jameson's view, "only Marxism can give us an adequate account of the essential mystery of the cultural past," and that, "only if the human adventure is one."[21] The salient contrast to be made here is not between "faithful" or "believing" history and its supposedly "godless" or "atheistic" opposite, but between an *artificial* immediacy, one produced by *collapsing* the past into the immediacy of the present, and an *expansive* history that understands past and present as distinct

---

17. Contrast the program of "postliberal" theology; e.g., Lindbeck, *The Nature of Doctrine*.

18. Fredriksen, *From Jesus to Christ*, 214–15.

19. Novenson, "Anti-Judaism and Philo-Judaism"; Barth, *Epistle to the Romans*, 2nd ed., 6–7.

20. See, e.g., Wright, *Paul in Fresh Perspective*, 16–18.

21. Jameson, *The Political Unconscious*, 18, 19.

Qui Bono?

moments in "a single great collective story," the "single vast unfinished plot" of human striving into which we, like our ancestors, are plunged.[22]

HISTORY AND THE UNDERTOW OF THEOLOGY

What it means to "do history" has changed as a result of the Shoah: rethinking historiography about the first century remains a work in progress. A general sense of what counts today as *historically probable* is different from what it was forty years ago.

In historical Jesus studies, scholars routinely note the shift, in the 1970s, from an earlier criterion of "double dissimilarity," which effectively *separated* Jesus from his Jewish context, to the criterion of "contextual credibility," which restored him to precisely that context—all in the name of historical probability.[23]

In Paul studies, E. P. Sanders acknowledged that he relied on the substantial work of predecessors like G. F. Moore, who had argued in his monumental three-volume work that from the ancient Jewish point of view, Paul's critique of the Torah was "inexplicable"; but there was no "post-Moore" era after the 1920s comparable to the "post-Sanders era" in which Paul scholars profess to work today.[24]

Clearly, *something happened* between the 1920s and the 1970s to change what counted as "history" in New Testament studies. Just as clearly, that "something" was the horrific Nazi project to exterminate European Jews and Judaism. Among other catastrophic effects, that project further distorted what was already a profoundly supersessionist and often anti-Jewish tendency in Christian biblical scholarship—an effect still only inconsistently and imperfectly apprehended by the scholarly guild today.

We may appreciate the difference in historiography by recalling the now-notorious example of Gerhard Kittel—a German New Testament scholar, perhaps best known to many New Testament scholars and students as the general editor of the *Theologisches Wörterbuch des Neuen Testaments*, in English parlance the *TDNT* or simply "Kittel." Gerhard Kittel was also

22. Jameson, *The Political Unconscious*, 19–20.

23. The classic statement of the criterion of dissimilarity was Bultmann, *History of the Synoptic Tradition*, esp. 205; see also Käsemann, "The Problem of the Historical Jesus." Prominent pushback came from Vermes (*Jesus the Jew*) and Sanders (*Jesus and Judaism*); see now Winter, "Saving the Quest for Authenticity from the Criterion of Dissimilarity." By 2012, Anthony Le Donne could write that "the criterion of double dissimilarity has all but fallen into obscurity": "The Criterion of Coherence," 108.

24. Sanders, *Paul in Palestinian Judaism*, 6, citing Moore, *Judaism in the First Centuries of the Christian Era*, 3:151.

an enthusiastic member of the Nazi Party after 1933; he participated as a scholar in the Reichsinstitut für Geschichte neuen Deutschlands after its founding in 1935, as a member of a research group on "the Jewish question." When, after the war, the Allies put him on trial for his activities as a Nazi, he protested in his self-defense that his scholarship had been purely scientific, and not dramatically different from the scholarship carried out by his peers in Great Britain or the United States.[25]

Kittel's defense was not just self-serving. From the sixteenth century onward, Protestants have relied on caricatures of *Jewish* legalism in their efforts to define themselves over against their depiction of *Roman Catholic* legalism. Figures like Jesus of Nazareth and the apostle Paul have been pressed into service as historical fulcrums, made to bear the weight of antagonistic theological formations.

If, looking back, we may appreciate how much has changed in the course of twentieth- and early-twenty-first-century New Testament scholarship, we should also bear in mind that *it took several decades* following World War II for questions about anti-Judaism to become a central academic preoccupation, notably following the publication of Rosemary Radford Ruether's bracing *Faith and Fratricide* in 1974. We should observe that the current represented in Ruether's work is not felt everywhere today with equal force. A deeper and more powerful theological undertow flows beneath much of Christian theology and practice, where the sanctity, completeness, and innocence of Christian scriptures and traditions are more usually presumed than interrogated.

That undertow should provoke caution regarding both the announced reversal of the "burden of proof" in historical argument and in its general application to "many or most" of the New Testament writings.

First, we should be leery of generalizations about "many or most" of the New Testament writings or about "the New Testament" as a bloc. The writings in our New Testament were variously composed in the late first or early second century, but clearly, none was intended to stand alongside others in what would, much later, be assembled as a sacred canon. Judgments regarding the original setting and purpose of any writing now found in the New Testament must be made on historical criteria, independent of judgments regarding other writings.

"Within Judaism" advocates note that an earlier scholarly view of the early and decisive "parting of the ways" between Judaism and Christianity

---

25. See Ericksen, "Theologian in the Third Reich"; on the *TDNT*, see Casey, "Some Anti-Semitic Assumptions."

has been successfully challenged.[26] They observe that we cannot conclusively document *Christianismos* or *Christianoi* as distinct social phenomena before the early second century.[27] But it does not follow that if we cannot attribute late-first-century writings to communities of self-conscious *Christians*, then we *must* attribute them to communities of *Jews*. That leap imagines only two possibilities—and these are categories derived from the Christian imagination of the second century.

Finally, generalizations about the character of "communities" that produced the Gospels (or other writings)—such as, for example, regarding the "Matthean" or "Lukan community"—bear scant weight. We simply do not know how, where, when, or by whom these writings were composed. All such judgments are necessarily inferential from the narratives themselves. Efforts to describe religious associations or other "communities that [wrote]" offer no corroboration to hypotheses that one or another Gospel represents the "theology" of one or another "church" or religious community, Jewish or otherwise.[28]

In short, the assertion that the burden of proof regarding the character of a writing now found in the New Testament should be shifted in favor of a context "within Judaism" seems premature. The implication that such judgment should be made before careful analysis of the argumentation or narrative and comparison with contemporary writings appears groundless. As Shelly Matthews has argued with regard to efforts to place Luke–Acts "within Judaism," it may be possible or *plausible* to imagine Jewish communities gathered in loyalty to Jesus, and embroiled in intra-Jewish controversy, late in the first century, as the context in which that narrative was composed. But historical judgment cannot prefer the *plausible* to the *probable*: in this case, that the Lucan narrative derives from the context it more clearly resembles, that of non-Jewish Christian circles in the early second

---

26. See Dunn, *The Parting of the Ways*; contra, Becker and Reed, eds., *The Ways That Never Parted*.

27. See Zetterholm, "The 'Within Judaism' Perspective," 10. Luke–Acts is routinely dated to the early second century; its reference to believers in Christ being first called "Christians" in Antioch (Acts 11:26) is likely a retrojection.

28. Richard Last's discussion of inscriptions authorized by religious and other associations ("Communities That Write") establishes that such practices happened. As refutation of Richard Bauckham's hypothesis regarding the Gospels being written for "the church" translocally (Bauckham, ed., *The Gospels for All Christians*), they seem superfluous; Bauckham's hypothesis is itself assertion in search of evidence. Last himself admits that "we do not know enough about the Christ-groups responsible for the gospels to label them defininitively as associations" (177)—or, indeed, to do more than *assert* that such "groups" were responsible for Gospel composition. His admission that "association writings are not generically analogous to the gospels" (178) appears fatal to the comparison he wishes to make.

century, for which we have ample direct evidence. The first option may be more congenial to an image of the Lukan narrative's origins as "innocent" of anti-Judaism, and that may be more appealing to Christian communities today. But the latter option frankly recognizes negative characterizations of Judaism, such as became the stuff of clearly self-defined *Christianismos*, early on.[29]

We may be tempted at this point to regard the work of history-making as determined by the interests of the contemporary collectives that carry it out. Indeed, in separate essays, James Crossley and Paula Fredriksen detect the limits imposed by conventional Christian theology in historical presentations that allow Jesus, or the apostle Paul, to be "Jewish, but not *too* Jewish."[30] Though such scholarship claims to contextualize these figures "within Judaism," they function rather to construe their subjects "within Protestantism," in ways congenial to its theological interests.[31]

The tension I describe continues to generate argument regarding how and to what extent early Christian figures and writings can be contextualized "within Judaism." While it is true, as Marxist historian Michel-Rolph Trouillot observed, that "collectivities" seek to gauge the credibility of "certain events and narratives" about the past "because it matters *to them* whether these events are true or false, whether these stories are fact or fiction,"[32] more is at stake in these debates than a contrast between competing tribes, "believing" scholars and their opposites, however these are identified—as "atheists," "humanists," "secularists," "modernists," "postmodernists," or as they might prefer to understand themselves, as objective historians.[33] Trouillot insisted that beyond the tension between "the mechanically 'realist'

---

29. I thank Professor Matthews for sharing a typescript of her response to papers on "Luke–Acts 'within Judaism'" in an Enoch Seminar session at the 2021 AAR/SBL Annual Meeting.

30. Crossley, "A 'Very Jewish' Jesus"; Fredriksen, "What Does It Mean to See Paul 'within Judaism'?"

31. Fredriksen ably traces the relative progress from earlier theological generalizations—Barth's or Käsemann's expostulations about the *homo religiosus* exemplified by the Jew (Barth, *Epistle to the Romans*; Käsemann, *Commentary on Romans*)—to the "New Perspective" of the 1980s, which opposed Paul to Jewish "ethnocentrism"; to what she christens "New Perspective 2.0," which seeks to affirm Paul's Judaism, but always within pointed limits or as its "fulfillment" or "transcendence" ("What Does It Mean to See Paul 'within Judaism'?" 361). She critiques, among others, Barclay, *Jews in the Mediterranean Diaspora*, 381–95, and Frey, "Paul's Jewish Identity." I offered similar criticisms in "The Question of Politics," chapter 9 in this volume.

32. Trouillot, *Silencing the Past*, 11.

33. A case in point is the recent debate sparked by Young, "Let's Take the Text Seriously"; Rowe's response, "What if It Were True?" and Crossley's counter-response, "On Kavin Rowe's Response to Stephen Young."

Qui Bono?

and naively 'constructivist' extremes" of doing history, "there is the more serious task of determining not what history is . . . but *how history works.*"[34]

HOW HISTORY WORKS

History "works," Trouillot observes, as the dialectic of power relations shapes what is included and excluded from its production. Because of this dialectic, "silences are inherent in history because any single event enters history with some of its constituent parts missing."[35] The generation of silences occurs, Trouillot argues, at "four crucial moments":

> the moment of fact creation (the making of *sources*); the moment of fact assembly (the making of *archives*); the moment of fact retrieval (the making of *narratives*); and the moment of retrospective significance (the making of *history* in the final instance).[36]

A full exposition of Trouillot's theory must awaits another occasion, along with its compatibility with Frederic Jameson's understanding of ideological closure and the repression of possibilities into "the political unconscious."[37] Here, I turn briefly to address the relevance of each of these four "moments" of historical production to our attempts to understand the New Testament writings "within Judaism." My treatment is admittedly a sketch, and focused on the Gospels, though as we shall see, a consideration of the apostle Paul according to Trouillot's approach is also important.

Silences in the Production of *Sources*

We may be so accustomed to thinking of the Gospels as primary sources of information about Jesus that it is difficult to recognize certain of their long-observed characteristics as "*erasures*" of historical fact. Consider an obvious and well-recognized intentional silence, the anonymity of all the Gospel authors. None of the Evangelists identifies himself, a place for himself within his own narrative, or (with the exception of the author of Luke) his temporal

---

34. Trouillot, *Silencing the Past*, 25; emphasis added.

35. Trouillot, *Silencing the Past*, 49. Trouillot's theorization is now amplified by Manjapra's compelling *Black Ghost of Empire*.

36. Trouillot, *Silencing the Past*, 26.

37. Jameson, *The Political Unconscious*. I address these questions in *Bodies of Christ: A Materialist Theology of the New Testament*, forthcoming.

connection to it;[38] and although the author of Luke declares his careful use of sources about the past, like a good Hellenistic historian (1:1–4), he never identifies these, or describes how he has used them. One consequence is that the ethnicity of any of these authors can only be inferred. Just as speculative is any hypothesis that a distinctive, yet anonymous Jewish-(Christian) *community* stood behind any of the Gospels (e.g., the "Johannine community"), since no such community is ever mentioned in any Gospel.[39] Thus, the hypothesis that any of the Gospels arose "within Judaism" will always depend on one or another interpreter's inferences from the content and perceived *Tendenz* of the narrative.

All four Evangelists rely on omniscient, rather than perspectival, narration, a technique that may generate in the reader a presumption of the narrative's self-sufficiency. It is all the more important, then, to note the absences of what we generally acknowledge as the profound events that shaped the Gospels. One weighty example is the peculiar disappearance of the enthusiastic crowd that surrounded Jesus as he entered Jerusalem in his last days, according to the Synoptics. We are not told how they were involved (if they were) in Jesus' action in the Temple, or how their motives in hailing Jesus as anointed deliverer related to his motives in that action (if they did), or whither the crowd went when Jesus and his disciples withdrew from the city afterward (if *they* did, as in Matthew and Mark). The Gospels do not describe how this crowd came to be replaced by the furious mob that appears before Pilate, calling for Jesus' death; or, if it is the *same* crowd, how their "wholesale defection" was brought about overnight—to use Paula Fredriksen's phrase for a plot development she has convincingly declared historically improbable.[40]

Fredriksen also notes that the Gospels' varying presentations of Pontius Pilate are "scarcely credible" as history. The procurator's actions as narrated would have constituted a breathtaking relinquishment of his imperial authority to a mob of those he was responsible to govern;

---

38. The "we-passages" in Acts are only an apparent exception to this generalization; the transition to first-person narration is abrupt and unexplained, and more probably a stylistic device than an autobiographical reference. The Fourth Gospel describes an eyewitness only at second hand, and anonymously (John 19:35; 21:24).

39. The previously mentioned Brown–Martyn hypothesis relied on correlating conjectured editorial layers in the Fourth Gospel with historical events read from the text of 1 John, for example. The authorial "we" at the end of the Gospel (John 21:24) is both unanticipated and anonymous.

40. Fredriksen, *From Jesus to Christ*, 116. See my essay "Jesus, the Crowds, and the Temple."

Qui Bono? 187

yet—incredibly—there is no record of any consequences for this reported dereliction of duty, other than the Gospel accounts of Jesus' death at the insistence of that mob.[41]

More to Trouillot's point: We learn from outside sources, especially Josephus, that subsequent decades brought a perilous escalation of Roman repression and convulsive popular uprisings against imperial rule in Judea, leading at last to a war in which Rome subdued Jerusalem and destroyed its Temple.[42] The Gospel authors were clearly familiar with these events, as, we may safely presume, were their readers. But *they narrate none of these facts*—preferring on occasion only to put mysteriously oblique predictions of coming "false prophets," or of "wars and rumors of wars," or of a "desolating sacrilege" on Jesus' lips. In various ways, it is a key purpose of all the Evangelists to portray the clearly intended, but never-mentioned events of 70 CE as direct consequences of the action taken *by the people of the city, and/or their leaders, against Jesus*, decades earlier.

This narrative fulcrum has long been at the center of debates over the *anti-Jewish* nature of one or another Gospel. More recently, it has been read as evidence that one or another Gospel arose "within Judaism"; that is, on the usual explanation, in one Jewish subgroup irreconcilably estranged from another, who has projected the characteristics of their enemies back onto Jesus' opponents as narrative foils. But again, no direct mention of such communal tensions ever appears in any Gospel; nor does any connecting narrative, however slight, ever bridge the decades-long gap between Jesus' death and the events of 70.[43]

There is little doubt that the creation of silences around these matters, and the shift of blame for Jesus' death to some ruling elite among the Jews and/or "the people of the city" as their pawns, were "very important theologically and politically" to the interests served by the Gospels. These erasures are also readily understood as "protective camouflage vis-à-vis Rome."[44] They are, then, immediately intelligible as the effects of power relations on the production of history.

41. Fredriksen, *From Jesus to Christ*, 120.

42. Josephus was also a biased and tendentious source, of course—and an effective one: his posing of a monolithic "Fourth Philosophy" as an inauthentic expression of Judaism remains persuasive in much New Testament scholarship today. See Horsley and Hanson, *Bandits, Prophets, and Messiahs*, and on the decades leading up to the revolt of 66 CE, Goodman, *The Ruling Class of Judaea*.

43. Luke-Acts is the only Gospel to extend a narrative beyond the appearances of the risen Jesus—yet even here the attention shifts decisively *away* from events in Jerusalem as its fate draws near.

44. Fredriksen, *From Jesus to Christ*, 120. Fredriksen does not think "protective camouflage" on the Evangelists' part suffices to explain the absence of direct evidence

The point is important. Whether or not any of us can elaborate a plausible explanation "within Judaism" for a Gospel's tendentious narrative of the past, we must recognize that *every Gospel narrative has obscured or erased actual Jewish experience of Roman rule*, from the time of Jesus' contemporaries through the tumultuous decades leading to the catastrophe of 70, and up to the time of its own composition. It is not too much to say that the production of such silences, and the deflection of the readers' attention to a plot centered on Jesus himself, is central to the purpose of the Gospels.

The Production of Silences in *Archives*

We may move more swiftly through the other "moments" Trouillot identifies. The long history of pious Christian appeals to the legitimacy and authority of the Gospels as sources for the life and significance of Jesus has made them into "archives" of Christian faith. Even in critical scholarship, we meet variations on the theme that the Gospels were composed *in order to assemble a factual record* (in Trouillot's phrase, an *archive*)—as the result of Jesus' own insistence that his disciples learn his teachings by heart, on the model of rabbinic schools;[45] or to ensure a Jesus tradition as the generation of eyewitnesses began to die off;[46] or as expressions of a widely perceived "gospel imperative" that the memory of Jesus be responsibly adapted to ever-new situations.[47] Such suggestions are obviously congenial to Christian theological interests, embedding Gospel production itself within the bosom of the watchful, more or less Jewish community of the Christ-believing faithful. They remain hypotheses, nonetheless, *without any explicit basis in the Gospels themselves*.[48]

An alternative explanation, based in actual historical comparison—such as Robyn Faith Walsh's argument that the Gospel narratives were composed by members of a tiny class of literate individuals, as much to entertain as to inform other members of that class—serves as something of a null hypothesis, satisfactorily explaining important aspects of the Gospels without requiring invisible communities of the pious to warrant their

---

Jesus that was a political agitator; but her argument overall clearly demonstrates that such camouflage *was* a prominent feature of the Gospels.

45. Gerhardsson, *Memory and Manuscript*.
46. Nickle, *The Synoptic Gospels*.
47. Watson, *Gospel Writing*.
48. One apparent exception, John 20:31, vaguely explains a motive for *excluding* information about Jesus, proving the rule.

authenticity.[49] Further, Paula Fredriksen and Oded Irshai remind us that such literary figures, particularly non-Jewish thinkers writing in the aftermath of the Judean War, played a prominent role in producing much of the earliest Christian literature.[50] It is appropriate, of course, even on these views to speak, in Trouillot's term, of "collectivities" around the Gospel narratives, but less as communities of pious vigilance guaranteeing a past deposit of the faith than as loose aggregates of curious readers in the narrators' present, with particular questions about events and figures at a chronological and geographic distance from themselves.

The transmission and reception of Gospels as "archives" was clearly the result of intentional processes. Just as clearly, these processes gave an aura of authenticity to the silences already created in the Gospels as sources.

Silences in the Production of *Narratives*

Under this term, Trouillot draws attention to the moments in which the past is "retrieved" in narration. He means more than what biblical scholars call "reception history." Trouillot draws attention to the regular, selective, highly affective, and often ceremonial deployments of ancient sources and archives in order to constitute communities in the present. Here it should suffice to point again to the prevalent context in which "within Judaism" scholarship is routinely deployed today, Sunday morning homilies and liturgies in Catholic and mainline Protestant churches. In my own experience as a priest in the Episcopal Church, this "moment" involves various techniques for reducing or softening the apparently anti-Jewish aspects of Gospel texts, for example during Holy Week, *while still reciting these Gospel texts as sacred and authoritative.*

The Production of Silences in *the Making of History*

Trouillot aims in this last "moment" at the work of professional interpreters. We "within Judaism" scholars may protest that our interpretive work is governed by standards of objectivity, at some remove from the liturgical contexts I've just named. At that moment, Trouillot observes that "the professionalization of the discipline" of history "is premised" on an imagined

---

49. Walsh, *The Origins of Early Christian Literature*. Walsh's fruitful work also deserves far greater discussion than is possible here.

50. Fredriksen and Irshai, "Christian Anti-Judaism."

distinction between active involvement in the flux of history and its dispassionate interpretation, between *agents* and *narrators*.[51]

Trouillot's theorization poses a challenge to our work. Do we, under the guise of neutral historiography, perpetuate the silences created in the production of the New Testament sources, their transformation into archives, and their ritual recitations in Christian worship? Do our explanations serve further to *enclose* ancient Judaism, *as the Gospels enclose it*, as a set of false expectations that led to a general rejection of Jesus on the part of most Jews—except for the bright exceptions who were the ancestors of Christians today? Does our work serve to acquit the Gospel narratives of anti-Judaism, even as they deflect attention and sympathy from the trauma of 70 CE?

A second direction takes seriously what Paula Fredriksen has called the "dynamic of expectation and disappointment" that decisively shaped belief in Jesus as messiah after his death, and determined the character of all the New Testament writings, even as the tradition about Jesus "grew away from its own past" within Judaism.[52] Fredriksen aptly describes Paul and his Christ-believing contemporaries as plunged into "a kind of eschatological twilight zone" already in the 40s, as disconfirming facts accumulated around them.[53] Under the growing pressure of historical reality—"the nonresponse of Israel, the reception of the Gentiles, the delay of the End"—that "twilight zone" gave way, not to the dawn of the messianic age, but to the "failure" of the movement's "central prophecy."[54] Placing the New Testament writings "within Judaism" requires explicating this fundamental failure, and the strategies to deflect attention from it, *as the hallmark of those writings*.

This perspective may seem to some antagonistic, even corrosive of Christian theology.[55] But it augurs an end of the Christian theological task only if that task is conceived as participating in and extending the silencing of history begun with the New Testament sources. An alternative theology—one enriched by the perspective of Marxist theory—recognizes precisely the crushing of messianic hopes by imperial power as a familiar enough pattern

---

51. Trouillot, *Silencing the Past*, 5.
52. Fredriksen, *From Jesus to Christ*, 135.
53. Fredriksen, *From Jesus to Christ*, 167.
54. Fredriksen, *From Jesus to Christ*, 135.

55. I recall, early in my faculty career, hearing New Testament colleagues express admiration for Fredriksen's *From Jesus to Christ* but insist, regretfully, that they could never use it in their introductory courses: "it would require too much damage control," they agreed. I presumed they meant it would raise disturbing questions in the minds of their Christian students, something I took as a vocational obligation.

in human history, and chooses solidarity with the vanquished, past and present, as its fixed point.

In our day, taking seriously the vast and increasing material disparities generated in "the killing fields of inequality"[56] is the challenge before any responsible theology, and especially any claiming the title "theology of liberation."[57] As Ivan Petrella observes, however, progressive theologies have too often drawn back from serious engagement with the creation, under neoliberalism, of "zones of social abandonment" and have contented themselves with liberal agendas of social inclusion. There is, I contend, a symmetry between that withdrawal and the tendency in recent Christian efforts toward a "post-supersessionist" theology that endorses recognition and acceptance of Judaism and Jews without rethinking "core Christological convictions."[58] To the extent such "convictions" include the fundamentally Jewish vocabulary concerning the *Christ*, that is, *Messiah*, Christian theology must grapple with the two-thousand-year failure of the messianic age, a failure for which "delay" seems a tendentious euphemism.

The *unrealized* horizon of messianic hope continues to haunt Christianity. It is of vital importance, then, not only to the task of history but to Christian theology itself, that we not allow "within Judaism" scholarship to close around the interpretive narratives suggested by the Gospels themselves. Rather, we must ever open up that scholarly perspective to the widest possible sociohistorical horizon and to a broad and deep human solidarity. In our days, the affirmation that another world is possible, indeed, necessary, is made beyond the reach of neoliberalism's ideology of necessity and inevitability, in global movements against it.[59] Fixing our eyes on *that* horizon may allow a genuine understanding of the hopes arising "within Judaism," in the ancient world as now, and beyond it; hopes for a genuine partnership in *tikkun 'olam*, the work of repairing the world we share.

56. Therborn, *The Killing Fields of Inequality*.

57. Petrella, *Beyond Liberation Theology*. I take up this agenda in Elliott, *Bodies of the Christ*, forthcoming.

58. For example, the Society for Post-Supersessionist Theology, founded in 2018, affirms "God's irrevocable covenant with the Jewish people," while also promoting "perspectives that remain faithful to core Christological convictions" and affirming "the ecclesia's identity as a table fellowship of Jews and Gentiles united in the Messiah" (see https://www.spostst.org). The Society's 2021 webinar, titled "Catholic Doctrines on the Jewish People after Vatican II," featured Gavin D'Costa's discussion of "Hebrew Catholics" as evidence of the church's fundamental innocence of anti-Judaism; see https://www.youtube.com/watch?v=A983VddpnFM.

59. These are the slogans of the World Social Forum, first organized in 2001 as an alternative to the World Economic Forum: see wsforum.net. On the compulsory illusion of capitalism's inevitability see Fisher, *Capitalist Realism*.

Bibliography

Ahmad, Eqbal, et al. *Terrorism, Theirs and Ours*. Open Media Pamphlet Series. New York: Seven Stories, 2001.

Alcock, Susan E. *Graecia Capta: The Landscapes of Roman Greece*. Cambridge: Cambridge University Press, 1993.

Ando, Clifford. *Imperial Ideology and Provincial Loyalty in the Roman Empire*. Classics and Contemporary Thought 6. Berkeley: University of California Press, 2000.

Ashton, John. *The Religion of Paul the Apostle*. New Haven: Yale University Press, 2000.

Auget, Roland. *Cruelty and Civilization: The Roman Games*. London: Allen & Unwin, 1972.

Aune, David E. *The New Testament in Its Literary Environment*. Library of Early Christianity 8. Philadelphia: Westminster, 1987.

Badiou, Alain. *Saint Paul: The Foundation of Universalism*. Translated by Ray Brassier. Cultural Memory in the Present. Stanford: Stanford University Press, 2003.

Barclay, John M. G. "'Do We Undermine the Law?' A Study of Romans 14:1—15:6." In *Paul and the Mosaic Law*, edited by James D. G. Dunn, 287–308. WUNT 89. Tübingen: Mohr Siebeck, 1996.

———. *Jews in the Mediterranean Diaspora: From Alexander to Trajan (332 BC—117 AD)*. Berkeley: University of California Press, 1996.

———. "'Neither Jew nor Greek': Multiculturalism and the New Perspective on Paul." In *Ethnicity and the Bible*, edited by Mark G. Brett, 197–214. BibInt 19. Leiden: Brill, 1996.

———. *Obeying the Truth: Paul's Ethics in Galatians*. Edinburgh: T. & T. Clark, 1988.

———. *Pauline Churches and Diaspora Jews*. WUNT 275. Tübingen: Mohr Siebeck, 2011.

———. "Why the Roman Empire Was Insignificant to Paul." Draft of a paper given in 2007 at the Society of Biblical Literature Annual Meeting. Subsequently published in revised form in Barclay, *Pauline Churches and Diaspora Jews*, 363–87.

Barrett, C. K. "Cephas and Corinth." In *Abraham unser Vater: Juden und Christen im Gespräch über die Bibel. Festschrift für Otto Michel zum 60. Geburtstag*, edited by Otto Betz, 1–12. Arbeiten zur Geschichte des Spätjudentums und Urchristentums 5. Leiden: Brill, 1963.

Bartchy, S. Scott. *Mallon Chrēsai: First-Century Slavery and the Interpretation of 1 Corinthians 7:21*. SBL Dissertation Series 11. 1973. Reprint, Eugene, OR: Wipf & Stock, 2003.

Barth, Karl. *The Epistle to the Romans.* 2nd ed. English ed. Translated from the 6th German edited by Edwyn C. Hoskyns. London: Oxford University Press, 1933.

Bassler, Jouette M., ed. *Pauline Theology I: Thessalonians, Philippians, Galatians, Philemon.* Minneapolis: Fortress, 1991.

Bauckham, Richard, ed. *The Gospels for All Christians: Rethinking the Gospel Audiences.* Grand Rapids: Eerdmans, 1998.

Baur, Ferdinand Christian. *Paul, the Apostle of Jesus Christ.* Edited by Peter C. Hodgson. Translated by Robert F. Brown. Eugene, OR: Cascade Books, 2021.

Becker, Adam H., and Annette Yoshiko Reed, eds. *The Ways That Never Parted: Jews and Christians in Late Antiquity and the Early Middle Ages.* Texte und Studien zum Antike Judentum 95. 2003. Reprint, Minneapolis: Fortress, 2007.

Beker, J. Christiaan. "The Faithfulness of God and the Priority of Israel in Paul's Letter to the Romans." *Harvard Theological Review* 79 (1986) 10–16.

———. *Paul the Apostle: The Triumph of God in Life and Thought.* Philadelphia: Fortress, 1980.

———. *The Triumph of God: The Essence of Paul's Thought.* Minneapolis: Fortress, 1990.

Betz, Hans Dieter. "Christianity as Religion: Paul's Attempt at Definition in Romans." *Journal of Religion* 71 (1991) 315–44. Republished in Betz, *Paulinische Studien*, 206–39. Tübingen: Mohr Siebeck, 1994.

———. *Galatians: A Commentary on Paul's Letter to the Churches in Galatia.* Hermeneia. Philadelphia: Fortress, 1979.

———. "The Literary Composition and Function of Paul's Letter to the Galatians." In *The Galatians Debate: Contemporary Issues in Rhetorical and Historical Interpretation*, edited by Mark D. Nanos, 3–28. Peabody, MA: Hendrickson, 2002.

Bhabha, Homi. *The Location of Culture.* London: Routledge, 1994.

Bitzer, L. F. "The Rhetorical Situation." *Philsophy & Rhetoric* 1 (1968) 1–14.

Blum, William. *Killing Hope: U.S. Military and CIA Interventions since World War II.* 2nd ed. Monroe, ME: Common Courage, 2004.

Blumenfeld, Bruno. *The Political Paul: Justice, Democracy, and Kingship in a Hellenistic Framework.* JSNTSup 210. Sheffield: Sheffield Academic, 2001.

Boccaccini, Gabrielle, and Carlos Segovia, eds. *Paul the Jew: Rereading the Apostle as a Figure of Second Temple Judaism.* Minneapolis: Fortress, 2016.

Boer, Martinus C. de. "Paul's Mythologizing Program in Romans 5–8." In *Apocalyptic Paul: Cosmos and Anthropos in Romans 5–8*, edited by Beverly Roberts Gaventa, 1–20. Waco, TX: Baylor University Press, 2013.

Boer, Roland. *Marxist Criticism of the Bible.* London: T. & T. Clark, 2003.

Bornkamm, Günther. *Paul.* Translated by D. M. G. Stalker. New York: Harper & Row, 1971.

Boswell, John. *Christianity, Social Tolerance, and Homosexuality: Gay People in Western Europe from the Beginning of the Christian Era to the Fourteenth Century.* Chicago: University of Chicago Press, 1981.

Botha, Peiter J. J. "Verbal Art of the Pauline Letters: Rhetoric, Performance, and Presence." In Rhetoric and the New Testament, edited by Stanley E. Porter and H. Thomas, 409–28. JSNTSup 90. Sheffield: Sheffield Academic, 1993.

Bowersock, Glen W. "Imperial Cult: Perceptions and Persistence." In *Jewish and Christian Self-Definition*, vol. 3: *Self-Definition in the Graeco-Roman World*, edited by Ben F. Meyer and E. P. Sanders, 171–82. Philadelphia: Fortress, 1980.

Bibliography

Boyarin, Daniel. *A Radical Jew: Paul and the Politics of Identity*. Berkeley: University of California Press, 1994.
Brown, Raymond E. *The Community of the Beloved Disciple*. New York: Paulist, 1979.
Brown, Robert McAfee, ed. *Kairos: Three Prophetic Challenges to the Church*. Grand Rapids: Eerdmans, 1990.
Brunt, P. A. "Laus Imperii." In *Roman Imperial Themes*, 288–323. Oxford: Clarendon, 1990.
———. *Roman Imperial Themes*. Oxford: Clarendon, 1990.
Bryan, Christopher. *Render to Caesar: Jesus, the Early Church, and the Roman Superpower*. Oxford: Oxford University Press, 2005.
Bultmann, Rudolf. *History of the Synoptic Tradition*. Translated by John Marsh. New York: Harper & Row, 1963.
———. *Theology of the New Testament*. 2 vols. Translated by Kendrick Grobel. New York: Scribner, 1951, 1954.
Burk, Denny. "Is Paul's Gospel Counterimperial? Evaluating the Prospects of the 'Fresh Perspective' for Evangelical Theology." *Journal of the Evangelical Theological Society* 51 (2008) 309–37.
Câmara, Dom Hélder. *Spiral of Violence*. Translated by Della Couling. Sheed & Ward Stagbooks. London: Sheed & Ward, 1971.
Campbell, William S. *Paul's Gospel in an Intercultural Context: Jew and Gentile in the Letter to the Romans*. Studies in the Intercultural History of Christianity 69. Frankfurt: Lang, 1992.
———. "Revisiting Romans." *Scripture Bulletin* 12 (1981) 2–10.
———. "The Rule of Faith in Romans 12:1—15:13: The Obligation of Humble Obedience to Christ as the Only Adequate Response to the Mercies of God." In *Pauline Theology III: Romans*, edited by David M. Hay and E. Elizabeth Johnson, 259–86. Minneapolis: Fortress, 1993.
———. "Why Did Paul Write Romans?" *Expository Times* 85 (1973/74) 264–69.
Carey, Greg. "Introduction and a Proposal: Culture, Power, and Identity in White New Testament Studies." In *Soundings in Cultural Criticism: Perspectives and Methods in Culture, Power, and Identity in the New Testament*, edited by Francisco Lozada and Greg Carey, 1–14. Soundings. Minneapolis: Fortress, 2013.
Carter, Warren. *The Roman Empire and the New Testament: An Essential Guide*. Abingdon Essential Guides. Nashville: Abingdon, 2006.
Casey, Maurice. "Some Anti-Semitic Assumptions in the *Theological Dictionary of the New Testament*." *NovT* 41 (1999) 280–91.
Castelli, Elizabeth A. *Imitating Paul: A Discourse of Power*. Louisville: Westminster John Knox, 1991.
———. "Interpretations of Power in 1 Corinthians." *Semeia* 54 (1991) 197–222.
Cavanaugh, William. *Torture and Eucharist*. Oxford: Blackwell, 1998.
Chancey, Mark. Foreword to E. P. Sanders, *Paul and Palestinian Judaism: Fortieth-Anniversary Edition*. Minneapolis: Fortress, 2017.
Charles, Ronald. *Paul and the Politics of Diaspora*. Paul in Critical Contexts. Minneapolis: Fortress, 2014.
Chomsky, Noam. *Deterring Democracy*. New York: Verso, 1994.
———. *Pirates and Emperors, Old and New: International Terrorism in the Real World*. New ed. London: Pluto, 2002.

Chow, John K. *Patronage and Power: A Study of Social Networks in Corinth*. JSNTSup 75. Sheffield: JSOT Press, 1992.

Classen, Carl Joachim. "St. Paul's Epistles and Ancient Greek and Roman Rhetoric." In *The Galatians Debate: Contemporary Issues in Rhetorical and Historical Interpretation*, edited by Mark D. Nanos, 95–113. Peabody, MA: Hendrickson, 2002.

Cohen, Shaye J. D.. *The Beginnings of Jewishness: Boundaries, Varieties, Uncertainties*. Hellenic Culture and Society 31. Berkeley: University of California Press, 1999.

Collins, Adela Yarbro, ed. *Early Christian Apocalypticism. Semeia* 36 (1986).

Collins, John J. *The Apocalyptic Imagination: An Introduction to the Jewish Matrix of Christianity*. New York: Crossroad, 1984.

———. *Scriptures and Sectarianism*. WUNT 332. Tübingen: Mohr Siebeck, 2014.

Colpe, Carsten. *Die religionsgeschichtliche Schule: Darstellung und Kritik ihres Bildes vom gnostischen Erlösermythus*. Forsuchungen zur Religon und Literatur des Alten und Neuen Testaments n.F. 60. Göttingen: Vandenhoeck & Ruprecht, 1961.

Colson, F. H., and G. H. Whitaker, trans. *Philo. Vol. 5: On Flight and Finding; On the change of Names; On Dreams*. Loeb Classical Library. New York: Putnam, 1934.

Consigny, Scott. "Rhetoric and Its Situations." *Philosophy & Rhetoric* 7 (1984) 175–86.

Conzelmann, Hans. *1 Corinthians: A Commentary on the First Epistle to the Corinthians*. Translated by James W. Leitch. Edited by George W. MacRae. Hermeneia. Philadelphia: Fortress, 1975.

Corradi, Juan E. et al., eds., *Fear at the Edge: State Terror and Resistance in Latin America*. Berkeley: University of California Press, 1992.

Countryman, William. *Dirt, Greed & Sex: Sexual Ethics in the New Testament and Thier Implications for Today*. Minneapolis: Fortress, 2007.

Cousar, Charles B. *A Theology of the Cross: The Death of Jesus in the Pauline Letters*. Overtures to Biblical Theology. Minneapolis: Fortress, 1990.

Crawford, M. H. "Greek Intellectuals and the Roman Aristocracy." In *Imperialism in the Ancient World: The Cambridge University Research Seminar in Ancient History*, edited by P. D. A. Garnsey and C. R. Whittaker, 193–208. Cambridge Classical Studies. Cambridge: Cambridge University Press, 1978.

Crossan, John Dominic. *The Historical Jesus: The Life of a Mediterranean Jewish Peasant*. San Francisco: Harper, 1998.

Crossley, James G. "A 'Very Jewish' Jesus: Perpetuating the Myth of Superiority." *Journal for the Study of the Historical Jesus* 11 (2013) 109–29.

Dahl, Nils Alstrup. "Anamnesis: Memory and Commemoration in the Early Church." In *Jesus in the Memory of the Early Church*. Minneapolis: Augsburg, 1976.

———. "The Future of Israel." In *Studies in Paul: Theology for the Early Christian Mission*, 137–58. 1977. Reprint, Eugene, OR: Wipf & Stock, 2002.

———. "Missionary Theology in the Epistle to the Romans." In *Studies in Paul: Theology for the Early Christian Mission*, 70–94. 1977. Reprint, Eugene, OR: Wipf & Stock, 2002.

———. "Romans 3.9: Text and Meaning." In *Paul and Paulinism: Essays in Honour of C. K. Barrett*, edited by Morna Hooker and Stephen G. Wilson, 184–204. London: SPCK, 1982.

———. *Studies in Paul: Theology for the Early Christian Mission*. 1977. Reprint, Eugene, OR: Wipf & Stock, 2002.

Danker, Frederick W. *Benefactor: Epigraphic Study of a Graeco-Roman and New Testament Semantic Field*. St. Louis: Clayton, 1982.

Das, A. Andrew. *Paul and the Stories of Israel: Grand Thematic Narratives in Galatians.* Minneapolis: Fortress, 2016.

———. *Solving the Romans Debate.* Minneapolis: Fortress, 2007.

Deidun, Thomas. "James Dunn and John Ziesler on Romans in New Perspective." *Heythrop Journal* 33 (1992) 79–94.

Deissmann, Adolf. *Licht vom Osten: Das neuen Testament und die neuentdeckten Texte der römischen-hellenistischen Welt.* Tübingen: Mohr, 1908. 4th ed., 1923. ET *Light from the Ancient East.* Translated by L. M. R. Strachan. London: Hodder and Stoughton, 1910. Reprint, Eugene, OR: Wipf & Stock, 2004.

de Lange, Nicolas. "Jewish Attitudes to the Roman Empire." In *Imperialism in the Ancient World: The Cambridge University Research Seminar in Ancient History,* edited by P. D. A. Garnsey and C. R. Whittaker, 255–81. Cambridge Classical Studies. Cambridge: Cambridge University Press, 1978.

Dettwiler, Andreas, Jean-Daniel Kaestli, and Daniel Marguerat, eds. *Paul, une théologie en construction.* Monde de la Bible 51. Geneva: Labor et Fides, 2004.

Dewey, Arthur J. "A Re-Hearing of Romans 10:1–15." *Semeia* 65 (1994) 109–27.

Dewey, Joanna. "Textuality in an Oral Culture: A Survey of the Pauline Traditions." *Semeia* 65 (1994) 37–65.

Donfried, Karl P. "The Cults of Thessalonica and the Thessalonian Correspondence." *NTS* 31 (1985) 336–56.

———, ed. *The Romans Debate.* Rev. and exp. ed. Peabody, MA: Hendrickson, 1991.

Donfried, Karl P., and Peter Richardson, eds. *Judaism and Christianity in First-Century Rome.* Grand Rapids: Eerdmans, 1998.

Doty, William G. *Letters in Primitive Christianity.* Guides to Biblical Scholarship: New Testament Series. 1971. Reprint, Eugene, OR: Wipf & Stock, 2014.

Downing, F. Gerald. *Cynics, Paul, and the Pauline Churches: Cynics and Christian Origins II.* London: Routledge, 1998.

DuBois, Page. *Torture and Truth.* New York: Routledge, 1990.

Duff, J. Wright, and Arnold M. Duff, trans. *Minor Latin Poets.* Loeb Classical Library. Cambridge: Harvard Univeristy Press, 1934.

Duff, Paul Brooks. "Apostolic Suffering and the Language of Processions in 2 Corinthians 4:7–10." *Biblical Theology Bulletin* 21 (1991) 158–65.

———. "Metaphor, Motif, and Meaning: The Rhetorical Strategy behind the Image 'Led in Triumph' in 2 Corinthians 2:14" *Catholic Biblical Quarterly* 53 (1991) 79–92.

Dunn, James D. G. *Jesus, Paul, and the Law: Studies in Mark and Galatians.* London: SPCK, 1990.

———. "The New Perspective on Paul." *Bulletin of the John Rylands Library* 65 (1983) 95–122.

———. *Romans.* 2 vols. Word Biblical Commentary 38A, 38B. Dallas: Word, 1988.

———. "Romans 13:1–7—A Charter for Political Quietism?" *Ex Auditu* 2 (1986) 55–68.

———. *The Parting of the Ways: Between Christianity and Judaism and Their Significance for the Character of Christianity.* London: SCM, 1991; 2nd ed. 2006.

———, ed. *Paul and the Mosaic Law.* WUNT 89. Tübingen: Mohr Siebeck, 1996.

———. *The Theology of Paul the Apostle.* Grand Rapids: Eerdmans, 1998.

Edwards, Douglas R. *Religion and Power: Pagans, Jews, and Christians in the Greek East.* New York: Oxford University Press, 1996.

Ehrensperger, Kathy, and J. Brian Tucker, eds. *Reading Paul in Context: Explorations in Identity Formation: Essays in Honour of William S. Campbell.* LNTS 428. London: T. & T. Clark, 2010.

Ehrman, Bart D. *The New Testament: A Historical Introduction to the Early Christian Writings.* 7th ed. New York: Oxford University Press, 2020.

Eisenbaum, Pamela. "Paul, Polemics, and the Problem of Esssentialism." *Biblical Interpretation* 13 (2005) 224–38.

———. *Paul Was not a Christian: The Original Message of a Misunderstood Apostle.* New York: HarperOne, 2009.

Elliott, Neil. "The Apostle Paul's Self-Presentation as Anti-Imperial Performance." In *Paul and the Roman Imperial Order*, edited by Richard A. Horsley, 67–88. Harrisburg, PA: Trinity, 2004.

———. *The Arrogance of Nations: Reading Romans in the Shadow of Empire.* Paul in Critical Contexts. Minneapolis: Fortress, 2008.

———. *Bodies of Christ: A Materialist Theology of the New Testament.* Forthcoming.

———. *Currents in the Interpretation of Paul: Collected Essays.* Eugene, OR: Cascade Books, 2024.

———. "Figure and Ground in the Interpretation of Romans 9–11." In *The Theological Interpretation of Scripture: Classic and Contemporary Readings*, edited by Stephen E. Fowl, 371–89. Blackwell Readings in Modern Theology. Oxford: Blackwell, 1997.

———. "Jesus, the Crowds, and the Temple: A Way Less Traveled." In *The New Testament and Class Struggle*, edited by Robert Myles, 15–52. Lanham, MD: Lexington Books/Fortress Academic, 2018.

———. *Liberating Paul: The Justice of God and the Politics of the Apostle.* 1994. Reprint, Minneapolis: Fortress, 2006.

———. *Paul against the Nations: Soundings in Romans.* Eugene, OR: Cascade Books, 2023.

———. *The Rhetoric of Romans: Argumentative Constraint and Strategy and Paul's Dialogue with Judaism.* JSNTSup 45. Sheffield: JSOT Press, 1990.

———. "Romans 13:1–7 in the Context of Imperial Propaganda." In *Paul and Empire: Religion and Power in Roman Imperial Society*, edited Richard A. Horsley, 184–204. Harrisburg, PA: Trinity, 1997.

Elliott, Neil, and Werner Kelber, eds. *Bridges in New Testament Interpretation: Interdisciplinary Advances.* Lanham, MD: Lexington Books/Fortress Academic, 2018.

Elliott, Neil, and Mark Reasoner. *Documents and Images for the Study of Paul.* Minneapolis: Fortress, 2010.

Engberg-Pedersen, Troels. *Paul and the Stoics.* Edinburgh: T. & T. Clark, 2000.

———, ed. *Paul beyond the Judaism/Hellenism Divide.* Louisville: Westminster John Knox, 2001.

———, ed. *Paul in His Hellenistic Context.* Minneapolis: Fortress, 1995.

Ericksen, Robert P. "Theologian in the Third Reich: The Case of Gerhard Kittel." *Journal of Contemporary History* 12 (1977) 595–622.

Esler, Philip F. *Conflict and Identity in Romans: The Social Setting of Paul's Letter.* Minneapolis: Fortress, 2003.

———. *Galatians.* New Testament Readings. London: Routledge, 1998.

Faludi, Susan. *Backlash: The Undeclared War against American Women.* New York: Anchor, 1992.

Bibliography

Fanon, Frantz. *Wretched of the Earth*. Translated by Constance Farrington. 1963. Reprint, New York: Grove, 2004.
Findlay, G. G. "St. Paul's Use of *Thriambeuo*." *Expositor* 10 (1879) 403–21.
Fisher, Mark. *Capitalist Realism: Is There No Alternative?* Washington, DC: Zero Books, 2009.
Fitzgerald, John T. *Cracks in an Earthen Vessel: An Examination of the Catalogues of Hardships in the Corinthian Correspondence*. SBL Dissertation Series 99. Chico: SBL, 1988.
Fitzmyer, Joseph A. *Paul and His Theology: A Brief Sketch*. Englewood Cliffs, NJ: Prentice Hall, 1989.
Fredriksen, Paula. "Did Jesus Oppose the Purity Laws?" *Bible Review* (June 1995) 19–25, 42–47.
———. *From Jesus to Christ: The Origins of the New Testament Images of Jesus*. New Haven: Yale University Press, 1988.
———. "Judaism, the Circumcision of Gentiles, and Apocalyptic Hope: Another Look at Galatians 1 and 2." *Journal of Theological Studies* 42 (1991) 533–64.
———. "What Does It Mean to See Paul 'within Judaism'?" *JBL* 141 (2022) 359–80.
———. "What You See Is What You Get: Context and Content in Current Research on the Historical Jesus." *Theology Today* 52 (1995) 75–97.
Fredriksen, Paula, and Oded Irshai. "Christian Anti-Judaism: Polemics and Policies, from the Second to the Seventh Century." In *The Cambridge History of Judaism*, Vol. 4: *The Late Roman-Rabbinic Period*, edited by Steven T. Katz, 977–1034. Cambridge: Cambridge University Press, 2008.
Frey, Jörg. "Paul's Jewish Identity." In *Jewish Identity in the Greco-Roman World*, edited by Jörg Frey et al., 285–321. Ancient Judaism and Early Christianity 71. Leiden: Brill, 2007.
Friedrich, Gerhard. "εὐαγγελίζεσθαι." In *TDNT* 2 (1964) 707–37.
Friesen, Steven J. "The Blessings of Hegemony: Poverty, Paul's Assemblies, and the Class Interests of the Professoriate." In *The Bible in the Public Square*, edited by Cynthia Briggs Kittredge et al. 117–28. Minneapolis: Fortress, 2008.
———. "Poverty in Pauline Studies: Beyond the So Called New Consensus." *JSNT* 26 (2004) 323–61.
Fruhling, Hugo. "Resistance to Fear in Chile: The Experience of the Vicaría de la Solidaridad." In *Fear at the Edge: State Terror and Resistance in Latin America*, edited by Juan E. Corradi et al., 121–41. Berkeley: University of California Press, 1992.
Funk, Robert W. "Apostolic Parousia: Form and Significance." In *Christian History and Interpretation: Studies Presented to John Knox*, edited by William Farmer et al., 249–68. Cambridge: Cambridge University Press, 1967.
Furnish, Victor Paul. *The Moral Teaching of Paul*. Nashville: Abingdon, 1979.
———. *II Corinthians*. Anchor Bible 32A. Garden City, NY: Doubleday, 1984.
———. *Theology and Ethics in Paul*. Nashville: Abingdon, 1968.
Gaca, Kathy L. *The Making of Fornication: Eros, Ethics, and Political Reform in Greek Philosophy and Early Christianity*. Hellenistic Culture and Society 40. Berkeley: University of California Press, 2003.
Gager, John G. *Kingdom and Community: The Social World of Early Christianity*. Prentice-Hall Studies in Religion Series. Englewood Cliffs, NJ: Prentice-Hall, 1975.

———. *The Origins of Anti-Semitism: Attitudes toward Judaism in Pagan and Christian Antiquity*. New York: Oxford University Press, 1983.
Galinsky, Karl. *Augustan Culture*. Princeton: Princeton University Press, 1998.
Gaston, Lloyd. *Paul and the Torah*. Vancouver: University of British Columbia Press, 1987.
Geertz, Clifford. *The Interpretation of Culutres*. New York: Basic Books, 1973.
George, Alexander, ed. *Western State Terrorism*. New York: Routledge, 1991.
Georgi, Dieter. *Die Geschichte der Kollekte des Paulus für Jerusalem*. Hamburg-Bergstet: Reich, 1965.
———. "Gott auf den Kopf stellen." In *Theokratie*, ed. Jacob Taubes. Paderborn: Schöning, 1987. ET *Theocracy in Paul's Praxis and Theology*.
———. *Theocracy in Paul's Praxis and Theology*. Translated by David Green. Minneapolis: Fortress, 1991.
Gerhardsson, Birger. *Memory and Manuscript: Oral Tradition and Written ransmission in Rabbinic Judaism and Early Christianity; with Tradition and Transmission in Early Christianity*. Grand Rapids: Eerdmans, 1998.
Goodenough, E. R. *An Introduction to Philo Judaeus*. 2nd ed. Oxford: Blackwell, 1962.
Goodman, Martin. *The Ruling Class of Judaea: The Origins of the Jewish Revolt against Rome, A.D. 66–70*. Cambridge: Cambridge University Press, 1987.
Gordon, Richard. "Veil of Power: Emperors, Sacrificers and Benefactors." In *Pagan Priests: Religion and Power in the Ancient World*, edited by Mary Beard and John North, 201–31. Ithaca: Cornell University Press, 1990.
Gottwald, Norman K. *The Politics of Ancient Israel*. Louisville: Westminster John Knox, 2001.
Hafemann, S. J. "Paul and His Interpreters." In *Dictionary of Paul and His Letters*, edited by Gerald F. Hawthorne et al., 666–89. Grand Rapids: Eerdmans, 1993.
Hamerton-Kelly, Robert G. *Sacred Violence: Paul's Hermeneutic of the Cross*. Minneapolis: Fortress, 1992.
Hamerton-Kelly, Robert, and Robin Scroggs, eds. *Jews, Greeks, and Christians: Religious Cultures in Late Antiquity: Essays in Honor of William David Davies*. SJLA 21. Leiden: Brill, 1976.
Hanson, Anthony Tyrrell. *The Paradox of the Cross in the Thought of St. Paul*. JSNTSup 17. Sheffield: JSOT Press, 1987.
Harrison, James R. *Paul and the Imperial Authorities at Thessalonica and Rome: A Study in the Conflict of Ideology*. WUNT 273. Tübingen: Mohr Siebeck, 2011.
———. *Reading Romans with Roman Eyes: Studies on the Social Perspective of Paul*. Paul in Critical Contexts. Lanham, MD: Lexington/Fortress Academic, 2020.
Hays, Richard B. *Echoes of Scripture in the Letters of Paul*. New Haven: Yale University Press, 1989.
———. *The Faith of Jesus Christ: The Narrative Substructure of Galatians 3:1—4:11*. Grand Rapids: Eerdmans, 1983; 2nd ed. 2002.
———. "The God of Mercy Who Rescues Us from the Present Evil Age." In *The Forgotten God*, edited by A. Andrew Das and Frank Matera, 123–43.
Hedner Zetterholm, Karin, and Anders Runesson, eds. *Within Judaism? Interpretive Trajectories in Judaism, Christianity, and Islam from the First to the Twenty-First Century*. Lanham, MD: Lexington Books/Fortress Academic, 2024.
———. "The 'Within Judaism' Perspective—An Emerging Paradigm Shift." In *Within Judaism? Interpretive Trajectories in Judaism, Christianity, and Islam from the*

First to the Twenty-First Century, edited by Karin Hedner Zetterholm and Anders Runesson, 1–6. Lanham, MD: Lexington Books/Fortress Academic, 2024.

Hendrix, Holland L. "Thessalonians Honor Romans." ThD diss., Harvard University, 1984.

Hengel, Martin. *The Cross of the Son of God*. Translated by John Bowden. London: SCM, 1986.

———. *Die Zeloten: Untersuchungen zur jüdischen Freiheitsbewegung in der Zeit von Herodes I. bis 70 n. Chr.* Arbeiten zur Geschichte des Spätjudentums und Urchristentums 1. Leiden: Brill, 1961.

Hennecke, Edgar. *New Testament Apocrypha: Gospels and Related Writings*. 3rd ed. 2 vols. Edited by Wilhelm Schneelcher and R. McL. Wilson. Translated by A. J. B. Higgins et al. London SCM 2012.

Herman, Edward S. *The Real Terror Network: Terrorism in Fact and Propaganda*. Boston: South End, 1982.

Herman, Edward S., and Noam Chomsky. *Manufacturing Consent: The Political Economy of the Mass Media*. New York: Pantheon, 2002.

Herman, Edward S., and Gerry O'Sullivan. *The "Terrorism" Industry: The Experts and Institutions That Shape Our View of Terror*. New York: Pantheon, 1989.

Heschel, Susannah. *The Aryan Jesus: Christian Theologians and the Bible in Nazi Germany*. Princeton: Princeton University Press, 2008.

Heyward, Carter. "Doing Theology in a Counterrevolutionary Situation." In *The Future of Liberation Theology: Essays in Honor of Gustavo Gutierrez*, edited by Marc H. Ellis and Otto Maduro, 397–407. Maryknoll, NY: Orbis, 1989.

Holmberg, Bengt. Paul and Power: The Structure of Authority in the Primitive Church as Reflected in the Pauline Epistles. Lund: Gleerup, 1978.

Horrell, David G. *The Social Ethos of the Corinthian Correspondence: Interests and Ideology from 1 Corinthians to 1 Clement*. Edinburgh: T. & T. Clark, 2000.

Horsley, Richard A., ed. *Christian Origins*. People's History of Christianity 1. Minneapolis: Fortress, 2005.

———, ed. *Hidden Transcripts and the Arts of Resistance: Applying the Work of James C. Scott to Jesus and Paul*. Semeia Studies 48. Atlanta: Society of Biblical Literature, 2004.

———. *Jesus and the Spiral of Violence: Popular Jewish Resistance in Roman Palestine*. 1987. Reprint, Minneapolis: Fortress, 1993.

———, ed. *Paul and Empire: Religion and Power in Roman Imperial Society*. Harrisburg, PA: Trinity, 1997.

———, ed. *Paul and Politics: Ekklesia, Israel, Imperium, Interpretation*. Harrisburg, PA: Trinity, 2000.

———, ed. *Paul and the Roman Imperial Order*. Harrisburg, PA: Trinity, 2004.

———. "Submerged Biblical Histories and Imperial Biblical Studies." In *The Postcolonial Bible*, edited by R. S. Sugirtharajah, 152–73. Bible and Postcolonialism 1. Sheffield: Sheffield Academic, 1998.

Horsley, Richard A., and Alan Callahan, eds., *Semeia 83/84: Slavery in Text and Interpretation* (2001).

Horsley, Richard A., and John S. Hanson. *Bandits, Prophets, and Messiahs: Popular Movements in the Time of Jesus*. 1985. Reprint, Harrisburg, PA: Trinity, 1999.

Horsley, Richard A., and Neil Asher Silberman. *The Message and the Kingdom: How Jesus and Paul Ignited a Revolution and Transformed the Ancient World.* 1997. Reprint, Minneapolis: Fortress, 2002.

Jameson, Fredric. *The Political Unconscious: Narrative as a Socially Symbolic Act.* Ithaca: Columbia University Press, 1981.

Jewett, Robert. *Paul the Apostle to America: Cultural Trends and Pauline Scholarship.* Louisville: Westminster John Knox, 1994.

———. *Romans: A Commentary.* Assisted by Roy D. Kotansky. Hermeneia. Minneapolis: Fortress, 2008.

———. "Romans as an Ambassadorial Letter." *Interpretation* 36 (1982) 5–20.

Johnson-DeBaufre, Melanie, and Laura Salah Nasrallah. "Beyond the Heroic Paul: Toward a Feminist and Decolonizing Approach to the Letters of Paul." In *The Colonized Apostle: Paul through Postcolonial Eyes*, edited by Christopher Stanley, 161–74. Paul in Critical Contexts. Minneapolis: Fortress, 2011.

Johnson, E. Elizabeth. "Divine Initiative and Human Response." In *The Theological Interpretation of Scripture*, edited by Stephen Fowl, 356–70.

———. "Romans 9–11: The Faithfulness and Impartiality of God." In *Pauline Theology III: Romans*, edited by David M. Hay and E. Elizabeth Johnson, 240–58. Minneapolis: Fortress, 1989.

———. "The Wisdom of God as Apocalyptic Power." In *Faith and History: Essays in Honor of Paul W. Meyer*, edited by John T. Carroll et al., 137–48. Scholars Press Homage Series 18. Atlanta: Scholars, 1990.

Jones, A. H. M. *The Later Roman Empire, 284–602: A Social Economic and Administrative Survey.* 2 vols. 1964. Reprint, Baltimore: Johns Hopkins University Press, 1986.

Juvenal. *Satires.* Translated by G. G. Ramsay in *Juvenal and Persius*. LCL. Cambridge: Harvard University Press, 1957.

Kahl, Brigitte. *Galatians Re-Imagined: Reading with the Eyes of the Vanquished.* Paul in Critical Contexts. Minneapolis: Fortress, 2010.

Kallas, James. "Romans XIII. 7: An Interpolation." *NTS* 11 (1964–65) 365–74.

Käsemann, Ernst. *Commentary on Romans.* Translated by Geoffrey Bromiley. Grand Rapids: Eerdmans, 1980.

———. *Essays on New Testament Themes.* Translated by W. J. Montague. Studies in Biblical Theology 1/41. Naperville, IL: Allenson, 1964.

———. *New Testament Questions of Today.* Translated by W. J. Montague. Philadelphia: Fortress, 1969.

———. *Perspectives on Paul.* Translated by Margaret Kohl. Philadelphia: Fortress, 1971.

———. "Principles of the Interpretation of Romans 13." In *New Testament Questions of Today*, 196–216. Translated by W. J. Montague. Philadelphia: Fortress, 1969.

———. "The Problem of the Historical Jesus." In *Essays on New Testament Themes*, 15–47. Translated by W. J. Montague. Studies in Biblical Theology 1/41. Naperville, IL: Allenson, 1964.

———. "The Righteousness of God in Paul." In *New Testament Questions of Today*, 168–82. Translated by W. J. Montague. Philadelphia: Fortress, 1969.

———. "The Saving Significance of Jesus' Death in Paul." In *Perspectives on Paul*, 32–59. Translated by Margaret Kohl. Philadelphia: Fortress, 1971.

Kautsky, John. *The Politics of Aristocratic Empires.* Chapel Hill: University of North Carolina Press, 1982.

Bibliography

Kazantzakis, Nikos. *The Last Temptation of Christ*. Translated by P. A. Bien. New York: Simon & Schuster, 1960.

Keck, Leander E. "What Makes Romans Tick?" In *Pauline Theology III: Romans*, edited by David M. Hay and E. Elizabeth Johnson, 3–29. Minneapolis: Fortress, 1995.

Kelber, Werner H. *The Oral and the Written Gospel: The Hermeneutics of Speaking and Writing in the Synoptic Tradition, Mark, Paul, and Q*. Philadelphia: Fortress, 1983.

Keller, Catherine. *Political Theology of the Earth: Our Planetary Emergency and the Struggle for a New Public*. Insurrections: Critical Studies in Religion, Politics, and Culture. New York: Columbia University Press, 2018.

Kim, Seyoon. *Christ and Caesar: The Gospel and the Roman Empire in the Writings of Paul and Luke*. Grand Rapids: Eerdmans, 2008.

———. *The Origin of Paul's Gospel*. Grand Rapids: Eerdmans, 2002.

Kittredge, Cynthia Briggs. *Community and Authority: The Rhetoric of Obedience in Pauline Tradition*. Harvard Theological Studies 45. Cambridge: Harvard University Press, 1998.

———. "Reconstructing 'Resistance' or Reading to Resist: James C. Scott and the Politics of Interpretation." In *Hidden Transcripts and the Arts of Resistance: Applying the Work of James C. Scott to Jesus and Paul*, edited by Richard A. Horsley, 145–55. Semeia Studies 48. Atlanta: Society of Biblical Literature, 2004.

Koester, Helmut. "Imperial Ideology and Paul's Eschatology in 1 Thessalonians." In *Paul and Empire: Religion and Power in Roman Imperial Society*, edited by Richard A. Horsley, 158–66. Harrisburg, PA: Trinity, 1997.

———. *Introduction to the New Testament*. 2nd ed. 2 vols. New York: de Gruyter, 2000.

Kovacs, Judith L. "Archons, the Spirit, and the Death of Christ: Do We Need the Hypothesis of Gnostic Opponents to Explain 1 Corinthians 2.2–26?" In *Apocalyptic and the New Testament: Essays in Honor of J. Louis Martyn*, edited by Marion L. Soards and Joel Marcus, 217–36. JSNTSup 24. Sheffield: JSOT Press, 1989.

Kraftchick, Steven J. "Death in Us, Life in You: The Apostolic Medium." In *Pauline Theology*, vol. 2: *1 & 2 Corinthians*, edited by David M. Hay, 156–81. Minneapolis: Fortress, 2002.

Lambrecht, Jan. "The Defeated Paul: Aroma of Christ. An Exegetical Study of 2 Corinthians 2:14–16b." *Louvain Studies* 20 (1995) 170–86.

Last, Richard. "Communities That Write: Christ-Groups, Associations, and Gospel Communities." *NTS* 58 (2012) 172–98.

Le Donne, Anthony. "The Criterion of Coherence: Its Development, Inevitability, and Historiographical Limitations." In *Jesus, Criteria, and the Demise of Authenticity*, edited by Chris Keith and Anthony Le Donne, 95–114. London: T. & T. Clark, 2012.

Lebram, J.-C. H. "Piety of the Jewish Apocalypticists." In *Apocalypticism in the Mediterranean World and the Near East: Proceedings of the International Colloquium on Apocalypticism, Uppsala, August 12–17, 1979*, edited by David Hellholm, 171–210. Tübingen: Mohr Siebeck, 1983.

Lenski, Gerhard E. *Power and Privilege: A Theory of Social Stratification*. New York: McGraw-Hill, 1966.

Levine, Amy-Jill. *The Misunderstood Jew: The Church and the Scandal of the Jewish Jesus*. San Francisco: HarperSanFrancisco, 2006.

Lindbeck, George A. *The Nature of Doctrine: Religion and Theology in a Postliberal Age*. Philadelphia: Westminster, 1984.

López, Davina A. *Apostle to the Conquered: Reimagining Paul's Mission.* Paul in Critical Contexts. Minneapolis: Fortress, 2008.

———. "Visual Perspectives." In *Studying Paul's Letters: Contemporary Perspectives and Methods*, edited by Joseph A. Marchal, 93–116. Minneapolis: Fortress, 2012.

López, Davina A., and Todd Penner. "Paul and Politics." *The Oxford Handbook of Pauline Studies*, ed. R. Barry Matlock, 580–97. New York: Oxford University Press, 2017.

MacMullen, Ramsay. *Paganism in the Roman Empire.* New Haven: Yale University Press, 1981.

———. *Roman Social Relations 50 B.C. to A.D. 284.* New Haven: Yale University Press, 1974.

———. *Romanization in the Time of Augustus.* New Haven: Yale University Press, 2000.

Malherbe, Abraham. "Ancient Epistolary Theorists." *Ohio Journal of ReligiousStudies* 5 (1977) 3–77.

———. *Social Aspects of Early Christianity.* 2nd ed. 1983. Reprint, Eugene, OR: Wipf & Stock, 2003.

Malina, Bruce J., and John J. Pilch. *Social-Science Commentary on the Letters of Paul.* Minneapolis: Fortress, 2006.

Manjapra, Kris. *Black Ghost of Empire: The Long Death of Slavery and the Failure of Emancipation.* New York: Simon & Schuster, 2023.

Marchal, Joseph A. *Appalling Bodies: Queer Figures before and after Paul's Letters.* New York and Oxford: Oxford University Press, 2020.

———. *The Politics of Heaven: Women, Gender, and Empire in the Study of Paul.* Paul in Critical Contexts. Minneapolis: Fortress, 2008.

———, ed. *Studying Paul's Letters: Contemporary Perspectives and Methods.* Minneapolis: Fortress, 2012.

Marguerat, Daniel. Introduction to Andreas Dettwiler, et al., eds., *Paul, une théologie en construction.* Monde de la Bible 51. Geneva: Labor et Fides, 2004.

Marshall, Peter. *Enmity in Corinth: Social Conventions in Paul's Relations with the Corinthians.* WUNT 2/23. Tübingen: Mohr Siebeck, 1987.

Martin, Dale B. *The Corinthian Body.* New Haven: Yale University Press, 1995.

———. "Heterosexism and the Interpretation of Romans 1:18–32." *Biblical Interpretation* 3 (1995) 332–55.

———. "Paul and the Judaism/Hellenism Dichotomy: Toward a Social History of the Question." In *Paul beyond the Judaism/Hellenism Divide*, edited by Troels Engberg-Pederen, 29–62. Louisville: Westminster John Knox, 2001.

———. *Sex and the Single Savior: Gender and Sexuality in Biblical Interpretation.* Louisville: Westminster John Knox, 2006.

Martín-Baró, Ignacio. *Writings for a Liberation Psychology.* Cambridge: Harvard University Press, 1994.

Martyn, J. Louis. "Events in Galatia: Modified Covenantal Nomism versus God's Invasions of the Cosmos in the Singular Gospel." In *Pauline Theology I*, edited by Jouette Bassler, 161–63.

———. *History and Theology in the Fourth Gospel.* 3rd ed. New Testament Library. Louisville: Westminster John Knox, 2003.

———. *Theological Issues in the Letters of Paul.* Nashville: Abingdon, 1997.

McKnight, Scot, and Joseph B. Modica, eds. *Jesus Is Lord, Caesar Is Not: Evaluating Empire in New Testament Studies.* Downers Grove, IL: IVP Academic, 2013.

McLean, B. Hudson. *The Cursed Christ: Mediterranean Expulsion Rituals and Pauline Soteriology*. JSNTSup 126. Sheffield: JSOT Press, 1996.

Meeks, Wayne A. *The First Urban Christians: The Social World of the Apostle Paul*. 2nd ed. New Haven: Yale University Press, 2003.

———. "Judgment and the Brother: Romans 14.1—15.13." In *Tradition and Interpretation in the New Testament*, edited by Gerald F. Hawthorne and Otto Betz, 290–92. Grand Rapids: Eerdmans, 1987.

Meeks, Wayne A., and John T. Fitzgerald, eds. *The Writings of St. Paul*. 2nd ed. Norton Critical Edition. New York: Norton, 2007.

Meggitt, Justin J. *Paul, Poverty, and Survival*. Studies of the New Testament and Its World. Edinburgh: T. & T. Clark, 1998.

Memmi, Albert. *The Colonizer and the Colonized: A Destructive Relationship*. Exp. ed. Boston: Beacon, 1991.

Miranda, José Porfírio. *Marx and the Bible: A Critique of the Philosophy of Oppression*. 1974. Reprint, Eugene, OR: Wipf & Stock, 2004.

Mitchell, Margaret M. *Paul and the Rhetoric of Reconciliation: An Exegetical Investigation of the Language and Composition of 1 Corinthians*. 1991. Reprint, Louisville: Westminster John Knox, 1993.

Moltmann, Jürgen. "The Resurrection of Christ: Hope for the World." In Gavin D'Costa, ed., *Resurrection Reconsidered*, 80–81. Oxford: Oneworld Publications, 1996.

Montefiore, C. G. *Judaism and St. Paul*. London: Goschen, 1914.

Moore, G. F. "Christian Writers on Judaism." *HTR* 14 (1921) 197–254.

———. *Judaism in the First Centuries of the Christian Era: The Age of the Tannaim*. 3 vols. Cambridge: Harvard University Press, 1927–30.

Moore, Stephen D. *Empire and Apocalypse: Postcolonialism and the New Testament*. Bible in the Modern World 12. Sheffield: Sheffield Phoenix, 2006.

———. "Paul and Empire." In *The Colonized Apostle: Paul through Postcolonial Eyes*, edited by Christopher Stanley, 9–23. Paul in Critical Contexts. Minneapolis: Fortress, 2011.

Munck, Johannes. *Christ and Israel: An Interpretation of Romans 9–11*. Translated by Ingeborg Nixon. Philadelphia: Fortress, 1967.

———. *Paul and the Salvation of Mankind*. Translated by Frank Clarke. Richmond: John Knox, 1959.

Nanos, Mark D. *The Mystery of Romans: The Jewish Context of Paul's Letter*. Minneapolis: Fortress, 1996.

———. "Paul's Relationship to Torah in Light of His Strategy 'to Become Everything to Everyone' (1 Corinthians 9:19–22)." In *Paul and Judaism: Crosscurrents in Pauline Exegesis and the Study of Jewish-Christian Relations*, edited by Reimund Bieringer and Didier Pollefeyt, 52–92. LNTS 463. London: T. & T. Clark, 2012.

Nanos, Mark D., and Magnus Zetterholm, eds. *Paul within Judaism: Restoring the First-Century Context to the Apostle*. Minneapolis: Fortress, 2015.

Nelson-Pallmeyer, Jack. *The War against the Poor: Low-Intensity Conflict and Christian Faith*. Maryknoll, NY: Orbis, 1989.

———. *School of Assassins: Guns, Greed, and Globalization*. Maryknoll, NY: Orbis, 2001.

Nickle, Keith F. *The Synoptic Gospels: An Introduction*. Rev. ed. Louisville: Westminster John Knox, 2001.

Nippel, Wilfried. *Public Order in Ancient Rome*. Key Themes in Ancient History. Cambridge: Cambridge University Press, 1995.

Nissinen, Martii. *Homoeroticism in the Biblical World: A Historical Perspective*. Translated by Kirsi Stjerna. Minneapolis: Fortress, 1999

Nostra Aetate. See Pope Paul VI.

Novak, Michael. *Will It Liberate? Questions about Liberation Theology*. New York: Paulist, 1986.

Novenson, Matthew V. "Anti-Judaism and Philo-Judaism in Pauline Studies, Then and Now." In *Protestant Bible Scholarship: Anti-Semitism, PhiloSemitism and Anti-Judaism*, edited by A. F. Baker et al., 106–24. Journal for the Study of Judaism Supplements 200. Leiden: Brill, 2022.

Nutton, V. "The Beneficial Ideology." In *Imperialism in the Ancient World: The Cambridge University Research Seminar in Ancient History*, edited by P. D. A. Garnsey and C. R. Whittaker, 209–22. Cambridge Classical Studies. Cambridge: Cambridge University Press, 1979.

Odell-Scott, David, ed. *Reading Romans with Contemporary Philosophers and Theologians*. New York: T. & T. Clark, 2007.

O'Neill, J. C. *Paul's Letter to the Romans*. Pelikan New Testament Commentaries. London: Penguin, 1975.

Pagels, Elaine. "Paul and Women: A Response to Recent Discussion." *Journal of the American Academy of Religion* 42 (1974) 538–49.

Paul VI, Pope. "Declaration on the Relation of the Church to non-Christian Religions." *Nostra Aetate* (1965), available online at https://www.vatican.va/archive/hist_councils/ii_vatican_council/documents/vat-ii_decl_19651028_nostra-aetate_en.html.

Peake, Arthur S. "The Quintessence of Paulinism." A Lecture Delivered at the John Rylands Library on the 11th of October, 1916.

Pearson, Birger. *The Pneumatikos-Psychikos Terminology in 1 Corinthians: A Study in the Theology of the Corinthian Opponents of Paul and Its Relation to Gnosticism*. SBL Dissertation Series 12. Missoula, MT: Society of Biblical Literature, 1973.

Penner, Todd, and Davina López. "Rhetorical Approaches: Introducing the Art of Persuasion in Paul and Pauline Studies." In *Studying Paul's Letters: Contemporary Perspectives and Methods*, edited by Joseph A. Marchal, 33–52. Minneapolis: Fortress, 2012.

Penner, Todd, and Caroline van der Stichele, eds. *Contextualizing Gender in Early Christian Discourse: Thinking beyond Thecla*. New York: Continuum, 2009.

―――, eds. *Her Master's Tools: Feminist and Post-colonial Engagements of Historical-Critical Discourse*. Global Perspectives on Biblical Scholarship 9. Atlanta: Society of Biblical Literature, 2007.

Perelman, C., and L. Olbrechts-Tyteca. *The New Rhetoric: A Treatise on Argumentation*. Translated by J. Wilkinson and P. Weaver. Notre Dame: University of Notre Dame Press, 1965.

Pervo, Richard. *The Making of Paul: Constructions of the Apostle in Early Christianity*. Minneapolis: Fortress, 2010.

Petersen, Norman R. *Rediscovering Paul: Philemon and the Sociology of Paul's Narrative World*. 1985. Reprint, Eugene, OR: Wipf & Stock, 2008.

Petrella, Ivan. *Beyond Liberation Theology: A Polemic*. London: SCM, 2008.

Petrément, Simone. *A Separate God: The Christian Origins of Gnosticism*. San Francisco: HarperSanFrancisco, 1990.
Pickett, Raymond. *The Cross in Corinth: The Social Significance of the Death of Jesus*. JSNTSup 143. Sheffield: Sheffield Academic, 1997.
Porter, Stanley E. "Ancient Rhetorical Analysis and Discourse Analysis of the Pauline Corpus." In *The Rheorical Analysis of Scripture: Essays from the 1995 London Conference*, edited by Thomas H. Olbricht, 249–74. JSNTSup 146. Sheffield: Sheffield Academic, 1997.
———. "Romans 13:1–7 as Pauline Rhetoric." *Filologia neotestamentaria* 3 (1990) 115–39.
———. "Theoretical Justification for Application of Rhetorical Categories toPauline Epistolary Literature." In *Rhetoric and the New Testament: Essays from the 1992 Heidelberg Conference*, edited by Stanley E. Porter and Thomas H. Olbricht, 100–122. JSNTSup 90. Sheffield: Sheffield Academic, 1993.
Porter, Stanley E., and Bryan R. Dyer, eds. *Paul and Ancient Rhetoric: Theory and Practice in the Hellenistic Context*. Cambridge: Cambridge University Press, 2016.
Porter, Stanley E., and Christopher D. Stanley, eds. *As It Is Written: Studying Paul's Use of Scripture*. SBL Symposium Series 50. Atlanta: SBL, 2008.
Porter, Stanley E., and Cynthia Long Westfall, eds. *Empire and the New Testament*. McMaster New Testament Studies. Eugene, OR: Pickwick Publications, 2011.
Price, S. R. F. *Rituals and Power: The Roman Imperial Cult in Asia Minor*. Cambridge: Cambride University Press, 1984.
Räisänen, Heikki. *Paul and the Law*. WUNT 29. Reprint, Philadelphia: Fortress, 1983.
Ramsay, William Mitchell. *The Cities of St. Paul: Their Influence on His Life and Thought. The Cities of Eastern Asia Minor*. Dale Memorial Lectures in Mansfield College, Oxford, 1907. London: Hodder & Stoughton, 1907.
Reasoner, Mark. *Romans in Full Circle: A History of Interpretation*. Louisville: Westminster John Knox, 2005.
———. *The "Strong" and the "Weak": Romans 14.1—15.13 in Context*. SNTSMS 103. Cambridge: Cambridge University Press, 1999.
Reed, Jeffrey T. "Using Ancient Rhetorical Categories to Interpret Paul's Letters: A Question of Genre." In *Rhetoric and the New Testament: Essays from the 1992 Heidelberg Conference*, edited by Stanley E. Porter and Thomas H. Olbricht, 292–324. JSNTSup 90. Sheffield: Sheffield Academic, 1993.
Reinhartz, Adele. *Befriending the Beloved Disciple: A Jewish Reading of the Gospel of John*. New York: Continuum, 2001.
———. *Cast Out of the Covenant: Jews and Anti-Judaism in the Gospel of John*. Lanham, MD: Lexington Books/Fortress Academic, 2018.
Richardson, Peter. "Augustan Era Synagogues in Rome." In *Judaism and Christianity in First-Century Rome*, edited by Karl Donfried and Peter Richardson, 17–29. Grand Rapids: Eerdmans, 1998.
———. *Herod: King of the Jews and Friend of the Romans*. Studies on the Personalities of the New Testament. 1996. Reprint, Minneapolis: Fortress, 1999.
Richardson, Peter, and David Granskou, eds. *Anti-Judaism in Early Christianity*. Vol. 1: *Paul and the Gospels*. Studies in Christianity and Judaism 2.Waterloo, ON: Wilfrid Laurier University Press, 1986.
Ridgeway, James, ed. *The Haiti Files: Decoding the Crisis*. Washington, DC: Essential Books, 1994.

Rieger, Joerg. *Theology in the Capitalocene: Ecology, Identity, Class, and Solidarity.* Dispatches. Minneapolis: Fortress, 2022.

Robbins, Jeffrey R. *Radical Theology: A Vision for Change.* Bloomington: Indiana University Press, 2016.

Robert, Louis. *Les gladiateurs dans L'Orient grec.* Bibliothèque de l'Ecole des hautes études. Sciences historiques et philologiques 278. Amsterdam: Hakkert, 1971.

Rodríguez, Rafael. *If You Call Yourself a Jew: Reappraising Paul's Letter to the Romans.* Eugene, OR: Cascade Books, 2014.

Roetzel, Calvin J. "'As Dying, and Beholdd We Live': Death and Resurrection in Paul's Theology." *Interpretation* 46 (1992) 5–18.

———. *The Letters of Paul: Conversations in Context.* 5th ed. Louisville: Westminster John Knox, 2009.

———. "No 'Race of Israel' in Paul." In *Putting Body and Soul Together: Essays in Honor of Robin Scroggs*, edited by Virginia Wiles et al., 230–44. Valley Forge, PA: Trinity, 1997.

———. *Paul: The Man and the Myth.* Studies in the Personalities of the New Testament. 1998. Reprint, Minneapolis: Fortress, 1999.

———. "*Oikoumene* and the Limits of Pluralism in Alexandrian Judaism and Paul."

———. *World That Shaped the New Testament.* Rev. ed. Louisville: Westminster John Knox, 2002.

Rowe, Kavin. "What If It Were True? Why Study the New Testament?" *NTS* 68 (2022) 144–55.

Ruden, Sarah. *Paul among the People: The Apostle Reinterpreted and Reimagined in His Own Time.* New York: Pantheon, 2010.

Ruether, Rosemary Radford. *Faith and Fratricide: The Christian Roots of Anti-Semitism.* 1974. Reprint, Eugene, OR: Wipf & Stock, 1996.

Runesson, Anders. "What Does It Mean to Read New Testament Texts 'within Judaism'?" *New Testament Studies* 69 (2023) 299–312.

Said, Edward. *Covering Islam: How the Media and the Experts Determine How We See the Rest of the World.* Rev. ed. New York: Vintage, 1997.

———. *Culture and Imperialism.* New York: Vintage, 1993.

———. *Orientalism.* New York: Pantheon, 1978.

Saldarini, Anthony J. *Pharisees, Scribes, and Sadducees in Palestinian Society: A Sociological Approach.* New ed. Grand Rapids: Eerdmans, 2001.

Sanders, E. P. "Jewish Association with Gentiles and Galatians 2:11–14." In *The Conversation Continues: Studies in Paul and John in Honor of J. Louis Martyn*, edited by Robert Fortna and Beverly Gaventa, 170–88. Nashville: Abingdon, 1985.

———. *Paul and Palestinian Judaism: A Comparison of Patterns of Religion.* Philadelphia: Fortress, 1977. 40th Anniversary edition 2013.

———. *Paul, the Law, and the Jewish People.* Philadelphia: Fortress, 1983.

Sawicki, Marianne. *Seeing the Lord: Resurrection and Early Christian Practices.* Minneapolis: Fortress, 1994.

Schäfer, Peter. *Judeophobia: Attitudes toward the Jews in the Ancient World.* Cambridge: Harvard University Press, 1997.

Schmithals, Walter. *Gnosticism in Corinth: An Investigation of the Letters to the Corinthians.* Nashville: Abingdon, 1971.

———. *Der Römerbrief als historisches Problem.* Studien zum Neuen Testament 9. Gütersloh: Gütersloher, 1975.

Schottroff, Luise. "'Give to Caesar What Belongs to Caesar and to God What Belongs to God': A Theological Response of the Early Christian Church to Its Social and Political Environment." In *The Love of Enemy and Nonretaliation in the New Testament*, edited by Willard M. Swartley, 223-57. Studies in Peace and Scripture 3. Louisville: Westminster John Knox, 1992.

Schürer, Emil. *The History of the Jewish People in the Age of Jesus Christ*. New English ed. by Geza Vermes, Fergus Millar, and Martin Goodman. 3 vols. Edinburgh: T. & T. Clark, 1973-1987.

Schüssler Fiorenza, Elisabeth. *But She Said: Feminist Practices of Biblical Interpretation*. Boston: Beacon, 1992.

———. "The Ethics of Biblical Interpretation." *JBL* 107 (1988) 3-17.

———. *In Memory of Her: A Feminist Theological Reconstruction of Christian Origins*. New York: Crossroad, 1983.

———. "Paul and the Politics of Interpretation." In *Paul and Politics: Ekklesia, Israel, Imperium, Interpretation*, edited by Richard A. Horsley, 40-57. Harrisburg, PA: Trinity, 2000.

———. "Rhetorical Situation and Historical Reconstruction in 1 Corinthians." *NTS* 33 (1987) 386-403.

Schweitzer, Albert. *The Quest of the Historical Jesus: A Critical Study of Its Progress from Reimarus to Wrede*. Translated by W. Montgomery. 1910. Reprint, New York: Macmillan, 1968.

Scott, James C. *Domination and the Arts of Resistance: Hidden Transcripts*. New Haven: Yale University Press, 1990.

———. "Protest and Profanation Agrarian Revolt and the Little Tradition, Part I." *Theory and Society* 4 (1977) 1-38.

———. "Protest and Profanation Agrarian Revolt and the Little Tradition, Part II." *Theory and Society* 4 (1977) 211-46.

———. *Weapons of the Weak: Everyday Forms of Peasant Resistance*. New Haven: Yale University Press, 1985.

Scroggs, Robin. *The New Testament and Homosexuality: Contextual Background for Contemporary Debate*. Philadelphia: Fortress, 1983.

———. "Paul and the Eschatological Woman." In *The Text and the Times: New Testament Essays for Today*, 69-95. Minneapolis: Fortress, 1993.

———. "Paul as Rhetorician: Two Homilies in Romans 1-11." In *Jews, Greeks, and Christians: Religious Cultures in Late Antiquity: Essays in Honor of William David Davies*, edited by Robert Hamerton-Kelly and Robin Scroggs, 271-99. SJLA 21. Leiden: Brill, 1976.

Segal, Alan F. *Paul the Convert: The Apostolate and Apostasy of Saul the Pharisee*. New Haven: Yale University Press, 1990.

———. "Universalism in Judaism and Christianity." In *Paul in His Hellenistic Context*, edited by Troels Engberg-Pedersen, 1-29. Minneapolis: Fortress, 1995

Segovia, Fernando F. "Criticism in Critical Times: Reflections on Vision and Task." *JBL* 134 (2015) 6-29.

Segundo, Juan Luis. *The Humanist Christology of Paul*. Translated by John Drury. 1986. Reprint, Eugene, OR: Wipf & Stock, 2007.

Slingerland, H. Dixon. *Claudian Policymaking and the Early Imperial Repression of Judaism at Rome*. South Florida Studies in the History of Judaism 160. Atlanta: Scholars, 1997.

Smallwood, E. Mary. *Jews under Roman Rule: From Pompey to Diocletian: A Study in Political Relations*. 2nd ed. SJLA 20. Leiden: Brill, 1981.

Snodgrass, Klyne R. "Justification by Grace—to the Doers: An Analysis of the Place of Romans 2 in the Theology of Paul." *New Testament Studies* 32 (1986) 72–93.

Sobrino, Jon. *Jesus in Latin America*. 1987. Reprint, Eugene, OR: Wipf & Stock, 2004.

Stanley, Christopher D. "'Neither Jew nor Greek: Ethnic Conflict in Graeco-Roman Society." *JSNT* 64 (1996) 101–24.

———, ed. *The Colonized Apostle: Paul through Postcolonial Eyes*. Paul in Critical Contexts. Minneapolis: Fortress, 2011.

———, ed. *Paul and Scripture: Extending the Conversation*. Early Christianity and Its Literature 9. Atlanta: SBL, 2012.

Ste. Croix, G. E. M. de. *Class Struggle in the Ancient Greek World*. Ithaca: Cornell University Press, 1981.

Stendahl, Krister. *Paul among Jews and Gentiles, and Other Essays*. Philadelphia: Fortress, 1976.

Stowers, Stanley K. *The Diatribe and Paul's Letter to the Romans*. SLBDS 57. Chico: Scholars, 1981.

———. *Letter-Writing in Greco-Roman Antiquity*. Library of Early Christianity 5. Philadelphia: Westminster, 1986.

———. *A Rereading of Romans: Gentiles, Jews, Justice*. New Haven: Yale University Press, 1994.

Stringfellow, William. *Conscience and Obedience: The Politics of Romans 13 and Revelation 13 in Light of the Second Coming*. 1977. Reprint, William Stringfield Library. Eugene, OR: Wipf & Stock, 2004.

———. *Ethic for Christians and Other Aliens in a Strange Land*. 1973. Reprint, William Stringfield Library. Eugene, OR: Wipf & Stock, 2004.

Tabor, James D. *Things Unutterable: Paul's Ascent to Paradise in Its Greco-Roman, Judaic, and Early Christian Contexts*. Studies in Judaism. Lanham, MD: University Press of America, 1986.

Támez, Elsa. *Contra Toda Condena: La Justificación por la Fe desde los Excluidos*. San José: Departmento Ecuménico de Investigaciones, Seminario Biblico Latinoamericano, 1991. ET *The Amnesty of Grace: Justification by Faith from a Latin American Perspective*. Nashville: Abingdon, 1991.

Taubes, Jacob. *The Politische Theologie des Paulus: Vorträge gehalten an der Forschungsstätte der evangelischen Studiengemeinschaft in Heidelberg, 23–27 Februar 1987*. Edited by Aleida Assmann et al. Munich: Fink, 1995. ET *The Political Theology of Paul*. Translated by Dana Hollander. Cultural Memory in the Present. Stanford: Stanford University Press, 2004.

Taylor, Mark Lewis. *The Theological and the Political: On the Weight of the World*. Minneapolis: Fortress, 2011.

Theissen, Gerd. *The Social Setting of Pauline Christianity: Essays on Corinth*. Translated by John Schütz. 1982. Reprint, Eugene, OR: Wipf & Stock, 2004.

Therborn, Göran. *The Killing Fields of Inequality*. Cambridge: Polity, 2013.

Tolbert, Mary Ann. "Social, Sociological, and Anthropological Methods." In *Searching the Scriptures*, vol. 1, edited by Elisabeth Schüssler Fiorenza, ed., 255–71. New York: Crossroad, 1993.

Trouillot, Michel-Rolph. *Silencing the Past: Power and the Production of History*. Boston: Beacon, 1995.

Bibliography

Tzaferis, Vassilios. "Jewish Tombs at and near Giv'at ha-Mivtar, Jerusalem." *Israel Exploration Journal* 20 (1970) 18–32.
Vermes, Geza. *The Complete Dead Sea Scrolls in English*. New York: Penguin, 1997.
——— . *The Dead Sea Scrolls in English*. 3rd ed. Sheffield: JSOT Press, 1987.
——— . *Jesus the Jew: A Historian's Reading of the Gospels*. Minneapolis: Fortress Press, 1981.
Virgil. *Aeneid*. Translated by H. Rushton Fairclough and revised by G. Goold. LCL. London: Heinemann, 1918.
Walsh, Robyn Faith. *The Origins of Early Christian Literature: Contextualizing the New Testament within Greco-Roman Literary Culture*. Cambridge: Cambridge University Press, 2021.
Wan, Sze-Kar. "Collection for the Saints as Anti-Colonial Act." In *Paul and Politics: Ekklesia, Israel, Imperium, Interpretation*, edited by Richard A. Horsley, 191–215. Harrisburg, PA: Trinity, 2000.
Ward, Richard. "Pauline Voice and Presence as Strategic Communication." *Semeia* 65 (1994) 102–3.
Watson, Francis S. *Gospel Writing: A Canonical Perspective*. Grand Rapids: Eerdmans, 2013.
——— . *Paul, Judaism, and the Gentiles: A Sociological Approach*. SNTSMS 56. Cambridge: Cambridge University Press, 1986.
Welborn, Larry L. *An End to Enmity: Paul and the "Wrongdoer" of Second Corinthians*. Beihefte zur Zeitschrift für die neutestamentliche Wissenschaft 185. Berlin: de Gruyter, 2011.
——— . *Paul's Summons to Messianic Life: Political Theology and the Coming Awakening*. New York: Columbia University Press, 2015.
——— . "'That There May Be Equality': The Contexts and Consequences of a Pauline Ideal." *NTS* 59 (2013) 73–90.
Wengst, Klaus. *Pax Romana and the Peace of Jesus Christ*. Translated by John Bowden. Philadelphia: Fortress, 1987.
West, Gerald O. *Academy of the Poor: Towards a Ddialogical Reading of the Bible*. Interventions. Sheffield: Sheffield Academic, 1999.
——— . "Disguising Defiance in Rituralisms of Subordination: Literary and Community-based Resources for Recovering Resistance Discourse within the Dominant Discourses of the Bible." In *Reading Communities Reading Scripture: Essays in Honor of Daniel Patte*, edited by Gary A. Phillips and Nicole Wilkinson Duran, 194–217. Harrisburg, PA: Trinity, 2002.
White, John L. *The Apostle of God: Paul and the Promise of Abraham*. Peabody, MA: Hendrickson, 1999.
White, L. Michael, ed. *Social Networks in the Early Christian Environment: Issues and Methods for Social History*. Semeia 56. Atlanta: Scholars, 1992.
Wiefel, Wolfgang. "The Jewish Community in Ancient Rome and the Origins of Roman Christianity." In *The Romans Debate*, edited by Karl P. Donfried, 85–101. Rev. and exp. ed. Peabody, MA: Hendrickson, 1991.
Williamson, Lamar. "Led in Triumph: Paul's Use of *Thriambeuo*." *Interpretation* 22 (1968) 317–22.
Wink, Walter. *Engaging the Powers: Discernment and Resistance in a World of Domination*. Minneapolis: Fortress, 1992.

———. *Naming the Powers: The Language of Power in the New Testament*. Philadelphia: Fortress, 1984.
———. *Unmasking the Powers: The Invisible Forces That Determine Human Existence*. Philadelphia: Fortress, 1986.
Winn, Adam, ed. *An Introduction to Empire in the New Testament*. Resources for Biblical Study 84. Atlanta: SBL Press, 2016.
Winter, Dagmar. "Saving the Quest for Authenticity from the Criterion of Dissimilarity: History and Plausibility." In *Jesus, Criteria, and the Demise of Authenticity*, edited by Chris Keith and Anthony Le Donne, 115–31. London: T. & T. Clark, 2012.
Wire, Antoinette Clark. *The Corinthian Women Prophets: A Reconstruction through Paul's Rhetoric*. 1990. Reprint, Eugene, OR: Wipf & Stock, 2003.
———. "Performance, Politics, and Power: A Response." *Semeia* 65 (1994) 129.
Woolf, Greg. *Becoming Roman: The Origins of Provincial Civilization in Gaul*. Cambridge: Cambridge University Press, 1998.
———. "Becoming Roman, Staying Greek: Culture, Identity and the Civilizing Process in the Roman East." *Proceedings of the Cambridge Philological Society* 40 (1994) 116–43.
World Council of Churches. *Theology of the Churches and the Jewish People*. Geneva: WCC Publications, 1988.
Wright, N. T. *The Climax of the Covenant: Christ and the Law in Pauline Theology*. Philadelphia: Fortress, 1991.
———. *Paul and His Recent Interpreters: Some Contemporary Debates*. Minneapolis: Fortress, 2015.
———. *Paul and the Faithfulness of God*, Parts I and II. Christian Origins and the Question of God 4. Minneapolis: Fortress, 2013.
———. "Paul's Gospel and Caesar's Empire." In *Paul and Politics*, edited by Richard A. Horsley, 160–83.
———. *Paul: In Fresh Perspective*. Minneapolis: Fortress, 2005.
Yamauchi, Edwin M. *Pre-Christian Gnosticism: A Survey of the Proposed Evidence*. London: Tyndale, 1973.
Young, Stephen L. "'Let's Take the Text Seriously': The Protectionist *Doxa* of Mainstream New Testament Studies." *Method and Theory in the Study of Religion* 32 (2020) 328–63.
Zanker, Paul. *The Power of Images in the Age of Augustus*. Translated by Alan Shapiro. Ann Arbor: University of Michigan Press, 1988.
Zerbe, Gordon M. *Citizenship: Paul on Peace and Politics*. Winnipeg: CMU Press, 2012.
Zetterholm, Magnus. *Approaches to Paul: A Student's Guide to Contemporary Scholarship*. Minneapolis: Fortress, 2009.
———. "The 'Within Judaism' Perspective—Why Does It Matter?" In *Within Judaism? Interpretive Trajectories in Judaism, Christianity, and Islam from the First to the Twenty-First Century*, edited by Karin Hedner Zetterholm and Anders Runesson, 9–21. Lanham, MD: Lexington Books/Fortress Academic, 2024.
Zias, Joseph, and Eliezer Sekeles. "The Crucified Man from Giv'at ha-Mivtar: A Reappraisal." *Israel Exploration Journal* 35 (1985) 22–27.
Žižek, Slavoj. *The Puppet and the Dwarf: The Perverse Core of Christianity*. Short Circuits. Cambridge: MIT Press, 2003.

Ancient Document Index

HEBREW BIBLE/ OLD TESTAMENT

Genesis
23:7	102

Numbers
23:9	162

Deuteronomy
21:22–23	153n27
32:8–9	65

Joshua
24:2–4	141

Isaiah
11:10	140
40:2	115n39
60	24

Jeremiah
20:8–9	12

Zecharaiah
9:12	115n39

Daniel
	5
2:37	59

2:44	59, 65
6	114n34
7:9–14	156
7:22	65
7:27	65
10:13	58
10:20	58

NEW TESTAMENT

Matthew
10:1–16	132
10:40–42	132

Luke
	183n26, 184, 187n43
1:1–4	186
1:1	30
10:1–12	132
21:12	16, 26, 31
23:13	58n21
23:35	58n21
24:20	58n21
24:36–43	34

John
7:26	58n21
19:35	186n38
20:26–29	34
20:31	188n48
21:1–14	34
21:24	186nn38, 39

Acts

	30, 128, 183–84, 187n43
1:8	26
4:8–10	58n21
4:26	58n21
5:34	15
9	31, 34
9:1–2	31
9:11	31
9:22	159
10:28	16
11:26	183n27
13:15ff	159
13:27–28	58n21
13:46	159
14:1	159
15:1–29	16
17:1f	159
17:10f	159
17:16–34	26
18:1–2	139
18:4	159
18:24–28	109
19:4	159
21	25
21:17–36	16
21:27–29	31
21:28–29	25
22–28	25
22	31, 34
22:3	15, 31
22:25–29	31
24–26	26
26	31, 34
28:17–22	26
28:21–22	31
28:30–31	31

Romans

	22, 30, 89
1–4	73
1–3	142, 167
1	141
1:1–5	10
1:5–6	24
1:5	110
1:9	93
1:13	10
1:14	150
1:15–32	141
1:16–17	88, 115
1:16	89, 110, 150, 158
1:17	90
1:18–32	74, 90, 91, 93
1:24–27	40, 91
2–3	20
2	160, 167
2:5	64
2:6–11	64
3	160
3:1	158
3:20	90
3:21–25	145
3:24–25	23
3:27–28	17
3:31	26, 63
4:2	17
4:4–6	17
4:5	141
4:13	141
5–8	62
5–6	23
5:1	114n34
5:12	65
5:18	65
6–7	63
6:1–5	53
6:2	63
6:3–11	21
6:6	63
6:12–20	93
6:13	115
6:15–19	91
6:17	57n17
6:19	93
6:20–23	91
7:1	63
7:4	63
7:7	16
7:12	63
7:22	63
7:25	63
8	65n42
8:4–17	91
8:11	119

8:18–25	58
8:20–22	68
8:20–21	65
8:22–23	66
8:28–39	21
8:35–39	65
8:35	65n41
8:38–39	63
8:38	65
9–11	20, 65, 139, 140, 142, 159
9	65n42
9:1–5	14, 66
9:1–4	16
9:30—10:6	145
9:31–32	15
9:32	16, 17
10:20–21	159
11	26, 89, 140, 159
11:6	17
11:13–32	20, 91
11:13–14	159
11:13	10
11:23–27	25
11:25–26	140, 159
11:26	87
12–15	91
12:1–2	24, 91
12:1	93
12:2	74
12:3	91
12:3–7	21
12:19–21	142
12:19–20	64
13:1–7	33, 36, 48, 73, 74, 88, 91, 92nn89–90; 124, 125
13:1	37
13:3	92
13:4	92, 142
13:6	92
13:11–14	91
14:14	16, 166
14:15	53
15:8–13	24
15:8	24
15:9–12	15
15:12	140
15:14–16	19, 93, 110
15:16–18	10
15:16–17	24
15:16	24n25
15:17	24
15:18–19	110, 115
15:25–28	19
15:25–26	24
15:27	19
16:1–7	32, 57n17
16:23	169

1 Corinthians

	22, 28, 30, 59, 122, 131
1:8	24n25
1:14–16	25
1:17–18	109, 117
1:18—2:16	173
1:26–29	137
1:26	132
1:28	68
2	59, 60, 63, 64, 132
2:1—3:15	25
2:1–6	27
2:1–5	109
2:2	57, 117
2:4–6	106
2:4	110, 117, 138
2:6–9	137
2:6–8	62n31, 63, 68
2:6	59, 60, 65
2:7	59
2:8	58, 59, 105
3:5	117
3:10–15	52
4	137
4:9–13	79, 113–14, 116, 138
4:10	138
4:15	28
4:19–20	109
5:1–8	28
5:7	23
5:9–13	27
5:9	29
6	136
6:9–10	40
7	27, 135
7:1–7	32
7:1	136
7:12–16	136

1 Corinthians (continued)

7:17–24	36, 37
7:17	136
7:20	136
7:21	34
7:24	136
7:28	136
7:31	62, 67, 68, 134, 137
8	27, 132, 134
8:11	53
8:4–12	134
9	27
9:8	11
9:19–23	166
9:19–21	16
9:22	136
10	132, 134
10:1–11	11
10:14–22	27, 135
11:17–34	21, 27, 132
10:23	136
11:2–16	110n20, 135
11:2	14, 57n17
11:3	135
11:4	135
11:22	67
11:23–26	14
11:26	53, 122, 135
12:31–13:13	21
12:4–30	21
12:6	38
14:33–34	32, 36, 79, 110n20
15	60, 63, 64
15:3–8	10
15:3–7	14
15:3	23
15:21	65
15:24–28	63, 137
15:24	59, 63, 65, 122
15:26	59, 63, 65
15:32	114
15:50	34
15:51–58	68
15:58–59	58
16:1–4	67

2 Corinthians

	22, 28, 30, 77, 117n43, 131, 133–34, 143
1–9	113
1:8–10	111, 112
1:8	113
1:9	112
1:15–17	112
1:23–2:4	112
2	114
2:4	113
2:8–9	66
2:12	112
2:13	113
2:14	112, 113
2:14–16	66, 79, 111, 112, 138
2:14	113
4:7–12	66
4:8–9	66
4:10–11	118
4:10	66, 79, 112, 113, 116
4:14	118
5:14	79, 112
6:3–4	113
6:4–10	79, 113
7:2	112, 113
7:5	113
8–9	111
8:13–14	138
9:13	139
9:22–23	30
10–13	138
10	115n39
10:3–6	115
10:9–10	27
10:10	109
11:1–6	27
11:2	24n25
11:4	27
11:23–27	116, 138
11:24	166
11:25	116n41
11:28	13, 24
12	18, 34, 155, 156
12:12	64, 110, 138
12:5	64

Galatians

	22, 30
1:4	173
1:6–9	27
1:11—2:10	37
1:11–16	145
1:12–14	145
1:13–17	12
1:13–14	13, 17
1:14	15, 76
1:15–16	105
2	19, 33, 87
2:1–9	16
2:8	10
2:11–14	16, 27
2:14	16
2:15–21	145
2:16	17
2:18	27
2:19–20	12
3	153
3:1–14	145
3:1	53, 117n42, 138
3:2	17
3:3–5	110
3:3	88
3:5	17
3:10	17
3:13	23, 153n27
3:28	34, 37
4:8	88
5:2–3	20
5:2	88
5:3	88
5:11	27, 88
6:12	88
6:13	88
6:17	116

Ephesians

	22, 64, 66
1:20–22	64n35
2:13–16	26, 33
3:1–6	26
5:22–24	36
6:5–9	34
6:5–8	36

Philippians

	22, 23, 30
1:10–11	24n25
2:6–8	21, 58
2:6	58
2:7	58
2:8	58, 68
2:15	74
3:17	28
3:2–9	145
3:4–7	37
3:5–6	15
3:7–9	145
3:9	15

Colossians

	22, 30, 64, 66
1:16	64
2:15	64n35, 65, 66
3:2	66
3:18—4:1	34
3:18	36
3:22–25	36
4:14	31
4:16	29

1 Thessalonians

	22, 30, 77
1:5	110
1:8–10	134
2:13	57n17
2:15–16	58
2:19	78
3:13	24n25, 78
4	64
4:13–18	27
5:1–11	58
5:23	24n25
5:3	78, 130

2 Thessalonians

	22, 30
3:10	38

1 Timothy

| | 22, 29, 32 |

1 Timothy (continued)

1:8–11	40
2:2	33
2:11–15	32, 36
4:1–4	32
5:3–16	34
6:1–2	34
6:1	35

2 Timothy

	22, 29
3:16	11

Titus

	22, 29
2:9–10	36

Philemon

	22, 23, 30, 34
8	27

Hebrews

30

PSEUDEPIGRAPHA

2 Baruch

146n8

1 Enoch

16

4 Ezra

	146n8
11.39–46	56

Jubilees

16

4 Maccabees

	74, 90, 82n103, 157, 91, 95, 165n72
1:2	99

1:11	100
1:15–18	100
5:34–38	90n80
6:20	90n80
9:23	90n80
12:11	90n80

Pseudo-Philo

Liber antiquitatum biblicarum

157

DEAD SEA SCROLLS

1QpHab

	99
3	91n87

11QH

5.18	16
8.12	16

RABBINIC WRITINGS

Mishnah

'Abodah Zarah

134

'Abot

3:2	85

Babylonian Talmud

Shabbat

33b	85

Midrash

Genesis Rabbah

65.1	91n87

Ancient Document Index

GRECO-ROMAN AUTHORS

Aristotle

Politics

1254a22–24	82n50

Rhetoric

1.1376	81n44
2.6.10	81n44

Augustus

Res Gestae

	141

Calpurnius Piso

Eclogue

1	142

Calpurnius Siculus

	142

Bucolica

	90n85

Cicero

De Provinciis consularibus

10	83n54

De Re publica

3	83n54
3.37	83
3.41	81
3.45	81n47
5.6	81

Pro Flacco

	81n47

Einsiedeln Eclogues

	90n85

Horace

Odes

3	91

Josephus

Against Apion

2.164–167	92n91
2.186–187	92n91
2.218–219	92n91

Antiquities

13.164	169
18.6–10	61
18.60–62	61
18.63–64	61
18.65–80	61n29
18.81–84	61n29
18.85–89	61

War

2.66–79	54
2.252–253	54
2.293–300	54
2.345–404	85
2.348	86n66
2.357	85
3.336–408	76
5.446–451	55
5.553–561	55
5.44.9	55n6
5.363–68	85
6.312–13	76

Philo

Embassy to Gaius

8–13	86
161	60
301–302	60
310	60

Life of Moses

2.49–51	92n91

On Dreams

2	100, 86n65
2.78–79	100
2.81–82	101
2.83–84	101
2.83	103
2.86–87	102
2.90	102
2.91	102
2.92–95	101
2.92	103, 130

Special Laws

3.159–63	101

Plutarch

Fortune of the Romans

316	84
318	81n48
323	84

Moralia

814F	84

Quintilian

Institutes

1.11	109n19

Seneca

	142

De Clementia 1.1

	83

Socrates

Apology

24A	89n79
29D	89n79
35A	89n79
38D	89n79

Suetonius

Claudius

25.4	139

Tiberius

36	61n29

Tacitus

Annals

	91n86
14.42–45	54

Histories

4.17.2	56, 91n87
5.10	94

Velleius Paterculus

History of Rome

2.126	81n48
2.99	91n86

Virgil

Aeneid

	141
6.113	139
8.720–23	24

Xenophon

Memorabilia

1.2.40–46	81n46

EARLY CHRISTIAN AUTHORS

Acts of Paul

	30, 32, 33, 34, 114n33, 136
3	112n28
7	1112n28
9	136
10.6	26

Ancient Document Index

Ascent of James
33

1 Clement
55.2 34

Clementine Recognitions
1.70–71 33

3 Corinthians
30, 34

Epistle to Barnabas
30

Epistle to the Laodiceans
29, 30

Epiphanius
Panarion 16.6–9 33

Eusebius
Eccl. Hist.
2.25.5 26

Hermas
Mandates
8.10 34

Similitudes
12.8 34

Ignatius
To Polycarp
4 34–35

Irenaeus
Against Heresies
1.26.2 33

John Chrysostom
Homily on Philemon
35

Letters of Paul and Seneca
29, 33

Martyrdom of Paul
33

Martyrdom of Polycarp
33

Tertullian
On Baptism
17 32

Author Index

Alcock, S. E., 72n58, 106nn8, 9
Ando, C., 106n9
Ashton, J., 12n2
Auguet, R., 114n32
Aune, D. E., 109n18
Aymer, M., 12n2
Badiou, A., 46n8
Balch, D., 83n54
Barclay, J. M. G., 74n14, 75n15, 77n22, 85n62, 86n67, 87n71, 97nn13–14; 111n24, 126n7, 127n9, 129, 161n55, 162nn56–61; 163nn62–65; 164nn66–68; 165n72, 166nn73–75, 77; 167nn78–80; 168n86, 171nn93–96; 172nn97–99; 173n100, 184n31
Barrett, C. K., 111n24, 13n5
Bartchy, S. S., 37n33, 79n38, 136n20
Barth, K., 180n19, 184n31
Bassler, J. M., 110n22
Bauckham, R., 183n28
Baur, F. C., 72n, 88n23, 146n10
Becker, A. H., 183n26
Beker, J. C., 44–5n3, 53n1, 55n6, 63, 63n32, 64n35, 67n46, 68n49, 118n46
Betz, H. D., 80n41, 109n19, 110n21, 117n42
Bhabha, H., 128n12, 166n68
Bitzer, L. F., 110n23
Blum, W., 120n52
Blumenfeld, B., 161n55
Boccaccini, G., 48n11
Bornkamm, G., 87n72

Boswell, J., 40n43
Botha, P. J. J., 109n18
Bowersock, G. W., 106n9, 107n10
Boyarin, D., 46n6, 73n9, 75n16, 87n71, 147nn12, 13
Bradley, K., 56n12
Brauch, M. T., 68n48
Breytenbach, J. C., 111n25
Brinton, T., 38
Brown, R. E., 175n2, 186n39
Brown, R. M., 5n8, 37n32
Brunt, P. A., 81n47, 84n57
Bryan, C., 161n55
Bultmann, R., 14n7, 59n22, 62n31, 181n23
Burk, D., 49n15

Callahan, A., 6n13, 93n95
Câmara, D. H. , 55n9
Campbell, W. S., 45n4, , 73n10, 89n77
Carey, G., 41, 42n49
Carter, W., 161n55
Casey, M., 182n25
Castelli, E. A., 41n48, 80n40, 109–10n20, 126n8
Cavanaugh, W., 93n94, 121nn54–56, 122n57, 123n58
Chancey, M., 43, 45
Charles, R., 166n68
Chomsky, N., 82n50, 92n91, 166n68
Chow, J. K., 77n24, 108n16
Classen, C. J., 80n42
Cohen, S. J. D., 151n21
Collins, A. Y., 60n26
Collins, J. J., 60n26, 179n13

Colpe, C., 59n23
Colson, F. H., 86n65
Consigny, S., 110n23
Conzelmann, H., 59n22
Corradi, J. E., 120n51
Countryman, W., 40n43
Cousar, C. B., 58n20
Crawford, M. H., 84n59
Crossan, J. D., 71n2
Crossley, J. G., 184nn30, 33

Dahl, N. A., 24n25, 109n19, 110n22
Danker, F. W., 77n23
de Boer, M. C., 146n8
de Lange, N., 85n63, 91n87
Deidun, J., 46n6, 72n8, 147n11, 179n12
Deissmann, A., 125n3
Detweiler, A., 44n2
Dewey, A. J., 109n18
Dewey, J., 109n18
Donfried, K. P., 78nn30, 33
Doty, W. F., 109n18
Downing, F. G., 80n76
DuBois, P., 81n44
Duff, A. M., 90n85
Duff, J. W., 90n85
Duff, P. B., 57n14, 66n44, 111n26, 112n27, 113nn30, 31
Dunn, J. D. G., 17n10, 45, 46, 72n8, 75n15, 89n75, 144n3, 183n26

Edwards, D. R., 78n36
Ehrman, B. D., 175n2
Eisenbaum, P., 19n16, 48n11, 144n2, 148nn14, 15
Elliott, N., 2n1, 5n10, 6n12, 8nn15, 16; 19n15, 20n19, 29n27, 30n28, 40n44, 46nn7, 8; 50n16, 63n33, 65nn42, 43; 73nn10, 11; 76n20, 77n21, 79nn37–39; 86n64, 89n78, 92n92, 93n93, 100n26, 110nn20, 22, 23; 126; 135n19, 136n20, 137nn23, 24; 139n26, 140nn29, 30; 141n31, 142n32, 143nn34, 36; 147n13, 150n18, 154n34, 157nn43, 44; 158nn45, 46; 160nn52–54; 161n55,

165n69, 167nn81, 82; 171n94, 184n31, 185n37, 186n40, 191n57
Engberg-Pedersen, T., 163n63
Ericksen, R. P., 182n25
Esler, P. F., 88n73

Faludi, S., 5n9, 36n31
Fanon, F., 96n12
Findlay, G. G., 111n24
Fisher, M., 191n59
Fitzgerald, J. T., 12n2
Fitzmyer, J. A., 57n17
Fredriksen, P., 18n1, 43n1, 51nn17–19, 52n20, 58n18, 71n3, 76n19, 77n22, 87n70, 95n4, 153nn26, 28, 30; 154nn31–34; 155n35, 156n40, 158n47, 179nn15, 16; 180n18, 184nn30, 31; 186n40, 187n41, 187n44, 189n50, 190nn152–55
Frey, J., 151, 152nn23–25; 153n27, 158n47, 158n47, 159nn49–51; 168, 184n31
Friedrich, G., 78n28
Friesen, S. J., 7, 8n14, 108n16
Fruhling, H., 121n55
Funk, R. W., 109n18
Furnish, V. P., 91n88, 111n26, 113n29, 118n44

Gaca, K. L., 24n24
Gager, J. G., 45, 47n10, 93n93, 95n6, 167n81, 168n87
Galinsky, K., 71n4
Garnsey, P. D. A., 72n5
Garrett, S. R., 114n36
Gaston, L., 20n18, 45, 47n101, 87n73, 88n74, 167n81, 168n87
Geertz, C., 107n10
George, A., 120n52
Georgi, D., 78nn28–31; 90n83, 104n1, 105n3, 108n16, 126n4
Gerhardsson, B., 188n45
Goodenough, E. R., 86nn64, 65, 102, 103n28
Goodman, M., 85n61
Gordon, R., 71n4, 104n2, 107nn13, 15
Gottwald, N. K., 128n11

Author Index

Hafemann, S. J., 111n25, 113n30, 146n10
Hamerton-Kelly, R., 46n7, 62n31, 67n45
Hanson, A. T., 114nn33, 34; 115nn37, 39
Hanson, G., 60n26
Hanson, J. S., 187n42
Harrison, J. R., 48n13, 131n16, 161n55
Hays, R. B., 68n48, 130n14, 147n13
Hedner Zetterholm, K., 174n1
Hendrix, H., 77n27, 104n1
Hengel, M., 54nn2, 3; 95n5
Hennecke, E., 112n28, 114n33
Herman, E. S., 120n52
Heschel, S., 178n10
Heyward, C., 3n4
Holmberg, B., 109n18, 110nn21, 22
Horrell, D. G., 108n16
Horsley, R. A., 6n13, 21n21, 49n14, 55n9, 56n11, 67n47, 71nn2, 4; 75n17, 76n20, 77n21, 78n30, 80n43, 93n95, 104n1, 108n16, 126n6, 128n10, 144n4, 161n55, 187n42

Irshai, O., 189n50

Jameson, F., 180n21, 181n22, 185n37
Jewett, R., 75n18, 87n29, 93n95
Johnson-DeBaufre, M., 41n46
Johnson, E. E., 59n24
Jones, A. H. M., 80n44

Kahl, B., 20n18, 168n87, 170
Kallas, J., 92n90
Käsemann, E., 58n19, 68n48, 92n90, 110n23, 115n38, 181n23, 184n31
Kautsky, J., 71n2, 81n45, 82n52, 83n56
Kazantzakis, N., 10n1
Keck, L. E., 92n89, 143n35
Kelber, W. H., 6n12, 110n22, 117n43
Keller, C., 8n16
Kim, S., 13n3, 49n15
King, Martin Luther, Jr., 36
Kittredge, C. B., 12n2, 41n48, 80n40, 131n16

Koester, H., 78n31
Kovacs, J. L., 59n25, 60n27, 64n38
Kraftchick, S. J., 109n20, 118n48

Lambrecht, J., 111n25, 115n37
Last, R., 183n28
Le Donne, Anthony, 181n23
Lebram, J.-C. H., 95n7
Lenski, G. E., 71n2
Levine, A.-J., 179n14
Lindbeck, G. A., 180n17
Lopez, D. A., 40n44

MacMullen, R., 106n8
Malherbe, A., 115n39
Malina, B. J., 149n16, 150nn17–19; 151nn20, 22
Manjapra, K., 185n35
Marchal, J., 41n48
Marguerat, D., 44n2
Marshall, P., 77n24, 108n16, 111n25, 116n40
Martin, D. B., 40n43, 84n60, 100n25, 137n22
Martín-Baró, I., 120n51
Martyn, J. L., 110nn22, 23; 175n2, 186n39
Matthews, S., 184n29
Mattison, M., 145n5
McKnight, S., 21n21, 126n7, 129n13, 161n55
McLean, B. H., 114n32
Meeks, W. A., 12n2, 13n4, 72n6, 109n19, 132n17
Meggitt, J. J., 7, 8n14, 72n6, 108n16, 132n18
Memmi, A., 96n12
Miranda, J. P., 90n82
Mitchell, M. M., 84n60
Modica, J. B., 21n21, 126n7, 129n13, 161n55
Moltmann, J., 119n50
Montefiore, C. G., 146n6
Moore, G. F., 45n4, 146n6, 181n24
Moore, S. D., 161n55
Moxnes, H., 73n12, 74n13, 91n88
Munck, J., 19n17, 87n73, 109n19

Nanos, M. D., 14n6, 19n17, 20n18, 21n22, 46n6, 48n11, 73n10, 75n16, 89n77, 93n93, 147n12, 148n14, 166n76
Nelson-Pallmeyer, J., 120nn52, 53
Nickle, K. F., 188n46
Nippel, W., 107n11, 114n35, 116n41
Nissinen, M., 40n42
Novak, M., 4n7
Novenson, M. V., 180n19
Nutton, V., 84n60

O'Neill, J. C., 92n90
O'Sullivan, G., 120n52
Olbrechts-Tyteca, L., 82n49, 92n91

Pagels, E., 73n11, 79n38
Paul VI, Pope, 178nn9, 11
Peake, A. S., 15n8
Pearson, B., 59n23
Penner, T., 47n9
Perelman, C., 82n49, 92n91
Pervo, R., 29n27, 35n30
Petersen, N. R., 79n38
Petrella, I., 191n57
Petrément, S., 59n23
Pickett, R., 78n35, 105n3, 110n22, 118nn45, 47; 122n58
Pilch, J. J., 149n16, 150nn17–19; 151nn20, 22
Porter, S. E., 80n42, 161n55
Price, S. R. F., 6n11, 71n4, 78n36, 88, 105nn4, 5; 107n10, 106nn5, 6, 9; 107nn12, 13

Räisänen, H., 47n9, 146n7, 158n48
Ramsay, W. M., 125n3
Reasoner, M., 29n27, 89n77
Reed, A. Y., 183n26
Reed, J. T., 80n42
Reinhartz, A., 179n14
Richardson, P., 85n61
Ridgeway, J., 4n5
Rieger, J., 8n16
Robbins, J. R., 109n18
Robert, L., 57n13
Roetzel, C. J., 72n8, 78n34, 87n40, 96nn8–10, 118n47
Rowe, K., 184n33

Ruden, S., 24n24, 40n43
Ruether, R. R., 17n9, 72n7, 177n6
Runesson, A., 174n1, 178n8

Said, E., 70n1, 82n50, 83n55, 125n1
Saldarini, A. J., 77n25
Saller, R., 72n5
Sánchez, D., 12n2
Sanders, E. P., 2, 17n2, 18n12, 43, 45n4, 46, 47, 48n12, 49, 68n48, 71n3, 72nn7, 8; 145n6, 146n7, 181n23, 181n24
Sawicki, M., 117n43, 118n49
Schäfer, P., 94n1
Schmithals, W., 13n5
Schneemelcher, W., 112n28, 114n33
Schottroff, L., 34n29, 90n81
Schürer, E., 65n43
Schüssler Fiorenza, E. , 41nn45, 48, 80n40, 93n95, 109–10n20, 110n21, 126n8
Schweitzer, A., 179n16
Scott, J. C., 6, 80n43, 96n11, 97nn15–17; 98nn18–23; 130n15
Scroggs, R., 40n43, 79n38
Segal, A. F., 18n14, 64n36, 77n21, 144n1, 155n36, 156nn37–41; 157nn42, 43
Segovia, F. F., 48n11
Segundo, J. L., 90n82
Sekeles, E., 153n29
Silberman, N., 76n20, 77n21
Slingerland, H. D., 95n3, 140n28, 144n4
Smallwood, E. M., 20n20, 94n2
Snodgrass, K. R., 64n37
Sobrino, J., 60n28
Stanley, C. D., 21n21, 161n55
Ste. Croix, G. E. M. de, 54n3, 55nn5, 7, 8; 57n15, 64n39, 72n5, 77n24, 80n44, 81n46, 82n51, 83n53, 84n58
Stendahl, K., 13n3, 17nn9, 11; 72n7
Stowers, S. K., 20n18, 89n76, 90nn83, 84; 104n1, 105n3, 109n18, 142n33, 165n70, 167nn81, 83, 84;, 168nn85, 87
Stringfellow, W., 3n3

Author Index

Tabor, J. D., 64n36
Támez, Elsa 38n37
Taubes, J., 126n4, 165n69
Taylor, M. L., 22n23
Theissen, G., 13nn4, 5; 77n24, 108n16, 132n17
Therborn, G., 191n56
Tolbert, M. A., 108n16
Trouillot, M. R., 184n32, 185nn34–36; 190n151
Tzaferis, V., 153n29

Vander Stichele, C., 47n9
Vermes, G., 91n87, 181n23
Walsh, R. F., 189n49

Wan, S.-K., 139n27
Ward, R. F., 109nn18, 19
Wasserman, F., 43n1
Watson, F. S., 188n47
Welborn, L. L., 139n25, 169nn88–91; 170n92
Wengst, K., 55n10, 126n4
West, G. O., 80n43
Westfall, C. L., 161n55
White, J. L., 78nn32, 34; 110n22

White, L. M., 77n24
Wiefel, W., 65n43, 160n53
Williamson, L., 111n25
Wink, W., 58n21, 65n40
Winn, A., 48n13, 125n2
Winter, D., 181n23
Wire, A. C., 13n5, 28n26, 41n47, 77n26, 109nn19, 20, 126n28, 136n21
Woolf, G., 72n5, 106n8, 165n71
World Council of Churches, 178n11
Wright, N. T., 42n50, 45, 48, 49n14, 58n19, 68nn48, 50; 78n29; 87nn68, 80; 129, 147n13, 171nn94, 95; 180n20

Yamauchi, E. M., 59n23
Young, S. L., 184n33

Zanker, P., 6n11, 71n4, 107n11
Zerbe, G. M., 39n41, 40n44
Zetterholm, M., 14n6, 21n22, 48n11, 145n5, 146n8, 174nn1, 2; 176n5, 177n7, 183n26
Zias, J., 153n29
Žižek, S., 46n8

www.ingramcontent.com/pod-product-compliance
Lightning Source LLC
Chambersburg PA
CBHW030825230426
43667CB00008B/1376